Operations Management in the Travel Industry

Operations Management in the Travel Industry

Edited by

Peter Robinson
University of Wolverhampton, UK

www.cabi.org

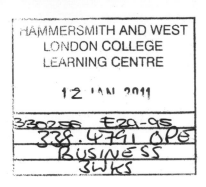
CABI is a trading name of CAB International

CABI Head Office
Nosworthy Way
Wallingford
Oxfordshire OX10 8DE
UK

Tel: +44 (0)1491 832111
Fax: +44 (0)1491 833508
E-mail: cabi@cabi.org
Website: www.cabi.org

CABI North American Office
875 Massachusetts Avenue
7th Floor
Cambridge, MA 02139
USA

Tel: +1 617 395 4056
Fax: +1 617 354 6875
E-mail: cabi-nao@cabi.org

A catalogue record for this book is available from the British Library, London, UK.

Library of Congress Cataloging-in-Publication Data

Operations management in the travel industry / edited by Peter Robinson.
      p. cm. -- (CABI tourism texts)
   Includes bibliographical references.
   ISBN 978-1-84593-503-0 (alk. paper)
1. Tourism--Management. I. Robinson, Peter, 1979- II. Title. III. Series.

G155.A1M2615 2009
910.68--dc22

2008037563

ISBN: 978 1 84593 503 0

Typeset by SPi, Pondicherry, India.
Printed and bound in the UK by Cambridge University Press, Cambridge.

The paper used for the text pages of this book is FSC certified. The FSC (Forest Stewardship Council) is an international network to promote responsible management of the world's forests.

Contents

Contributors

Peter Robinson is a senior lecturer at the University of Wolverhampton, a member of the Tourism Society and Associate of the Tourism Management Institute. He is Course Leader for Tourism Management, Entertainment Industries Management and Work Based Learning, which includes the Foundation Degree in Travel Operations Management. Previous experience in the public, private and voluntary sectors includes working in senior management teams in a range of roles that have included Tourism Development Officer, Visitor Services Manager and Tourism Projects Manager. His research interest lies in the field of operations management and sociology of tourism. He has produced a range of small local publications for business stakeholders, and has developed and delivered training courses and consultancy projects.

Crispin Dale is a Principal Lecturer and has taught Strategic Management for Tourism at undergraduate and postgraduate level for a number of years. He has published widely in peer-reviewed journals on strategic management for tourism businesses. His research has focused upon the competitive environment of travel businesses in the tour operating industry and the strategic networks of travel e-mediaries. He has also researched the impact of contemporary strategic management issues on small tourism enterprises in the expanding European Union. As a consequence of his expertise in the field, he was invited to write a resource guide on strategic management for the hospitality, leisure, sport and tourism subject network of the Higher Education Academy.

Steve Gelder is a Senior Lecturer at the University of Wolverhampton and has worked as a Principal Local Government Officer within the Leisure and Community Department. He has a Master's degree in Business Administration and focuses his teaching and research in policy, planning and operations management within the leisure and lifestyle industries. He cites the 'inclusion agenda' as close to his heart and of fundamental importance in ensuring equality of access to the service industry.

Sine Heitmann has been teaching tourism and leisure students at both undergraduate and postgraduate level after graduating with an MBA in Tourism. Work experience includes organizations within the public and private tourism and hospitality industries, from which her interest in human resource management derives. Current research areas include the sustainability of tourism, the relationship between tourism and media, tourism and accessibility and cultural tourism – the latter has been subject of papers presented in conferences.

Ade Oriade is a Senior Lecturer in Tourism and Postgraduate Programmes Course Leader at the University of Wolverhampton. Having worked in the industry in different capacities, he brought these experiences to bear in delivering customer service, quality management and operations modules. He specializes in Quality Management in Tourism, he also has special interest in Tourism/Hospitality Education and Career Analysis and Transportation for Tourism. His interest in the travel industry was fuelled by his research findings when he was studying for a Postgraduate Diploma in Transport Studies. His current research works focus on quality perception and career development in travel and tourism.

Ghislaine Povey is a Senior Lecturer within the School of Sport, Performing Arts and Leisure. She holds an MSc in Tourism and Hospitality Education from the University of Surrey (1996).

She joined the University of Wolverhampton in 1992, and has been a member of School of Sport, Performing Arts and Leisure (SSPAL) since its inception. Prior to that, she was a lecturer in tourism at Bourneville College of Further Education. She has extensive international industrial experience, having worked in the travel industry in four continents, in both public and private sectors. She wrote a regular regional food recipe column in the *Express and Star* newspaper for 2 years, and has made numerous appearances on television and radio discussing heritage, tourist experiences and regional food.

Christine Roberts is a Lecturer in Sport Management, having completed her MSc in Applied Sport and Exercise Science. Alongside maintaining an international athletic career and multi-regional coaching employment, she has established long-term work experience in the public, private and voluntary sport and leisure industries, whereby her interest in human relations and the management of human resources developed.

Debra Wale is an experienced marketing professional, who has been involved in local and national marketing projects in the public, private and voluntary sectors within the leisure and lifestyles industry. Her work history includes holding the position of Brand Manager within the Whitbread Group. She moved into academia 5 years ago and has complimented her industry experience by developing and writing Foundation Degree courses and associated materials. She is a Senior Lecturer who specializes in Marketing in Leisure Industries.

Caroline A. Wiscombe is an exceptional practitioner who has operated as an entrepreneur for some 20 years. An outstanding professional and current trustee of a major industry partner, she regularly makes decisions that have contributed to a £7.5 million turnover. Recently negotiating capital assets of £1.5 million, the business continues to strive for professional standards. A late blossomer in academic terms, she has provided a unique insight into applying business to practice. Publications include: (i) But why do I need training? A case study approach; (ii) On-licensed retail training philosophies amongst tenants, lessees and free-house operators; (iii) Foundation Degree (Arts) Professional Licensed Retailing: Innovations in Design and Delivery; (iv) Training for the Responsible Service of Alcohol: Guidelines for the Responsible Service of Alcohol. Brussels: The Amsterdam Group: the European Forum for Sensible Drinking.

Preface

When the staff team of Leisure Industries at the University of Wolverhampton were asked to develop and deliver modules for a Foundation Degree in Travel Operations Management, in partnership with Coventry University and University College Birmingham, it quickly became apparent that there was not much information available that was specifically focused on travel. For the most part, travel tended to be discussed as a part of tourism, in the same way that 20 years ago tourism was discussed in terms of generic business studies. Travel as a sector is only now becoming clearly separate from tourism.

The Foundation Degree was designed for staff working in the industry, people who may have years of experience, or who may be new to the world of work. Many of the students who started the Foundation Degree happily agreed that it had provided a multitude of opportunities to look outside their businesses, to consider the wider external environment and to have tools and models available to support research and analysis.

At the same time there are numerous examples of best practice that are happening in the industry, new approaches to management and new ideas for products and services that should be shared and developed. The University of Wolverhampton had numerous industry contacts and many of them contributed to this book with case studies. While students were the original focus of the book, our students are all practitioners, and the book is most certainly as useful in the workplace at it is in the classroom.

What we have created then is a book that offers a mix of theory, concepts, frameworks, case studies, review questions, practical suggestions and guides for further research. It is the creation of the Leisure Industries staff at Wolverhampton and the shared expertise of lecturers with significant industry experience and academic understanding of operations management, quality, logistics, finance, strategy, marketing and employability. We have strived to write an innovative and informative text with just the right balance of all the components that go into creating a really useful book. To clarify, the book has the following objectives:

- to provide an insight into all aspects of operational management in the travel industry;
- to demonstrate the role of operations through a range of business functions;
- to take the theory, apply it to practice and demonstrate its application through case studies;
- to enhance the learning opportunities presented through a range of tasks and activities to support self-reflection, group work and class activities; and
- to be as useful to students as it is to practitioners.

As suggested already, the book relies upon real-life case studies to deliver a text that has academic and practical grounding, and our grateful appreciation is extended to all our industry contributors, who are acknowledged in each chapter, and to the students from TUI UK plc who have studied the new Foundation Degree in Travel Operations Management and have shared their experiences in this book.

We hope that you enjoy reading this book as much as our staff team enjoyed writing it! We have learnt much more than we already knew from sharing each other's chapters as we prepared the final manuscript, and would like to also acknowledge the support we have received from the staff at CABI.

Peter Robinson BA, MA, MTS, MTMI
Wolverhampton, UK
2008

1 Travel and Management: an Introduction

PETER ROBINSON

Objectives of the Chapter

This chapter is divided into three sections. The first, Part A, outlines the structure and focus of this book. The second, Part B, explains and investigates the definitions of travel, describing the nature and scope of travel as a service industry. The third, Part C, goes on to explore the theories of management and organizational structure that underpin the subject area and contextualize the industry. The chapter objectives are to:

- explain the structure and approach of the book;
- explain the nature and scope of the travel industry;
- provide current trends, features and characteristics of the industry; and
- provide underpinning concepts of management, organizational structure and culture.

PART A: STRUCTURE OF THE BOOK

In the writing of this book, there has been considerable debate about the topic content, detail and coverage, and the need to ensure it remains operational in its focus. The publication is designed for students of Travel and Tourism qualifications, but also for practitioners and, although focused on operations, does profile all aspects of the workings of a travel business. Throughout each chapter, theories and concepts are illustrated with case studies and debated within the text. All the chapters have a mixture of tasks, activities and questions to support the factual content and a set of review questions at the end, which can be used by lecturers or by the individual reader. A brief guide is also given at the end of each chapter for additional sources and reading material, in addition to the comprehensive reference lists that provide some of the quotes and ideas that are discussed and debated in each chapter.

This chapter commences with an explanation of travel, giving clear definitions to explain the industry and to differentiate it from related subject areas such as tourism and hospitality. Of course, none of these industry sectors is totally separate, in fact they interrelate all the time. A passenger buying food on an aircraft is involved in travel, tourism and hospitality, but it is important to identify what defines and characterizes travel. The chapter then goes on to explore the scope of the industry and profiles some of the key segments within the travel sector.

This chapter also considers management. This book was never intended to be a management volume, but it did become clear in its writing that it needed to introduce a few concepts that are discussed in subsequent chapters. The introduction here to management theory considers approaches to management, organizational structure and organizational culture. Without this, however, it is much harder to understand, for example, the relationship between planning and implementation or the challenges managers face in consulting and communicating across a business.

Chapter 2 starts with an overview of careers in the travel industry. This chapter is also divided into two sections. The first deals with career planning and takes the reader through the different stages of employment planning, with a critique of the challenges that working in travel presents to its loyal, dedicated and hard-working workforce. There is no question that working in travel is challenging and demanding, but the rewards, satisfaction and fun that can be had make the experience worthwhile. The second section considers individual skills that are needed and discusses personal development planning to help take steps into management and up the management ladder.

Chapter 3 builds on this 'human' element of the travel business and looks at human resource (HR) management functions. People are unquestionably the most important asset to the travel business. When it is all going wrong, the hotel is overbooked, the flights are late and the coach has broken down, travellers have nowhere else to turn but the holiday representative. A friendly face may be all that is needed to take control of the situation, calm frayed nerves and sooth tempers. Staff have to be looked after and feel valued if they are to be motivated to deliver high standards of service. This HR chapter describes the whole range of functions covered in the topic area and considers not just the role of the HR department, but also the responsibility everybody in the business has to recognize, reward, motivate and support their staff and colleagues.

Chapter 4 then starts to look in detail at operations management. It sets out to define and characterize the systems and processes that support the organization and its people to ensure that the end product or service is effective. Time is also spent looking at operational strategy and its role within the business, and a range of revenue, performance and productivity measures are presented which enable managers to better understand what is happening in the workplace. In addition to health and safety, legislation and facilities design are also discussed. This content is also supported by Chapter 5, which focuses upon logistics and supply chain management. Logistics are a part of operations management so it may seem at odds to separate them. However, logistics is such a crucial part of the travel business that it needs this level of depth, which also allows the chapter to look at quality and establish the link between effective logistics management and the delivery of a quality service, together with the development of supply chain management strategies to improve financial performance.

Although the book is focused on operations – and this by its very nature is relatively short-term in its viewpoint, managing and reacting to day-to-day issues – it is essential to see operations within a strategic context, and this is provided in Chapter 6. Here a range of models and frameworks around which to plan strategically are presented. Consideration is given throughout to the relationship between strategic and operational management. Chapter 7 discusses the role of marketing and provides a further set of tools and frameworks that can be easily applied to all sectors of a business, but are best explained in marketing terms. Marketing is essential for businesses to promote themselves, and opportunities for advertising are becoming broader through the development of new technologies. As a relatively young industry, the travel sector is capitalizing on many of these new innovations.

Chapter 8 then underpins everything that has preceded it. Again divided into Parts A and B, it focuses on finance, and all aspects of strategy, operations, marketing and human resources are ultimately governed by the financial bottom line. Travel businesses generally operate within the private sector, but some are charities and voluntary sector businesses and their financial management is different. The first section of the chapter looks at types of accounts and explains accounting in a simple and straightforward manner. The second section is more concerned with finance at a strategic level and strong relationships exist here between operations and strategy as the chapter explains how finances inform and influence the business, and how financial data can be used for performance management.

The final two chapters are more concerned with emerging themes and current research in travel. Chapter 9 discusses sustainability, and as the environment moves up the political and social agendas, it does not attempt to preach about environmental responsibility so much as to define the delicate balance that exists between business, management and the natural resources upon which many destinations depend for their commercial and social existence. This chapter relies very heavily on tourism theory and concepts as less research exists that relates to travel, but there are many ideas here that are developed into travel concepts, combined with examples of good practice from the travel industry. In Chapter 10 the reader is introduced to more complex social theory as the book explains culture and society. This helps to underpin some of the challenges outlined in the sustainability chapter, but also establishes some of the prosaic frameworks that explain why people travel, how they make their travel decisions and the conflicts between host and visitor communities.

There is a short concluding essay before the index, an epilogue in many ways, which talks about the future of travel and some of the trends that can be expected in the future. Indeed many of these trends will probably shape the next edition of this publication!

PART B: TRAVEL

Introduction

The travel industry as it is known today can be traced back to the 17th century. Before this time, tourism certainly existed and was manifested by pilgrimages to cathedrals and shrines, but it would be hard to define this as travel, as most movement was on foot or horseback, and although there was a hospitality industry, there was no formal travel business. However, growing knowledge of the world and an increasingly accessible European continent promised opportunities for young aristocrats, who would travel across Europe on a Grand Tour for between 6 and 12 months, visiting places considered to be tasteful and from where fashions developed in architecture, clothing, garden design and furniture. Many young architects and designers would also visit what were considered to be highly cultured European cities (Italy, Greece) and the North African coast.

Travel would, however, remain elitist for many more years, through the Agricultural and Industrial Revolutions, until in 1840 Thomas Cook planned the first train trip, facilitated by the completion of the London to Manchester Railway. Increasing welfare issues, holidays, bank holidays and holy days, as well as increasing wealth, started to open up travel opportunities for the masses. After World War I, Billy Butlin and Fred Pontin developed the first holiday camps, the forerunners of today's resorts, and after World War II, the development of commercial aircraft finally offered opportunities for mass air travel, opening up the world and transforming the travel and tourism industries.

The Travel Industry

The travel industry was historically associated with poor pay and unsociable hours. However, new qualifications, greater rewards and staff benefits are now reversing this trend. Many roles in the travel sector require people with general sales and customer service skills and a positive disposition. This combination of skills and characteristics will hold an individual in much better stead than a formal academic qualification within lower-paid roles, but as individuals look to progress up the management ladder a lack of education and understanding of academic and business principles is likely to considerably slow progression and promotional opportunities.

Travel as a Service Industry

Travel, tourism and hospitality are service sector businesses. This is defined by five characteristics.

Intangibility: Services are not tangible, they cannot be touched or sensed. For example, the holiday package cannot be looked out and tested before the customer experiences it.

Heterogeneity: Every experience is different to different individuals. Two people in the same restaurant may have very different ideas about the level and quality of service, based usually on their previous experiences which can be used to measure the experience.

Perishability: Services cannot be stockpiled. A holiday that is available from 1 April to 1 May cannot be kept and sold on 5 May because there are spaces left on the aircraft.

Inseparabilty: The service has to be used where it is bought – it cannot be taken home for later.

Lack of ownership: Because of the intangible nature of the industry, services which are bought do not confer ownership. A hotel customer who books a room does not own the bed or the room, just the opportunity to use it and to expect to receive a certain level of service.

Defining Travel

The difference between travel and tourism is not necessarily clear, and the two often merge. Some would argue that travel is a part of tourism; others would suggest travel is a key component or part of the definition for tourism. Tourism has been described as 'a multidimensional, multifaceted activity which touches many lives and many different economic activities' (Cooper *et al.*, 2000, p. 8), which was a development of the earlier definitions that focused on movement and struggled to identify the relationship between the industry and those involved in it as participants or as hosts. One of these earlier definitions was the 'movement of people away from their normal place of residence' (Holloway, 1995, p. 1). The problem with these definitions is that they would include non-touristic activity because of the notion of movement away from a normal place of residence. Would travelling away from a place of residence to look at a new car be considered to be tourism and those involved to be tourists?

The characteristics of the industry help to define it better than some of the definitions. It usually involves travel to a different location to spend time away from home and with some form of expenditure taking place. It is likely to be an activity which will be enjoyable or interesting for those involved and may also include accommodation, activities and attractions, which cover all elements of tourism, travel, hospitality, events and leisure. All of these definitions demonstrate significant interrelationships.

Travel, however, also involves some other components which are easier to define. In many situations, travel encompasses tour operations and holiday packages. Yale (1998) describes a tour operator as 'a person or company who purchases different items that make up an inclusive holiday in bulk, combines them together and then sells the final products to the public either directly or through travel agencies'. This is supported by Medlik and Middleton (1973, in Middleton, 1988) who define it thus:

> As far as the tourist is concerned, the product covers the whole experience from the time he leaves home to the time he returns from it....[T]he tourist product is not an airline seat or a hotel bed or relaxing on a sunny beach...but rather an amalgam of many components....Airline seats and hotel beds are merely elements or components of a total tourist product which is a composite product.

The interrelationship between the travel agent and the tour is explained by Holloway (1994, p. 5) describing the 'organisation selling and managing this type of product is usually a tour operator, although the product may be sold through a travel agent, who also manage the package, or elements of the package through resort reps'.

The role of the travel agent has changed over the years and continues to do so. The travel agent is described as 'one who acts on behalf of a principal, i.e. the original provider of tourist services such as a holiday company, airline, tour operator, shipping company' by Burkhart and Medlik (1974).

Structure of the Travel Industry

The travel industry is complex in its component parts: tour operators, travel agents, transport, accommodation, activities, events and attractions.

Businesses in the travel industry may be defined by size:

- Multinationals are the market leaders, and include AMEX (AE), Thomas Cook and TUI AG. Many independents (see below) are owned by these major operators and fulfil the more niche-market offerings.
- National multiples are those businesses which are based across the UK, and include Leger and Midland Counties Cooperative.
- Regional multiples are those businesses operating within a region, such as the West Midlands or London.
- Independents are the individual operators of generally very small businesses and often specialists.

Businesses operating in this sector each have distinct characteristics. Travel agents and tour operators have been defined earlier in the chapter, so this section concentrates on the actual operating companies involved in the industry.

Accommodation: Accommodation in this sector can cover a multitude of businesses and business models. It includes hotels, self-catering cottages, guest houses, farm holidays, bed and breakfast, camping and caravanning and resorts. The range of businesses involved is a result of the broadening scope of the travel industry. There was a time in the early period of the industry where accommodation really referred to hotels set up for the package holiday market, but there are so many businesses offering tailor-made packages that all sectors of the hotel business can now be associated with the travel industry.

Airline: The airline industry has in recent years been dominated by the growth in low-cost airlines and cheap flights. There are, however, still a number of more traditional charter flights for the package holiday market and traditional carriers still have scheduled services with different ticket levels, usually economy, business and club class. Most recent developments in this sector include the development of very large aircraft such as the Airbus A380 and the increased risk of terrorism.

Attractions: Attractions encompass a broad scope of 'things to do'. Of particular relevance here is the way that attractions are used. They include ruins, historic buildings, gardens, theme parks and children's activity parks. Some package holidays include visits to attractions as part of the package. Some sectors use attractions as add-ons, hence excursions from cruise ships and resorts. Very often they are a key part of the independent traveller's itinerary and provide a focus for special interest sectors.

Coaches: Pre-booked coaches are used for excursions and trips. Some coach companies offer their own holiday packages and many of the market leaders own their own hotels or have contracts with overseas hotels. Some people will choose to travel by coach as part of the holiday, often on scheduled services, and there is the decreasingly popular domestic day trip on coaches.

Cruise: Cruise operators traditionally offered high-end holidays but are widening the appeal and lowering the price of the experience. Some cruise companies also recognize that developing cruise markets may be unsure about what to expect so offer taster cruises to broaden the appeal. Cruise companies usually plan a number of excursions at different ports of call.

Ferry: Ferry companies are generally industry suppliers, providing coach companies with transport to overseas destinations and offering transport for individual and commercial travellers. There are some instances where the ferry company acts as a travel agent or tour operator, in particular to offshore locations. UK examples of this practice include Red Funnel and Wightlink (Isle of Wight) and Condor Ferries (Channel Islands).

Taxi: The taxi and private hire industry presents the biggest challenge for the reputation of the industry as so many small local operators exist; many tourists in overseas locations are charged more than they should be, and customer care is not seen as being as important to the operators. Some luxury private hire companies and limousine companies have entered this market and have improved service standards, but prices reflect this because of the higher-quality vehicles that are used. Many cities and destinations across the world also have service standards and training courses for the taxi sector, but not yet for the private hire business.

Train: This sector is one of the most complex. It encompasses a whole variety of combinations of business. The simplest structure at national level is individual or

P. Robinson

group travel to a specific location, with a combination of economy and first-class ticket options. These national carriers include GNER, Virgin and First Great Western. There are, in addition, a myriad of local train operators. While the overall standard and quality of national travel has changed and improved drastically over recent years, this has been less noticeable on provincial railways. Some train operators provide packages for city breaks, and some travellers choose to tour different countries by train. There is also a large market for nostalgic steam-hauled train travel in the UK and across Europe managed by companies including the famous Venice-Simplon Orient Express.

The sector can also be defined by the typologies of the business that it is involved with.

Business travel: This encompasses travel for the purpose of work. International business travel is under threat from the growth in technology and affordability of communications technology. Traditionally, business travellers tend to purchase higher-class tickets which are very profitable for operators, but with increasing security risks and easy use of satellite and web technologies which facilitate communication and reduce travel time to zero, the market, although stable now, could face decline in the future. Short-haul business travellers are increasingly using low-cost airlines, although on trains first-class tickets are still popular with business travel.

Mass-market travel: Still the most popular form of travel, this sector is trying to improve its image. It includes a diverse range of businesses, from Club 18–30 to high-end ski holidays and everything in between. The industry is increasingly defending its environmental credentials and impacts on host communities. Businesses commonly operate as travel agents and tour operators, using charter flights and contracted hotels, with the experience being managed by overseas resort representatives. Some businesses in this sector, such as TUI AG, have bought specialist companies to offer niche-market package travel while still delivering mass-market travel under traditional brands. Some of these large players also now own their own aircraft, reducing the needs to rely on suppliers, but increasing the responsibility and cost of running the business.

Niche-market travel: This refers to more specialist travel motives. These may be packages or independent travel and often focus on particular interests. Common niche-market products include holidays to learn new skills, such as languages, art or adventure skills, or to explore emerging destinations. Over time, many of these sectors grow to the mass-market model as emerging destinations develop in popularity or niche-market interests (historically skiing is such an example) reach mainstream markets and as a result become increasingly affordable for a wider range of people.

Sustainable, green and eco-travel: There is considerable debate around these concepts, which will be discussed in more detail in a later chapter. It is sufficient here to identify that an increasing awareness of environmental issues combined with a desire to become more environmentally aware has raised all sorts of issues in the industry. There are travellers who believe in purchasing holidays which benefit local communities, and others who avoid heavily polluting forms of transport. There are resorts seeking accreditation from local, regional, national and international environmental standards agencies such as Green Globe, and there are others that are trying to change the way they work to appeal to a more environmentally aware consumer base.

Independent and specialist travel: The independent market is growing in popularity from its early beginning in the 1980s, pioneered by specialist companies such as

Travelbag; customers are able to have an entire holiday planned in every detail, taking away the worry of organizing flights and checking travel requirements, but still being able to travel when and where desired.

Domestic travel: A simple definition will suffice here, that domestic travel is within the traveller's country of origin using local, regional and national suppliers. This should not be taken, however, to mean short distances, as domestic travel for the US market could be a significant distance for a long holiday.

PART C: MANAGEMENT

Introduction

Management theory has evolved considerably over time and the style and approach of management vary across different industries. Approaches to management are discussed here to provide background to some of the detail that is discussed in subsequent chapters. First, it is crucial to understand what an organizational structure may look like, and a generic example is given in Fig. 1.1.

The structure of an organization provides the framework of order and command through which the activities of the organization can be planned, organized, directed and controlled. In a very small organization such as an independent travel agency, there will be very few if any structural problems. The distribution of the work, which staff have responsibility and authority, and the relationship between members of the organization can be established on a personal and informal basis.

It must be organized for business performance: The more direct and simple the structure, the more efficient it is. Individual performance can be easily assessed and altered if necessary to achieve a good result.

The structure should have the least possible levels: The chain of command should be as short as possible. Every additional level makes for difficulties in direction, communication and understanding. It sets up additional stresses, creates inertia on the part of those below and makes it more difficult for future managers to move up through the chain.

Any organization structure must make possible the training and testing of future top management: Future managers must be tested as they strive to reach the top. They should be given the freedom to make decisions while still young enough to benefit from

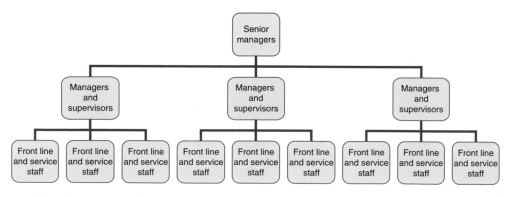

Fig. 1.1. Organizational structure.

the new experience. They should also have the opportunity to observe the operation of the business as a whole and not remain as a functional specialist for too long. An example of this would be an overseas tour operator. Resort managers have to work their way up from the post of first-year representative, so that by the time they reach management, they have experienced all aspects of the roles that they will be managing.

Classical management

Management has been traced back to the organization of early cultures such as the Romans and Egyptians who would have been coordinating the building of roads and pyramids, but it was during the agricultural and industrial revolution that the most significant changes took place in the way that people worked, as mechanization took over and people started to move to cities to work in factories. Classical management describes three approaches to management, developed from the 1860s to the 1920s.

The scientific approach: This was developed by Frederick Taylor (1856–1915) and suggested that jobs could be broken down into specific tasks and those tasks carried out in a prescribed manner. Staff are trained to carry out these very specific roles and managers check that procedures are followed. Elements of this approach are still used in the travel industry, in particular in retail and service environments where staff will follow systems, procedures and guidelines while selling a product or trying to understand a problem. Critics of this approach cite demoralization and lack of opportunity for personal development as major issues.

The bureaucratic approach: This is characterized perfectly by the example of organizational structure given above, and bureaucracy is a feature of many modern workplaces. It refers to the idea that everything operates within a very structured environment with clear rules, responsibilities and lines of authority explained through an organizational structure. Individuals in the business have specific roles and tasks and a specific communication and reporting system. The approach has been criticized because it creates an over-reliance on paperwork and limits opportunities for change. Imagine working on the front line and having an idea about how to improve service. This would be communicated back up the organization to the relevant manager, who would then have to make a decision and pass it on to another department for implementation. This explains why many large businesses are slow to change and adapt.

The administrative approach: This describes management in five elements: forecasting and planning, organizing, commanding; coordination; and controlling. Again it is a very structured approach and naturally fits with bureaucracy in the way that the business is organized, controlled and directed.

Human relations approach

Later studies into management considered the role of people within the organization as individuals. Much of this research was carried out by Mary Parker Follett (1868–1933) and focuses upon studies into individual attitudes, behaviours and group processes, concluding that workers respond primarily to the social context of work. Key findings of the research include:

- an emphasis on the importance of motivation at work;
- inappropriateness of workers to perform a task in a prescribed way;
- the need for managers to coordinate and harmonize group efforts;
- the need to replace bureaucratic institutions with group networks; and
- the need to optimize production but recognizing that scientific principles are not the right way to achieve this.

Further research was carried out by Elton Mayo in a series of experiments into working conditions, testing the impacts of lighting, heating, rest periods, working hours and group incentive schemes. Mayo reached two conclusions:

1. Work satisfaction is dependent on social factors such as friendliness, cooperation between group members, feeling of doing something worthwhile and relations with the supervisor.
2. The social factors had a far greater impact on output than physical conditions.

This led to the notion of different groups in the business. These are formal (as indicated by the organizational structure) and informal (where people get on well with others from different positions and departments in the business).

In summary, the human relations approach recognizes:

- motivation of people by more than pay and conditions alone;
- work as a group activity, and individuals should be seen as group members;
- the need for recognition, security and a sense of belonging in maintaining morale and productivity;
- power and influence of the informal work group; and
- awareness of an individual's social needs.

Systems approach

The systems approach treats all the processes in an organization as a system. The example given below is a closed system (Fig. 1.2). An open system, which includes the external environment, is demonstrated in Chapter 4.

The systems approach was an attempt at reconciling the classical and human relations approaches to management. It tries to also give a pictorial demonstration of what is happening in the business and so can be a particularly useful tool for operations managers. It demonstrates the components going into the business and the transformation of those components to create outputs.

The difference between the open and closed systems is simply the fact that an open system considers the wider operating environment and the external factors which impact upon the business. These are discussed in considerable detail in Chapter 4.

Contingency approach

This approach is probably the one most commonly used in the travel sector as it identifies and analyses a problem to create the best solution (Huczynski and Buchanan, 2001). Ultimately, this approach brings together elements of all the other approaches discussed (Fig. 1.3), so sometimes scientific approaches are effective, perhaps when

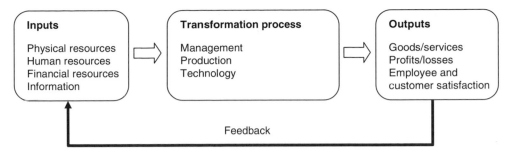

Fig. 1.2. A closed system. (Adapted from Mullins, 1999.)

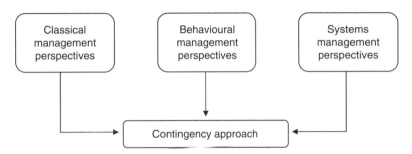

Fig. 1.3. Synergies of approaches to management.

trying to deliver a standard level and process for customer service, but when staff are engaged in a 'boring' activity, the use of social interaction can be a good motivator, as suggested in the human relations approach.

Organizational Culture

Organizational culture describes the norms and values that govern behaviour in an organization. Culture is usually unique to a given business and can be defined as a set of values, beliefs, understandings and norms within a business (Daft, 2000).

Some elements of organizational culture are visible and may be transmitted as dress styles, office layout, equipment and training courses, while below the surface there exist norms, values and morals which govern behaviour. Organizational culture tends to be positive and 'glues' employees together, by helping them to identify more closely with their fellow-workers, giving a sense of purpose and identity (adapted from Huczynski and Buchanan, 2001, p. 647).

Summary

This introductory chapter has defined what is understood by travel and the scale and scope of the industry. Everything that is discussed here will be investigated in more detail throughout the book, offering readers the opportunity to understand some of the complex factors which affect the industry and demonstrating why a range of skills and knowledge will ensure success in a dynamic, flexible and ever-changing operating environment.

Further Research

Beech, J. and Chadwick, S. (eds) (2006) *The Business of Tourism Management*. Financial Times/Prentice-Hall, Harlow, UK.

Huczynski, A. and Buchanan, D. (2001) *Organizational Behaviour: An Introductory Text*, 4th edn. Pearson Education, Harlow, UK.

Mullins, L.J. (2002) *Management and Organisational Behaviour*, 6th edn. Pearson Education, Harlow, UK.

Web Sites

www.abta.com
www.iata.co.uk
www.traveltourismguild.com
www.atta.co.uk
www.pata.co.uk

Review Questions

1. Compare travel agency to tour operations – what are the main similarities and differences?

2. Describe the structure of the travel industry.

3. Outline what you believe to be the key threats to the development of the industry.

4. Describe two characteristics of tour operators and travel agency. How do these sectors differ from tourism?

5. Based on the definitions presented here write your own definitions for travel, tour operations and tourism.

References

Burkhart, A.J. and Medlik, S. (1974) *Tourism*. William Heinemann, London.

Cooper, C., Fletcher, J., Wanhill, S., Gilbert, D. and Shepherd, R. (2000) *Tourism: Principles and Practice*, 2nd edn. Financial Times/Prentice-Hall, Harlow, UK.

Daft, R.L. (2000) *Management*. Harcourt College Publishers, Fort Worth, Texas.

Holloway, J.C. (1993) *The Business of Tourism,* 4th edn. Financial Times/Prentice-Hall, Harlow, UK.

Huczynski, A. and Buchanan, D. (2001) *Organizational Behaviour: An Introductory Text*, 4th edn. Pearson Education, Harlow, UK.

Middleton, V. T.C. (1988) *Marketing in Travel and Tourism*. Butterworth-Heinemann, Oxford.

Mullins, L.J. (1999) *Management and Organisational Behaviour*, 5th edn. Pearson Education, Harlow, UK.

Yale (1998) *From Tourist Attractions to Heritage Tourism*, 2nd edn. Elm Publications, Huntingdon, UK.

2 Career Development Skills and Strategies in the Travel Industry

GHISLAINE POVEY AND ADE ORIADE

Objectives of the Chapter

This chapter is split into two sections: Part A focuses on employment opportunities and Part B on the skills and strategies needed to adopt and develop a fulfilling, successful career in the travel industry. Topics covered include: skills auditing; personal development planning; curriculum vitae (CV) building; and the progression of effective verbal and written communication skills. Furthermore, the chapter addresses teamworking abilities, alongside team performance analysis, information searching, critical and analytical thinking and the effective use of information for decision making. Self-management, career planning, objective- and target-setting are also investigated. The objective for Part A is to:

- demonstrate an understanding of the theoretical basis for career development in the travel industry.

The objectives for Part B are to:

- identify the skills required by employers in the travel industry; and
- demonstrate an understanding of the strategies needed to adopt a progressive and fulfilling career.

PART A: CAREER STRATEGIES IN TRAVEL OPERATIONS

Introduction

The tourism industry is reputed to be one of the largest industries globally. Job opportunities within tourism and allied sectors are characteristically plentiful, often labelled as the 'employment of the future'. Yet the concept of developing these jobs into careers is a relatively new phenomenon, and not always given sufficient attention (Ayres, 2006). While the topic of career development has been exhaustively explored in some disciplines, particularly those pertaining to hospitality, little focus has been given to tourism and travel operations. There is no doubt that prospective students enter higher and further education with aspirations towards employment opportunities with progressive careers. The issue here is not whether it is worth pursuing a career in tourism or the availability of jobs – the very fact that there is a continuation of investment within the industry is indicative of this assumption. Organizations will, therefore, persist in their attempts to attract those with the skills necessary to take care of company interests. Candidates capable of contributing towards organizational aims will be sought after and are likely to make it to the top of their career. The issue dealt with here relates to the following questions:

- What are the skills needed to meet organizational aims?
- How will people develop these skills?
- How can they convince employers that they possess such qualities?

It is believed, rightly or wrongly, that relatively few graduates of tourism- and leisure-related disciplines make it to the top of their careers. Evidence has shown that non-progression is attributed to a number of factors. Chief among them are: non-development of appropriate career skills; lack of ability to formulate career planning; and limitations in organizational strategies needed to aid survival in today's competitive work environment. To overcome these problems, prospective candidates looking towards working within the travel industry must acquire professional skills and map out their career strategies. This chapter principally deals with these two major issues in career development.

Dominant Issues in Careers and Career Development

As a first step, it is important to fully understand the notions of career development and the individual career itself. There are numerous career and career-related definitions within the existing body of literature. Traditionally, the term 'career path' denotes the upward movement of a person within an organization or number of organizations within an industry. Given the trend in modern society and particularly the characteristics of the tourism industry, it will not be sufficient to view career from a bureaucratic perspective where emphasis is on the traditional acceptance of qualification, regular incremental advancement and degree of career-enhancing prospects (Ayres, 2006). In its simplest form, the term 'career' can be seen as 'the outcome of, on the one hand, human ability and ambition, and on the other hand, the opportunity available to the individual' (Ladkin and Juwaheer, 2000, p. 123). However, the understanding of 'career' has moved away from its original and generic definition; individual traits are now incorporated within different organizations, allowing for a heterogenic understanding of the term (Boon, 2006). Irrespective of 'career' terminology advancement, there remains a clear indication that individuals have a prominent role to play in charting the course of their careers.

Career development represents career outcomes for individuals and companies, and includes salient issues like economics, job transitions, mobility, career withdrawal and career compromise (Riley and Ladkin, 1994). Undoubtedly career patterns differ from individual to individual, profession to profession and industry to industry. Industry professionals must adopt a good understanding of career development, as this is crucial in enhancing the ability to manage careers effectively. Some of these elements include career planning, career mobility, career strategy, mentoring, decision making, human capital, career pattern and so on. For the purpose of this chapter, our major focus will be on three main elements. These are discussed below and they include career planning, career strategy and skills required by employers in the travel industry. It is pertinent to know that these cannot be discussed in isolation; occasional reference will be made to other related concepts.

Education

There are a number of qualifications available for people working or intending to work in the travel industry. The range of qualifications spans from 14 to 16 diplomas and postgraduate degrees in tourism and travel and allied subjects. For some, acquisition of qualification(s) as a strategy for moving up the career ladder is a starting point, while for others it is something to be achieved after successful establishment in a particular vocation. For example, completion of a 3-year BA degree is increasingly becoming a popular method of initiating, or progressing in, a successful career. It is becoming increasingly important that any individual aiming to get to the top must acquire one form of qualification or the other which will equip them with the kind of business skills needed in today's competitive and global market.

Acquiring qualifications as a means to progressing in a chosen career is well documented in career literature. Although it may not be seen primarily as a strategy (as its main purpose is to acquire skills which are not easily learnt in work environment), numerous individuals have achieved career-enhancing abilities and promotion from the acquisition of relevant qualifications.

It is advisable that individuals are strategic in their quest for acquisition of qualification.

There are many schemes aimed at select individuals who already possess certain qualifications, allowing for a fast-track route to a management position. CHME's (2001) report on graduate careers in hospitality management found that education is a prerequisite for getting to some managerial positions. In Ladkin's (2000) work on vocational education and food and beverage experience, possessing a relevant qualification was also found to be a key factor in maximum progression within a chosen career.

Issues in Travel Careers

There is a range of factors that influence the industry and impact upon employment patterns and the knowledge and skill requirements of those working in the industry:

- **Domination by major employers:** There are a number of major operators in the travel sector, such as Touristik Union International (TUI) and Thomas Cook, who offer a full range of services directly or through smaller specialist subsidiaries. Other businesses in the sector are either specialist (P&O or Great North Eastern Railway (GNER)) or small businesses.
- **Relatively low wages, seasonality, unsocial hours and work patterns:** Many jobs in the industry are low-paid, or seasonal or a combination. This presents a challenge in attracting people to work in the business. This is combined with long hours at peak times of the year, then quiet periods out of season.
- **Lack of any significant trade union press:** There is little union representation for the travel industry. Some sectors are covered by individual unions, but there is no overarching union for the industry as there is in teaching: British Air Line Pilots Association (BALPA; www.balpa.org.uk), National Union of Rail, Maritime and Transport Workers (RMT; www.rmt.org.uk), Transport Salaried Staffs' Association (TSSA; www.tssa.org.uk) and Transport and General Workers' Union (TGWU; www.tgwu.org.uk).
- **High levels of labour turnover:** Frequent staff turnover is sometimes attributable to the low-pay/long-hours issue, but is often symptomatic of a business where seasonal staff do not return or get offered full-time work halfway through their contract.

- **Lack of skills and understanding of the industry:** A lack of adequately skilled people in the accessible labour market at all levels of the travel business, combined with a skills gap where the current workforce sometimes has lower skills than necessary, sometimes through a lack of experience.
- **Perceived image of the industry:** The low-pay/long-hours image of the business does little to promote it to would-be employees.
- **Other recruitment difficulties:** This is an umbrella term incorporating all other forms of employer recruitment problems, except for skills shortage and skills gap as defined above. Such problems can be caused by poor recruitment practices, poor perceived image of the industry, low remuneration or poor terms and conditions of employment. These can occur where there are sufficient skilled individuals available and accessible for work.

Jobs in the Travel Industry

This section of the chapter considers some of the roles which exist within travel. This is far from an exhaustive list, and many businesses employ people for the same roles, but may give that role a different title. Alongside all of these jobs are the support functions in the business, including Human Resources, Finance and IT Support.

Train operations: Train Managers – This role, carried out on board the train, involves the overall management of staff on the train, checking tickets, keeping passengers updated about delays and issues affecting their journey, while trying to resolve problems quickly and efficiently and ensuring a high standard of customer care is delivered. Station Managers – This role encompasses overall management of station activities, including ticket sales, catering (or franchise) management, safety, security, maintenance and development of station facilities.

Coach and bus operations: Coach and Bus Operators – Roles in this sector vary greatly from local contract services (Arriva) to national travel (National Express), from private hire and schools work to professional tour operators (WAShearings), with the type of business dictating the roles that exist, which will include drivers, tour managers and couriers.

Airline operations: Supply Chain Team Leader – This role within the Engineering and Maintenance Division of the airline provides spares when an aircraft is undergoing maintenance, or has broken down or developed a fault. The ability to supply the necessary parts dictates if an aircraft is able to fly. It may be the case that a part is needed for a plane sitting on the ground, laden with passengers waiting to take-off. Base Performance Manager – This role involves the management of the operations and crew at airports; day-to-day responsibilities include meeting targets such as early departures, delays and revenue. Performances of suppliers, handling agents and airport services are also a part of this role. Weekly meetings take place with suppliers; audits need to be conducted and daily reports sent to the head office.

Overseas resort: Team Manager – This role involves managing and running an overseas resort. It includes training and developing new and existing resort representatives, airport revenue development, health and safety and customer service.

Travel agency: General and Regional Sales Managers and Retail Managers – This role involves managing Regional Sales Managers, who themselves manage groups of shops. The role requires excellent leadership and management skills, the ability to communicate effectively and to be entirely results-driven and customer-focused. These skills are essential throughout the retail sector, from Shop Manager to Director of Sales. The Regional and Shop Manager jobs also include managing and maintaining shop standards, ensuring processes and procedures are adhered to. Assistant Retail Manager – The Assistant Manager is responsible for assisting the Manager with the day-to-day running of the office and for the complete running of shop and staff in the Manager's absence. The role includes keeping records of cancellations, payments outstanding from holiday bookings and authorizing discounts, assisting the staff in any sales enquiries and keeping staff focused and motivated to reach targets and driving the sales through the store.

Editorial services: Editorial Executive – This role involves writing creative copy for holiday brochures and web sites, developing materials to support nationwide marketing campaigns, writing recruitment advertisements and public relations (PR) features.

Customer services: Customer Liaison Executive – Customer Liaison Executives provide 24-hour customer support and are responsible for monitoring and communication of operations issues overseas and/or airline disruption directly to customers or internal and external representatives of airline ground handling agents and UK/overseas tour operator, colleagues and representatives.

Business operations: Commercial Executives and Managers – Development of strong working relationships with key third-party operators accounts. The roles support and deliver key campaigns and communication to third-party agents and involve negotiation process with third parties.

Chapter 1 (this volume) discusses many of the roles that exist in the industry, although these are many and varied, and may have different job titles within different businesses.

Career Planning

Planning is an integral part of career development. For career success to be achieved, individuals will have to get involved in a process of defining their career goal, establishing means to achieve them and continually appraising their performance. It is not uncommon for external agencies to get involved in an individual career planning process; however, the starting point is the individual.

Individual roles

The changing work environment emphasizes that individuals self-manage their careers. Career moves in the travel and tourism industry are found to be predominantly self-directed, so the role of individuals in shaping and developing their career within the industry cannot be overemphasized. A number of theories have been utilized to analyse the individual in career development; one of the more prominent theories refers to 'self-concept', which denotes the aggregate of attitudes, beliefs and values about an individual in relation to his environment. Jersild (1960 in Pietrofesa and Splete, 1975, p. 12) submits that the self 'is a person's inner world. It is a composite of a person's thoughts and feelings, strivings and hopes, fears and fantasies, his view of what he is, what he has been, what he might become, and his attitudes pertaining to his worth.'

The genuine starting point of an enjoyable and successful career lies within the individual's ability to hold a good knowledge of his/her own 'self' in terms of skill, interests, preferences and disposition. All these have a major influence on individual aspirations, setting career objectives and goal acquisition.

Aspirations and expectations

Personality plays a strong role in career aspirations, acting as a driving force in determining individual goals (both long- and short-term), the length of time spent on attaining goals and how each goal will be achieved. Traditional goal-setting theory suggests that the individual should have a long-term goal in mind (such as a managerial role in his/her organization), and this goal should be achieved by the attainment of smaller, short-term goals (for instance, progression to a slightly more senior role than his/her current position).

A number of studies have been conducted in the area of career aspiration and expectation of tourism (and allied subjects) students (see Jenkins, 2001; Hjalager, 2003; Akis and Oztin, 2007). It is not uncommon for students to build their aspirations on unachievable career paths within the industry. Factors that may influence the level of individual realistic aspirations include socio-economic status, value, ability to perform perceived roles and measured intelligence (Pietrofesa and Splete, 1975). It is important that individuals have realistic and attainable goal within an appropriately measured time frame. Individuals with low aspirations are also relatively common. This again is highly influenced by personality, social learning and environmental influences. Through an educated and thorough examination of career prospects, these individuals should be able to understand and appreciate the possibilities of their own futures.

Mobility

Career mobility (when examined as a concept and research focus) can help to provide a better understanding of how individuals make use of the labour market. It also helps to provide the knowledge needed to reach a particular post in a given industry. It may also provide scope into the variety of tasks to be undertaken prior to starting work (see Ladkin and Juwaheer, 2000 for detail). In this chapter, we consider mobility as a strategy (adoptable by an individual aspiring to develop his or her career). Our focus is particularly on job mobility. However, applicants must also consider the other categories of labour mobility. These include:

- occupational mobility;
- inter-industry mobility; and
- geographical mobility.

Due to the industry's fragmented nature, career mobility is commonplace (Ayres, 2006). Mobility in this sense simply denotes the willingness and ability of an individual to make use of the labour market to optimize his/her career prospects. This task must be undertaken while bearing in mind his/her stock of productive skills and technical knowledge. According to Tuma's (1976, in Riley *et al.*, 2002) Reward–Resource Model, individuals seek to ensure that their stock of productive skills and technical knowledge

---

is proportional to their job reward; assuming that individuals have unrestricted opportunity to balance their resources and the reward for their job. Although some individuals may have restricted opportunities (such as lack of appropriate qualifications, lack of adequate skills, limited immigration status, etc.), mobility will always be an option.

McKercher *et al.* (1995 in Ayres, 2006) pointed out that career progression could be enhanced by the individual's willingness to change employers as well as being geographically mobile. It is safe to say that individuals with relevant stock of productive skills and technical knowledge (who are also willing to move to any geographical location) are likely to be able to negotiate a better deal on working conditions, pay and possibly position for themselves.

When making a decision to change employment, Riley *et al.* (2002) suggest that individuals should employ a cost–benefit evaluation. Their suggestion is in line with the guideline provided by Adam Smith in 1776. An individual changing his/her job must put into consideration the following points:

- the agreeableness or disagreeableness of the employment, the hardship involved and the honourableness or dishonourableness of the employment;
- the difficulty and expense of learning;
- the constancy and security of employment;
- the trust reposed in those who perform the job; and
- the probability of success in the job.

Planning for success

Acknowledgement of one's goals is the first step to successful career-orientated goal-setting. However, establishing these goals is far more difficult. Common goal-setting theory states that the individual will be far more successful with a realistic and sustainable plan, hence the phrase 'failing to plan is planning to fail'. Such plans, alongside important objectives, must also take into account goal-manoeuvrability and unforeseen circumstances. A good start for any goal-setting plan is to adopt the SMART approach. This commonly used acronym has been applied to many aspects of goal-attainment, and will be used to establish a successful plan in career development. 'SMART' stands for Specificity, Measurability, Achievability, Relevance and Time specificity. Career development, like any other project in life, requires an individual to set goals, objectives and/or targets; as a matter of fact, it should be the starting point. All the characteristics mentioned above are applicable to setting career goals and targets. Individual aspirations no doubt inform his/her career goals but people's career objectives/targets need to be well defined and focused.

An individual who sets a goal of becoming a successful practitioner in the travel trade in the next 10 years has not succeeded in charting a well-defined course for himself or herself. While there is time specificity to this, in the first place, it simply means he or she could become anything in the industry in the next 10 years – this is leaving things to chances rather than knowing exactly what to pursue. In the second place, it will be right to question the yardstick used in measuring 'successful practitioner'. In setting objectives and target, an individual should first look inward at self (as discussed above), consider his or her strengths and weaknesses, fears and hopes, likes and dislikes to determine what he or she can achieve. Then objectives based on this assessment should be set stating specifically what is to be achieved within a given time frame with corresponding success criteria bearing currency and relevance in mind. For example, it might be useful to draw a graphic picture of the number of positions, with time frame, to pass through to become an operations manager in air transport catering logistics. This type of target should be monitored and revised when necessary and if possible can be discussed with the employer.

Role of employer

It will be merely stating the obvious to say that organizations always want to recruit and retain employees with requisite skills. But it may not be so apparent to some applicants that organizations sometimes support their staff to develop their careers in order to achieve the objectives of attracting and retaining skilful workers. The tight labour market in most developed countries dictates organizations to attract, motivate and retain employees, and one way of meeting the challenge is to support employees to plan and develop their careers, and increase their career satisfaction (Barnett and Bradley, 2007). Organizational career management and organizational sponsorship are names given to the support offered within career development. This could take the form of programmes, projects, processes and assistance that are geared towards developing employees' careers. It is not uncommon for employers to ask potential employees about their career plans during interview sessions. It is also a common feature of the recruitment process for organizations to specify what role they will play in the career development of an individual; this may be through training, continuing professional development (CPD) and support to undertake further and higher education. Whatever form it takes, some employers prefer to see the written plan with associated action to be taken within a stipulated time. In some organizations, this is a continuous activity that is reviewed annually, referred to as appraisals (for further explanation on appraisals, see Chapter 3, this volume).

Career Strategies

Riley *et al.* (2002) refer to career strategies as tactical manoeuvres employed by individuals in ensuring advancement in their career. In this chapter, career strategies are considered through a discussion about employment procedures, gaining and using qualifications and mobility.

Some people find it hard getting their dream job simply because they have not taken time to understand and master the techniques involved in searching for jobs. This section explores techniques involved in searching for and securing desired employment. Issues explored here include establishing first contact, writing applications and curriculum vitae, attending interviews and assessment centres, and aptitude/psychometric tests.

Information search

The very first thing to do in starting a new career or changing job is to research opportunities that are available in your chosen industry or sector that will help in achieving your objectives. Information is powerful; acquisition or lack of a piece of information may determine your getting a job or not. While there is a wide range of

---

sources of information, it is worth noting that it is quality that matters, not quantity. Searching the right source and the right item will go a long way in helping to prepare your way into a career or up the ladder. Stumpf *et al.* (1983 in Riley *et al.*, 2002) identified six elements of information search:

- **The source of the information:** For example, employment fairs, Internet, job centres and newspapers; it must be noted that the type of post sought will to a very large extent determine the source of information. For instance, one is not likely to find job information for a travel operations manager of a multinational tour operating firm in the window of a corner shop.
- **The method of exploration:** This involves tactics employed in the search, comprising timing (daily, weekly or fortnightly) and networking (newsletter, mailshot, career fairs and friends and family).
- **The amount and scope of information required:** The type of position sought will determine the breadth and depth of information an individual may need to seek and process. For instance, an individual applying for the position of regional customer service manager will need to search more broadly than an entry-level range.
- **Individual commitment on the search process:** This has to do with an individual's motivation and aspiration. The role of commitment goes a long way in the achievement of goals in human endeavour.
- **Individual's confidence regarding the success of the job search:** It is about having a sense of searching the right sources and possessing the pertinent qualities required for the type of position sought.
- **The stress of the search process:** This is another factor that has a vital relationship with individual personality and motivation. A person who is not about to give up until his/her goals are achieved is not likely to feel stressed by the search process.

There are a large number of specialist web sites which specialize in advertising travel jobs (e.g. www.traveljobsearch.com), as well as trade publications which feature vacancies (e.g. www.travelweekly.co.uk) and specialist recruitment agencies who are often recruited to find or headhunt for senior management roles.

In order for the information search process to be worthwhile, the information gathered needs to be processed and put to use. For instance, job requirements must be matched with applicants' situation and qualification, so businesses increasingly include the person specifications with the job details.

The job advertisement

Job advertisements tend to try to attract interest through eye-catching titles and exciting content. To get a really good understanding of what the job is, it is best to get the job description and person specification. This example advertisement illustrates this point well. It does not make the job title or role clear, but it does sound exciting, and certainly worth finding out more details.

Exciting opportunity for creative travel experts!
Do you love travel? Do you want to see the world?
Our exciting new independent travel agency is seeking an enthusiastic and motivated business travel consultant to work with existing and new clients. A passion for the job, combined with a total commitment to providing the highest levels of customer

G. Povey and A. Oriade

service, is essential. If you think you can add value to our existing team then we will offer you a competitive salary and excellent prospects, with generous holiday and discounted travel.

Call us today!

Applying for a new position: establishing first contact

For many applicants, applying for a new position is a very scary process. It is important that we acknowledge our strengths and abilities. Successful applications are those who stand out for the right reasons. A key aspect of the job application is the package that prospective employees send to the employer, either in response to a job advertisement or speculatively, on the hopes that they are looking for new staff. This package is essentially a personal advertising brochure, and its contents and format form the first impression made with the organization. The two key components are the curriculum vitae (CV) and the application letter.

Curriculum vitae

A curriculum vitae is very much a personal brochure. It is the document that sells an individual to the rest of the world. It is the first communication that the prospective employer will see. It is generally considered that a recruiter scans each CV for 30 seconds before making the initial screening, which does not give the candidate very long to make that all-important first impression. The contents of the CV are much debated but essentially there are some key considerations. The CV needs to highlight the applicant's skills and give some explanation of evidence used in the candidate's self-evaluation.

CASE STUDY AND ACTIVITY: EXAMPLE OF A CURRICULUM VITAE

Questions

Imagine that you are recruiting assistant chalet staff for your company's operations at a ski resort in France. Your job advertisement asked prospective candidates to send their CV for consideration. Your company does not use application forms. The key roles outlined in the job description for the chalet staff are cooking and serving food to the guests and keeping the chalet clean. Key skills include the ability to cook a dinner party for a minimum of 12 people, being confident and independent with a strong desire to live in another culture away from home and family. The successful candidates will also have to drive to the local town to get the supplies for their chalet. They need to be organized, and be able to manage a chalet budget. The CV below has been sent to you for consideration.

1. Is it easy to see whether this is a suitable applicant? How readily can you spot the information you need? How can this CV be improved?

After answering this question please turn to p. 25 for some hints.

2. How does your own CV stand up to scrutiny?

Continued

Jane Doe
22 Wonderful Close
Miracletown
MT3 3AA
01837 99878
doe-eyed-goddess@theinternet.com

Profile
A Tour Operations Management Student who is keen to find a position as a Chalet Slave. Reliable, trustworthy, numerate and meticulous. Worked for Wellknown Hotel Group last summer and gained good understanding of what is required in housekeeping, and food service departments. Able to work on own initiativce or as a part of a team and can deal competently with admministrative duties.

Date of Birth: 12th June 1988
Marital Status: Single
Driving License: Full clean UK

Work Experience
2007-2008 General Worker, Wellknown Hotel, Miracletown – Full-time summer job. Assisted in various duties as needed by the managers including bar, restaurant and housekeeping. Full time.

2005 -7 Waitress, The Inn, Miracletown – Part time
Waiting on the tables in the restaurant and bar, for normal dinning, parties and weddings.

2003 – 4 Checkout Operator – The Miraclemart – Part time

Education
1994-2004 Miracletown High School
9 GCSE's
Mathematics B Chemistry C
Physics C Food Technology A
Geography C IT C
English Language B French A
Spanish A

3 GCSE A levels
Home Economics A
French C
Spanish C

2005-2008 University of Miracletown

BA(hons) Travel Operations Management

Interests
I regularly run, and enjoy snow boarding and skiing. My other hobbies are going to the cinema, and socializing with my friends. I also enjoy reading and watching television. At University I ran a charity quiz which raised £5000.

Referees:
Ghislaine Povey University of Miracletown, Library Road, Magicshire.
Ade Oriade, Wellknown Hotel, Comfortable Street, Miracletown.

Continued

CV question hints

- This CV needs to be much better organized.
- Jane Doe needs to use her computer skills to make it look much smarter using bold and including tables to organize her information.
- She needs to make a number of her skills more explicit; for example, to work as a waitress in a restaurant or hotel she must have a basic food hygiene certificate, which is not listed on the CV. She also fails to highlight her linguistic skills – she has 2 A levels in languages, and also makes no reference to her cooking abilities – yet she has an A level in home economics.
- Her personal interests also make her sound dull – it is generally considered best not to include activities that most normal humans do, such as socializing with friends, reading and watching television. Their inclusion detracts from the really good aspects such as the raising money for charity which would benefit from expansion.
- It would be a good idea for her to have stated what the relationship between her referees and herself was.
- Jane also needs to ensure that she has used a spellcheck.

More controversial points are:

Should she also consider changing her e-mail address? 'doe-eyed-goddess@theinternet.com' may be great for flirting in chat rooms, but she should consider whether it is the image she wants to project to her prospective employer. 'janedoe@theinternet.com' is much more professional.

Should she have included age and marital status? Some critics say that now that there are anti-ageism laws, it is wrong to include age, and that it is against equal opportunities to state personal circumstances such as marital status, as these should be irrelevant.

Application letter

When applying for any post, a CV needs to be accompanied by a letter. This letter is there for several reasons:

- It allows for inclusion of information not in the CV, and draws the employer's attention to the applicant's personal qualities
- It provides the prospective employer the chance to see the candidate's ability to write a lucid, coherent letter. This showcases your communication abilities.
- It helps to highlight key aspects of the CV and sell the applicant's strongest features.

The application letter is essentially a business letter, and it follows a logical structure, as set out in Table 2.1 below.

The format of the letter is, in the travel operations industry, best kept reasonably formal and conservative. The letter should be word-processed and printed on good quality paper. When writing the letter, consider who will be reading it. Use a font which is simple, professional in appearance and easy to read.

A sample application letter format is outlined in Fig. 2.1.

Table 2.1. The structure of an application letter.

Component	Description
The introduction	Details the job you are applying for (or seeking, if this is a speculative approach), and in what circumstances you are writing (is it purely speculation? Did someone suggest you write? Are you responding to a job advertisement?).
The main body	This is where you can sell yourself to the employer. It is important to include all the information needed in two or three short, hard-hitting paragraphs.
	• Outline why you want the job and why you wish to move from your present employer
	• Accentuate the key reasons why you are suitable for this particular post and emphasize your key skills
	• Highlight the personal qualities that you would bring to the role
	• Respond to clues about the challenges faced by the successful applicant in the job advertisement and description
The conclusion	This needs to pull the letter together, leaving the recruiter with a memorable, affirmative impression of you.
	Pick up each of the strands you developed in the main body where you sell yourself.
	Refer to enclosed documents such as your CV and copies of qualifications or testimonials.
	End with a statement which invites the reader to contact you for further information if you need it.

Activity

Find an advertisement for a position to which you aspire. Read the advertisement and job description. Write an application letter for that job, referring to the skills self-audit which you have undertaken earlier in this chapter and rewrite your CV to accompany it.

The interview

There are different forms of interview processes, all dependent on the nature of the job and how necessary skills are most appropriately assessed. However, preparation for each interview style can be undertaken relatively similarly, as demonstrated in the phases of the interview preparation model (Fig. 2.2).

Aptitude/psychometrics

Aptitude or psychometric tests can appear to be intimidating; however, in reality, they are simply ways for companies to ensure that they get the employee who is best suited to the company and, moreover, the position for which they have a vacancy. From an applicant's point of view, it is worth remembering that failure to meet criteria is not simply a matter of the individual performing insufficiently; failing such a test may also indicate that the job is simply not suited to that individual, and thus that person is saved from the harrowing experience of being unhappy and

G. Povey and A. Oriade

Your home address
Your telephone number
Your e-mail address
Today's date

Name of recruiter
Job title of recipient
Name of organization
Address of organization

Re: Title of job you are applying for

Introductory paragraph: this paragraph states what position you are applying for, and where you learned about the opportunity.

Main body paragraph 1: here you need to explain the reason you are interested in this post, and/or why you want to work for their organization. You need to show that you know what the role entails and that you can offer the employer the skills that they need to fulfil the job.

Main body paragraph 2: outline why the employer needs to interview you. Include references to your CV and to specific, relevant qualifications that make you suitable for the post.

Conclusion paragraph: Conclude with a positive image of yourself and what you have to offer. Mention to the employer any dates that you are not available for interview. State that you would be happy for the employer to contact you for more information. Refer to any enclosures as outlined above.

Yours sincerely

Your handwritten Signature

Your name (typed)

Enclosures: List enclosures here.

Fig. 2.1. Format of a typical application letter.

unsuccessful at work. Examples of psychometric tests are the Myers-Briggs Type Indicator and the Belbin Teamwork Role Indicator (discussed later in this chapter). Tests of this nature are also designed to detect guess work. Therefore, it is pointless to offer an answer which one believes will impress the employer. Candidates can, however, score better on some of these tests if adequate preparation is made and relevant experience acquired. It is now possible for prospective employees to practise aptitude/psychometric tests online. University or college careers team may also be able to help students to practise.

Assessment centres

Assessment centres are commonly used during graduate employment procedures, aiming to select the values of the candidate to the values of an organization. Organizations often aim to test a range of skills in an assessment centre. They are often used to test a set of skills which cannot be determined by talking to and asking a candidate a set of questions in under 30–50 minutes of an interview (or less in some cases). Sometimes the assessment centre precedes the main interview or is incorporated within the interview phase in the form of aptitude/psychometric tests, group activities and/or oral presentations. There is often (and quite naturally expected) the danger of applicants trying to outshine one another, which can often lead to the individual's detriment; it must be noted that candidates are assessed

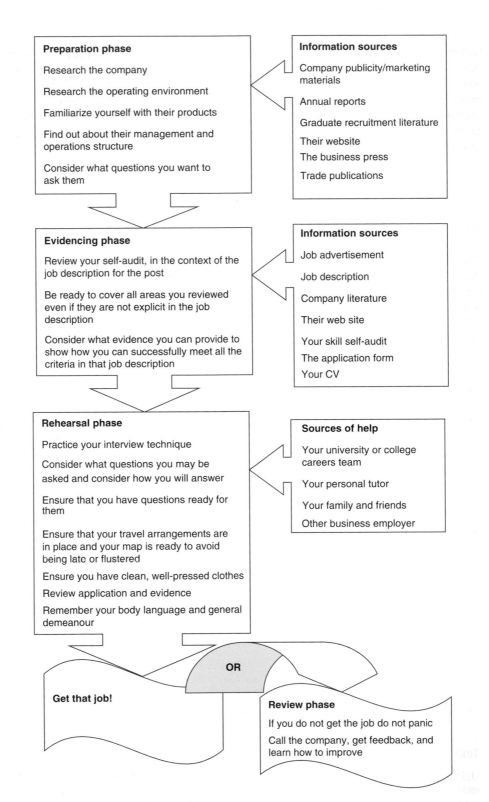

Preparation phase

Research the company

Research the operating environment

Familiarize yourself with their products

Find out about their management and operations structure

Consider what questions you want to ask them

Information sources

Company publicity/marketing materials

Annual reports

Graduate recruitment literature

Their website

The business press

Trade publications

Evidencing phase

Review your self-audit, in the context of the job description for the post

Be ready to cover all areas you reviewed even if they are not explicit in the job description

Consider what evidence you can provide to show how you can successfully meet all the criteria in that job description

Information sources

Job advertisement

Job description

Company literature

Their web site

Your skill self-audit

The application form

Your CV

Rehearsal phase

Practice your interview technique

Consider what questions you may be asked and consider how you will answer

Ensure that you have questions ready for them

Ensure that your travel arrangements are in place and your map is ready to avoid being late or flustered

Ensure you have clean, well-pressed clothes

Review application and evidence

Remember your body language and general demeanour

Sources of help

Your university or college careers team

Your personal tutor

Your family and friends

Other business employer

OR

Get that job!

Review phase

If you do not get the job do not panic

Call the company, get feedback, and learn how to improve

Fig. 2.2. Interview preparation model.

according to criteria predetermined by the organization and not by other applicant's characteristics and skills. The most important thing particularly with a group task is how much an applicant can help the *group* complete a task – his/her ability in persuading and encouraging the team member in accomplishing the objective(s). An assessment centre may last for half a day, a day or two. If not instructed about a particular mode of dressing, it is advised to dress smartly and attend with credentials and writing materials.

PART B: SKILLS FOR TRAVEL OPERATIONS

Introduction

There is a general consensus across all sectors that every role requires a corresponding 'skill set', which enables individuals to carry out their duty efficiently. This section explores various skills required by employers in the travel industry and goes further to suggest how the skills can be assessed and acquired. The skills to be discussed in following sub-sections include personal effectiveness, communication, teamwork, critical thinking and decision making.

Personal Effectiveness

Personal effectiveness is something that we need to develop throughout our working lives. The more effective an individual is, the easier that person's job becomes; hence, promotion is more likely to occur. To improve personal effectiveness one needs to understand one's own strengths and weaknesses. A key tool in this process is the skills self-audit.

Skills self-audit

Self-auditing is an ongoing task. Regardless of which stage an individual is positioned within his/her career, it is always beneficial to reassess and prevent stagnation. There are numerous models that can be used in this endeavour; however, the skills being audited are generally very similar. The challenge is mainly to find a format likeable enough to work with. Some of the books suggested for further reading at the end of this chapter are a source of help with this task. To audit skills successfully, it is important that the individual assesses the long-term goal (where he/she wishes to eventually progress to) and focuses on the skills needed to meet the requirements of that job. The appraisal system in the workplace (Chapter 3, this volume) provides opportunities to identify how these skills will be attained.

Task

Using the skills checklist below (Table 2.2), attempt to evaluate your current position within employment. Tick the boxes that are appropriate to you, and consider how you can evidence these abilities.

Table 2.2. Skills checklist.

Skills self-evaluation of travel operations professionals

	Skill	Home/ education ✓	Work ✓	Social ✓	Evidence
People skills	Teamworking				
	Leadership				
	Interpersonal				
	Empathy with customers/ colleagues				
	Written communication				
	Oral communication				
	Cultural diversity awareness				
	Networking				
General skills	Critical thinking				
	Problem solving				
	Computer literacy				
	Flexibility				
	Dedication				
Self-reliance skills	Confidence				
	Determination				
	Self-marketing skills				
	Initiative				
	Drive and motivation				
	Willingness to learn				
	Time management				
	Organization				
	Emotional intelligence				
Industry-specific skills	Understanding company procedures				
	Awareness of company mission and goals				
	Industry knowledge				
	Use of industry-specific software				
	Foreign languages abilities				
	Skill you identify yourself				
	Skill you identify yourself				

Once the evaluation process is regularly adopted, individuals will be in a strong position to develop themselves and their careers. Whatever model is chosen, it is worth ensuring that evidence is correctly identified, as this will be of interest to prospective employers.

Communication Skills

Communication, both verbal and non-verbal, is largely governed by our culture. In Chapter 10 (this volume), we discuss how our cultural heritage changes our perspectives on any situation. The way in which we communicate is also very culturally specific. We can however adopt strategies that help to ensure that our communication is received as we intended it to be. This skill is crucial to those wishing to enter and maintain employment within the travel and tourism industries, as cultural differences/ beliefs and mannerisms are largely dynamic.

Written communication skills are very important to travel operations professionals. It is fundamentally important that we write grammatically correctly and that, wherever possible, spelling is checked. Several of the books recommended as further reading will ensure that this is undertaken correctly.

The spoken voice

Our verbal skills are also of key importance. In the travel operations industry, we are often in situations where we are dealing with customers who have had bad experiences due to circumstances that are out of our control, such as bad weather delaying flights or the behaviour of other customers. Our use of language and the tone of our voices in these situations are very important. Language that is perceived by the recipient to indicate that you do not care (or, even worse, that is thought to be aggressive) will cause the situation to spiral out of control and even to escalate. Before being put into these situations, the employer should offer training to all employees; employees may also wish to ask for additional training in these areas. Whenever dealing with customers, employees must consider the tone and speed of their speech. This is, again, particularly important within the travel and tourism industry, as staff and customers may not share the same first languages.

Non-verbal communication

Non-verbal communication, which includes dress codes and body language, is also very important. The cleanliness and tidiness of clothes (whether they are a uniform or own choice) are paramount, and slovenliness will clearly indicate a lack of interest. Scruffiness is often perceived as an indicator of low self-esteem, and indicates poor working practices. If staff dress down when dealing with clients, it can be perceived as a lack of respect. If they are overdressed, especially in the context of the holiday situation, they can be perceived as aloof or unapproachable. In circumstances where individuals choose their own clothes, consideration must be paid to the nature of the job, and attire must be chosen accordingly.

Body language

Body language is as every bit as important as verbal communication. Similarly to the language we choose to use, our physical stance can send very clear messages to the people we are dealing with. Aggressive body language can make difficult exchanges spiral out of control, whereas neutral body language can help to soothe the situation. Individuals should also be aware of the perception of body language by local residents when working overseas. It is, for example, considered rude to blow your nose in public in some Middle Eastern cultures, whereas in English culture, it is considered much more polite than sniffling.

Teamwork

Teamwork is important in any industry, but in travel operations management it is vital. There are numerous models that can be used to discuss the concept of teamwork, which assigns different roles to individuals. These can be a useful tool when putting groups of people together in the workplace (to avoid conflict and ensure work is completed), but it must be remembered that environmental factors may affect the way people work together. The travel industry, at all levels, from front line staff to managers, needs to be able to work effectively individually and as part of team.

Decision Making

When we make a decision, we participate in a thought process; we consider a range of alternative actions, weigh up the advantages and disadvantages of each and then logically conclude upon which the best is. Sometimes, in the home and within social surroundings (in not-so-crucial situations), we simply flip a coin to assist us with decisions. However, in our professional lives, we need to be more logical in our approach. Much of what is studied in this book provides information and tools which can be used to aid decision making. This is generally undertaken through what is called 'cognitive bias'.

Types of cognitive bias

If we were all as logical as computers then we would not have any problems with decisions; however, in reality, we all have personalities, and we can all be influenced by extrinsic factors. There are different types of cognitive bias, which are as follows:

- **Attribution bias:** we attribute our success to our abilities and talents but our failures to bad luck and external factors, while attributing the success of others to good luck and external influences, and their failures to their abilities and talents.
- **Groupthink:** we conform to the viewpoints held by the group, sometimes getting a vastly overestimated understanding of our organization's abilities.
- **Source credibility:** we can reject information because of personal bias against the source and thus form a skewed picture of the situation.
- **Wishful thinking:** we tend to want to see things in the best light and can sometimes be blind to problems.

- **Selective search for evidence:** we ignore evidence that we do not like and only give value to that which we do like.
- **Selective perception:** we screen out information that we consider irrelevant.
- **Self-fulfilling prophecy:** we conform to preconceived ideas of what decision some-one in our position would make.

How we approach decision making is very important. We all have unique, individual approaches to the process. Isabel Briggs Myers, a behaviouralist, developed the Myers-Briggs Type Indicator, which is a tool to identify an individual's decision-making processes. It is based on whether individuals tend to *think* or *feel*, whether they are *extrovert* or *introvert*, use *judgement* or *perception* or prefer to use *sense* or *intuition*. How we score on these indices indicates our likelihood to make decisions a certain way. This test provides a useful insight into your skills and is usually available on the Internet at a small cost or in university or college careers centres.

Critical thinking

The art of thinking critically is a process where an individual uses his/her judgement to assess and analyse any given situation or decision. According to Metcalfe (2006), this skill is central to graduates and is what sets them apart from others. He goes on however to state that this is useless unless it is applied in the workplace. Critical thinking is a skill that can be acquired by anyone; however, it may take some practice until you get used to it. Numerous authors have suggested ways that this can be achieved.

A particularly interesting approach is that taken by Eduardo de Bono, who proposes that the use of six differently coloured hats can enhance how we structure thinking, both as an individual and in teamwork. According to de Bono (2006), this approach can encourage creative and lateral thinking, enhance the thought process and speed-up decisions. The hats can be any shape you wish; however, in Fig. 2.3, we have used wizards' 'cones'. This approach forces the participant to think about the situation or problem, and helps to stimulate creativity, enabling us to create a credible solution or generate critical discussion. It helps the thinker to consider the holistic view. Critics of de Bono say that this oversimplifies some aspects of your thinking such as the analysis of data (the remit of the white hat) and objectivity and critique (the remit of the black hat), while overemphasizing areas which are of less use to professionals such as the positive aspects (the remit of the yellow hat) and personal feelings (remit of the red hat). It is, however, a good starting point to develop an awareness of how to think critically.

To use this technique, you need to consider a problem or situation you have to deal with, then, metaphorically (or actually, if you wish to make six coloured hats), put on each hat and note down what your thoughts are from the aspect covered by that hat. You then compare and merge the thoughts generated to develop the solution or see the situation differently.

Questions

Use de Bono's six hats to consider the layout of a CV. Discuss the experience of using this technique with your peer group: was their experience similar to yours?

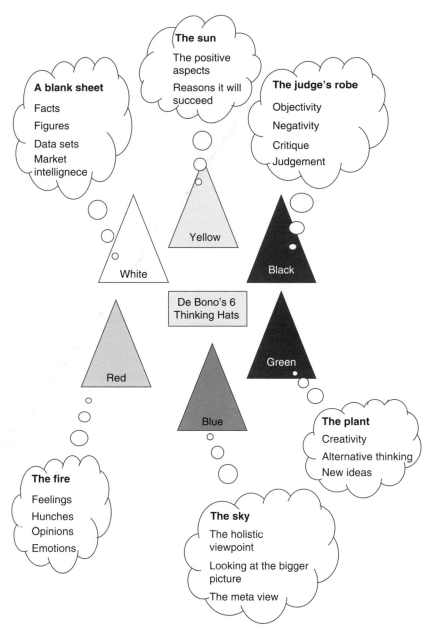

Fig. 2.3. de Bono's six thinking hats. (Adapted from de Bono, 2006.)

Role model adoption

The discussion on career development will not be complete without inclusion of the significance of role model adoption. It is an important element, which many have used to shape their career development process. The identification and adoption of a suitable role model will go a long way in influencing individual career behaviour. It is safe to say that aspiring to take after a successful manager or business entrepreneur will have a positive impact on an individual. There is no doubt that people draw from their bank of memory what they have seen to work for some people in the past when they are about to make important career decisions. Learning through, and about how, others have been successful in their careers in order to educate the younger generation has been the rationale for many research studies and these studies have provided valuable guidelines and suggestions to individuals on how to manage their careers. No experience can be more valuable than first-hand experience.

Stepping into Management

In order to successfully climb the career ladder to step up to management level, we propose that individuals should adopt a barrier-breaking goal-getting strategy. Kroll *et al.* (1970 in Pietrofesa and Splete, 1975, p. 11) submit that:

> Career development is a balancing operation – recognising and meeting the needs of the individual while recognising and responding to outer forces and lifelong process of working out a synthesis between the self and the reality opportunities and limitations of the world.

This statement cannot be truer of the modern-day work environment. Individuals must be able to identify the opportunities and barriers that exist in the work environment, take advantage of their strengths to optimize opportunities and find ways of breaking the barriers in order to reach their goals. Individuals must understand that in trying to make it to the top of their careers within an organization, they are contending with limited resources, ownership interest, aspirations of fellow employees and their own personalities where they need to make changes in their lives; changes in terms of developing realistic aspirations and acquiring new skills (see Fig. 2.4). It is only those employees that break these barriers who will be able to reach their goals.

There are three ways in which individuals step up to management:

- **Progressing through the ranks if an individual entered into an organization as operative staff:** The need to be much more focused and strategic then becomes imperative if the individual must get to the top, for which the adoption of a barrier-breaking goal-getting strategy becomes essential.
- **Progression through management trainee programme:** This option is only open to individuals with qualification up to degree level; sometimes higher qualifications are given consideration. Organizations set up many schemes that enable people with certain qualifications to join a fast-track route to management positions. Most forward-looking organizations go down this route of attracting and recruiting quality employees, and often get involved in the employees' development. It is not uncommon for such companies to demand that individual employees have a comprehensive career plan, which is jointly reviewed by the organization and the employee annually.
- **Transferring to another organization within the sector or industry:** An individual whose career aspiration and goal is not satisfied after a prolonged period of time in a given organization, even with 'organizational sponsorship', needs to look elsewhere. It is worth saying here that due consideration must be given to the points discussed in the mobility section.

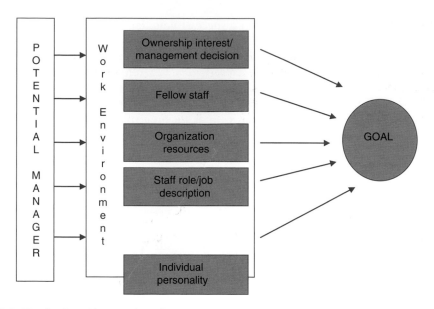

Fig. 2.4. Barrier-breaking goal-getting.

Another avenue involved with stepping up to management is for individuals to set up their own businesses. The travel and tourism industry is a multi-sectorial industry made up of several small- to medium-sized enterprises (SMEs). The set-up cost for some of the businesses, for example an independent travel agency, is not prohibitive compared to small business in other industries. However, any individual looking forward to being self-employed must develop, in addition to the skills stated above, entrepreneurial skills. Many further and higher education institutions teach how to develop these skills. Also, a number of short-term courses are available as CPD run by consultants and training organizations. At some time, schemes are set up by various tiers of government, local, regional, national and supranational, to encourage and support individuals who are interested in setting up their own business particularly in the travel and tourism trade. Interested individuals must be ready to conduct information search that will enable them get support. Support can be available in form of grants, training or mentoring.

Summary

Pursuing a career in the travel industry is not new but has never been given much attention in the past. As the industry is getting bigger and people are starting to realize that tourism is not only a big business but also a business for the serious-minded, there has been a shift in people's disposition to tourism jobs. There has been increase in the demand for skills required to work in the industry because organizations have to protect their investments. One thing that has become clear is that individuals working in the industry need to learn how to manage their careers as competition and the search for quality employees become intense. The secret to having a fulfilled career is in acquiring the industry's sought-after skills and developing strategies to ensure that the individual human capital is commensurably remunerated.

G. Povey and A. Oriade

Further Research

Cottrell, S. (2008) *The Study Skills Handbook*, 3rd edn. Palgrave Macmillan, Hampshire, UK.
De Bono, E. (2006) *de Bono's Thinking Course: Powerful Tools to Transform Your Thinking*. BBC, London.
Goleman, D. (2006) *Emotional Intelligence*. Bantam Books, London.
Metcalfe, M. (2006) *Reading Critically at University*. Sage Publications, London.

Review Questions

1. Which of Belbin's nine team roles most closely relate to the areas of thought which come under de Bono's six Thinking Hats? How does knowing your team role(s) help you to develop your critical thinking?
2. Considering the major features of planning, how does planning aid career development?

References

Akis, R. and Oztin, P. (2007) Career perceptions of undergraduate tourism students: a case study in Turkey. *Journal of Hospitality, Leisure, Sport and Tourism Education* 6(1), 4–17.

Ayres, H. (2006) Career development in tourism and leisure: an exploratory study of the influence of mobility and metoring. *Journal of Hospitality and Tourism Management* 13(2), 113–123.

Barnett, B.R. and Bradley, L. (2007) The impact of organizational support for career development on career satisfaction. *Career Development International* 12(7), 617–636.

Boon, B. (2006) When leisure and work are allies: the case of skiers and the tourist resort hotels. *Career Development International* 11(7), 594–608.

CHME (2001) *Getting Ahead: Graduate Careers in Hospitality Management*. HEFCE, Bristol, UK.

de Bono, E. (2006) *de Bono's Thinking Course: Powerful Tools to Transform Your Thinking*. BBC, London.

Hjalager, A. (2003) Global tourism career? Opportunity and dilemmas facing higher education in tourism. *Journal of Hospitality, Leisure, Sport and Tourism Education* 2(2), 26–38.

Jenkins, A.K. (2001) Making a career of it? Hospitality students' future perspective: an Anglo–Dutch study. *International Journal of Contemporary Hospitality Management* 13(1), 13–20.

Ladkin, A. (2000) Vocational education and food and beverage experience: issues for career development. *International Journal of Contemporary Hospitality Management* 12, 226–233.

Ladkin, A. and Juwaheer, T.D. (2000) The career path of hotel general managers in Mauritius. *International Journal of Contemporary Hospitality Management* 12(2), 119–125.

Metcalfe, M. (2006) *Reading Critically at University*. Sage Publications, London.

Pietrofesa, J.J. and Splete, H. (1975) *Career Development: Theory and Research*. Grune & Stratton, New York.

Riley, M. and Ladkin, A. (1994) Career theory and tourism: the development of a basic analytical framework. *Progress in Tourism, Recreation and Hospitality Management* 6, 225–237.

Riley, M., Ladkin, A. and Szivas, E. (2002) *Tourism Employment: Analysis and Planning*. Channel View Publications, Clevedon, UK.

3 Human Resource Management for Travel and Tourism

Sine Heitmann and Christine Roberts

Objectives of the Chapter

This chapter addresses the nature of human resource management (HRM) theories, processes and concepts in the context of the travel industry and travel organizations. Key topics include theories of motivation and leadership, empowerment of employees, human resources (HR) planning, recruitment and selection, training and development, grievance and discipline as well as key issues such as legislation and labour market realities. The ideas are analysed and discussed in the context of their application and usefulness in practice, supported by a range of different case studies to show the importance of the key concepts for managers in an increasingly competitive and diverse working environment.

At the end of the chapter, students should be able to:

- explain the nature and importance of HRM within travel organizations;
- understand key theories and concepts of HRM; and
- provide guidance for managers within the industry.

Introduction

People are seen as a strategic resource for achieving competitive advantage. Thus, the management of HR is crucial to most medium and large companies, and most key organizations within the sector have large HR departments responsible for looking after employees, from recruitment and training through to grievance and disciplinary procedures. Usually, HR will also manage the organizations' equal opportunities, health and safety, occupational health and other legal requirements. Staff will be well trained in employment law and will help both employees and the employer to follow correct procedures.

HRM used to be called personnel management (in some organizations, it is still referred to as the personnel department); however, the change to HR is about more than just a change of name. Personnel management refers to the old-fashioned, rather inflexible administration of people management, which follows much-defined policies and procedures. Having a very narrow functional outlook, it was often seen to merely be a buffer between the employer and the employees. This resulted in personnel department having a low status and low importance within the business, and therefore lacked credibility. By contrast, HRM is about taking a long-term view of the HR requirements of the business. HR recognizes the importance of individuals to business performance and usually rewards staff well when the business is performing effectively. It recognizes that a competitive advantage can be gained through people and often offers staff greater flexibility, which encourages greater commitment from employees. HRM recognizes organizational structure and supports supervisory and line management positions.

Ultimately the HR department's purpose should be to contribute to the overall business performance through effective HRM and by developing effective staff performance management. Some examples of HRM objectives are:

- management of staffing objectives (future growth of the business, new specialist staff to manage new technology);
- performance objectives (to ensure staff are working well and to address any training needs or disciplinary matters);
- change of management objectives (most organizations have to constantly adapt and change, which can be stressful for employees; the HR department can provide support for staff affected by change); and
- administration objectives (ensuring the business is well supported).

Human Resource Management Cycle

The HRM cycle (Fig. 3.1) outlines the various stages and tasks for any HR department and provides the basis for the structure of the following sections. Starting with recruitment and selection, the key issues involved with these processes are outlined, followed by maintaining the workforce through motivational strategies, and finally, development of the workforce through training strategies.

Human resource planning

In essence, human resource planning (HRP) is about having the right people, with the right skills, in the right place, at the right time, at the right price! HRP is concerned

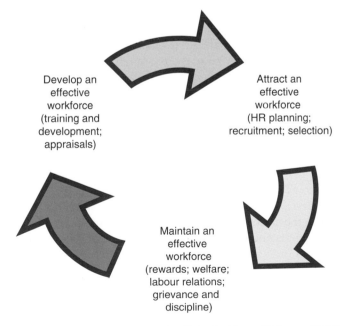

Develop an effective workforce (training and development; appraisals)

Attract an effective workforce (HR planning; recruitment; selection)

Maintain an effective workforce (rewards; welfare; labour relations; grievance and discipline)

Fig. 3.1. Human resource management cycle. (Adapted from Nickson, 2007.)

with the demand and supply of labour and problems arising from the process of reconciling these factors. From this emerge the HR practices of recruitment and selection, training and development needs, rewards, employee relations – thus influencing
each stage in the HRM cycle (see Fig. 3.1). HRP is important as it encourages clear
links between business and human resource plans, enabling organizations to make
more informed judgements. Furthermore, demand and supply can be analysed
through internal and external sources.

HRP should not be seen in isolation as it takes place within the wider environmental, business and societal context and in turn organizational resourcing aspects also
shape the environmental, business and societal context. HRP is an integral part of the
broader process of corporate planning and should be linked to the development of the
organization as a whole, its corporate objectives and the organizational culture and
climate. For example, if it is the main goal of an organization to make profit, too many
staff could increase wage bills while too few staff may result in less profit. In any travel
organization, customer service plays an important role – too few staff may result in
poor customer service and poor staff morale/motivation. Furthermore, suitable people
are needed to present the company, stressing the point that the right skills are needed
in order to provide high customer service (see emotional/aesthetic labour below).

Strategic HRP demonstrates the importance of planning and ensures people are
appropriate for the organizations needs, and that there are links to the mission and
values of the organization. While originally HRP was treated from a quantitative
perspective (how many employees are needed?), it has become more crucial to include
more qualitative aspects (what skills are needed?).

HRP is a strategy for the acquisition, utilization, improvement and preservation
of an enterprise's HR; directed to minimize uncertainty and surprise and to eliminate
mistakes and wastage. It aims to maintain and improve the ability of the organization in achieving corporate objectives through the development of strategies, which
enhance the contribution of HR at all times in the foreseeable future while monitoring and managing the flow of people into, through and out of the organization.
Furthermore, HRP is a systematic and continuous process concerned with: analysing
the needs of the organization (in relation to organizational goals); recognizing and
acting upon the changing external conditions; organizing and implementing systems
and structures to achieve organizational goals; and developing policies to meet long-
and short-term requirements (Rahman and Eldridge, 1998). Thus, HRP deals with
forecasting the future needs of the organization in terms of skills, expertise and
competences, while analysing the availability and supply of people. Furthermore,
HRP is concerned with the drawing up of plans that match supply to demand and
monitoring the implementation of the human resource plan (Armstrong, 2003). The
stages of HRP are outlined in Fig. 3.2.

HRP can involve different aspects: recruitment plans are drawn up in order to
avoid labour shortages; training needs are identified to avoid skill depletion; succession planning is important to avoid managerial shortages, which provides a basis for
the career planning of individual employees; and, finally, industrial relations plans are
drawn up in order to avoid industrial unrest.

Information needed for an effective analysis in each stage comprises: employee
(and the whole workforce) profiles; reasons and rate of labour turnover; demographic changes; changes in local external labour supply; and employee aspirations
and developments, etc. Sources of information for the HRP process can be either

S. Heitmann and C. Roberts

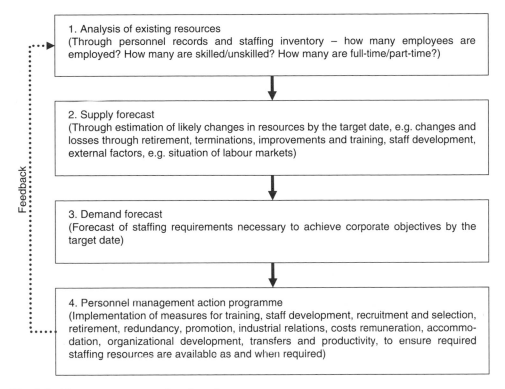

Feedback

1. Analysis of existing resources
(Through personnel records and staffing inventory – how many employees are employed? How many are skilled/unskilled? How many are full-time/part-time?)

2. Supply forecast
(Through estimation of likely changes in resources by the target date, e.g. changes and losses through retirement, terminations, improvements and training, staff development, external factors, e.g. situation of labour markets)

3. Demand forecast
(Forecast of staffing requirements necessary to achieve corporate objectives by the target date)

4. Personnel management action programme
(Implementation of measures for training, staff development, recruitment and selection, retirement, redundancy, promotion, industrial relations, costs remuneration, accommodation, organizational development, transfers and productivity, to ensure required staffing resources are available as and when required)

Fig. 3.2. Human resources planning stages.

internal (staffing tables, skill inventories, composition of workforce) or external (demographic changes, changes in educational system, changes in working structures, competition, government initiatives and legislation, developments in technology; Baum, 2006).

Most tour operators will begin their recruitment process from late autumn for the following summer season and it may last all the way through to the following spring and even longer if not enough quality staff are found. Ski companies will start their recruitment during the summer ready for the winter season. Another potential reason for the recruitment process being drawn out is due to commercial activity. Sometimes a particular resort has sold very well for a tour operator. This has led to more 'beds' being contracted within that resort, subsequently increasing the number of staff needed since the initial intake of new representatives.

Despite the importance of having a long-term perspective in HRP, HRP within the travel industry tends to be rather short term. Possible explanations for this are that both recruitment and redundancy echo the seasonal nature of the industry and that the travel industry is a rather dynamic and turbulent sector with a high labour turnover rate. Furthermore, although the importance of HRP is highlighted, it has to be noted that predicting future events is difficult as extrapolation (taking past events to predict future) is often inappropriate, insufficient records are kept, lack of strategic planning within the industry generally, and it is expensive and time-consuming.

Recruitment and Selection

Recruitment and selection are important aspects of HRM, as poor practices can result in a range of negative impacts on the organization. Productivity and quality can be affected by recruiting the wrong number of people or the wrongly skilled people. Constant recruitment can also cost the organization a significant amount of money. Existing staff can be affected as they are overloaded with work when usual work routines are disrupted, resulting in the possibility of the overall working morale being negatively affected. Recruitment and selection can be a time-consuming process for the manager who could use the time more effectively elsewhere. Finally, the appointee can be negatively affected by unprofessional practices, leading to stress, uncertainty and frustration. Human resource professionals spend a lot of time on recruitment and selection because getting the right people, in an industry that works through people, is a baseline fundamental.

Recruitment

Finding the right staff for a job is a complicated and often lengthy process, especially in larger organizations where budgets have to be signed off and a business case made for recruiting new staff. The process is often affected by the decentralization of the organization. For example, travel agents may allow branch managers to decide when new staff are needed, or in a more centralized organization it may be an area manager who has to make this decision.

Once a post is identified as a need, the right candidates have to be attracted. Not only must they be able to do the job accordingly, but also they need to understand the business and fit the image of the organization. This is a difficult requirement to comply with because of issues surrounding the legal requirements of equal opportunities (discussed later in the section 'Welfare Within the Workplace'). However, if a company such as Club 18–30 is employing staff, there are clearly people who would be better suited to the business culture. A tour operator representative would need to fulfil certain criteria in order to meet the expectations of customers.

Figure 3.3 depicts the different stages of the recruitment and selection process, starting with assessing the needs when a vacancy arises. The three main questions to be answered are:

- What does the job consist of?
- What are the aspects of the job that specify the type of candidate?
- What are the key aspects of the job that the ideal candidate wants to know before applying?

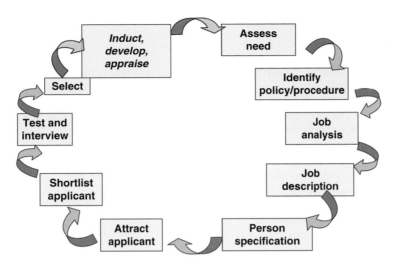

Fig. 3.3. Recruitment and selection process.

The answers to these questions lie in the job analysis, job description and person specification.

Job analysis is the process of collecting, analysing and setting out information about the contents of jobs and provides the basis for the job description and data for recruitment, training, job evaluation and performance management (Nickson, 2007). A job analysis is not necessary every time a vacancy arises, but allows examination of appropriateness for future needs. Any job can be analysed through a variety of methods, such as observation of the job, work diaries, interviews with jobholders, questionnaires and checklists.

The job description is the document that outlines the 'what' elements of the job, such as: purposes of the job; tasks involved; duties and responsibilities; performance of objectives; reporting relationships; and terms and conditions (remuneration, hours of work). It should be a clear and realistic preview of the job and can also be seen as a marketing document in that it also advertises the job.

The person specification, or competency profile, considers the 'who' of the job. It provides a profile of the ideal person for the job and describes personal skills and characteristics, usually under two headings: 'essential' – minimum standard expected, basis for potentially rejecting applicants; and 'desirable' – over and above minimum, basis for selection. There are two useful person specification models: Rodger Seven-point Plan and Fraser Fivefold Framework (Table 3.1).

The job has to be advertised. Possibilities include papers, job centres, specialist magazines, the company web site or on other web sites. Sometimes a recruitment consultant or agency is used to find the right person (often consultants are used for more senior positions and for small businesses with no HR function). Good job advertisements should appeal to the potential candidate, sell the company, sell the job, attract the right staff, have realistic expectations as well as information on salary and benefits and contact details.

Table 3.1. Person specification models.

Rodger Seven-point Plan	Fraser Fivefold Framework
Physical make-up (health, physique, appearance, bearing, speech)	Impact on others (appearance, speech, manner, self-confidence)
Attainments (education, training, experience, degree of success in each)	Acquired knowledge or qualifications (education, training, work experience)
General intelligence (ability to define and solve problems)	Innate abilities (speed of perception, special aptitudes)
Special aptitudes (mechanical, numerical, verbal, drawing, musical, manual)	Motivation (goals, consistency, initiative, practical effectiveness)
Interests (intellectual, practical, social, artistic, physical)	Emotional adjustment (ability to stand up to stress, coping with difficult customers)
Disposition (acceptability, influence, dependability, self-reliance)	
Circumstances (domestic, family, special)	

CASE STUDY: CABIN CREW PERSONNEL SPECIFICATION DOCUMENT

Cabin Crew at CS Airlines
Ref: CCXO4423
Location: Midlands – United Kingdom
Competitive salary, Full-time Temporary

The customers who fly with CS Airlines come from different backgrounds and have high standards of customer service – we like to cater for these demands with the people we recruit to work for us as cabin crew.

So whatever you're doing now, if you're looking for a challenge and an opportunity to provide a high level of customer service, we'd be happy to hear from you.

Our airline staff, and particularly our cabin crew, are the face and personality of our business. You will play a vital role in establishing how we're perceived by the millions of customer CS Airlines carries around the world every year.

At the moment we're looking for enthusiastic people to join our team for Summer 2009. You'll join us on a seasonal basis on a fixed term contract running from March until the middle of November.

Ideally, you should have a high level of personal presentation, with superb communication skills and unlimited energy and motivation. You should be flexible, attentive to individual customer needs and prepared to work hard, and of course you should have a great personality.

To join us, you must also be:

- Aged 18 or over
- Between 5'2" (1.58 m) and 6'3" (1.9 m) in height
- Physically fit
- Able to swim 25m
- Able to fit comfortably into a crew seat without modification
- Educated to GCSE level or equivalent, including Maths and English at grade C or above
- Demonstrable customer service experience working with a diverse range of customers' profiles

Continued

S. Heitmann and C. Roberts

- Excellent communication skills
- Articulate with a good sense of humour and an open and warm personality
- Strong team player
- Flexibility to work weekends, bank holidays and a variety of hours including night duties
- In possession of a valid UK or EEA passport permitting unrestricted travel worldwide
- Entitled to live and work in the UK indefinitely

What can we offer you in return?

In addition to a competitive basic salary, you'll receive flight allowances and sales commission on all goods sold onboard. Other benefits include discounted travel opportunities (including for your friends and family), free car parking, extensive four week training (free, unlike our competitors), uniform and dry cleaning vouchers as well as on-board meals.

And as all our cabin crew will testify, this is not just a job – you will join a unique working environment and experience our 'Top Notch' culture!

Our flights depart seven days a week, mornings and evenings, so you could be flying to Zante at 8 o'clock on a Monday morning or to Lanzarote at 10 o'clock on a Friday night. But you'll have plenty of spare time during the week; you can go shopping when others are working, socialize with friends at lunchtime or visit grandma for tea and crumpets.

When your friends are getting up at the same old time, wondering what to wear and preparing to battle through the rush hour, you could already be well on your way to any number of destinations; for you, the journey to work will have been quick and easy, outside the daily rush.

Life is always exciting when you work as cabin crew and you'll make new friends for life. You'll meet different customers every day and the skills you'll learn in training will enable you to deal confidently with the variety of situations that you'll encounter.

Apply now – fly further with CS Airlines!

Questions

1. Highlight the skills and characteristics according to the model by Roger or Fraser (Table 3.1).
2. What type of person is CS Airlines trying to attract?

Selection

As with recruitment, the approach to selection will reflect the organizations' strategy and philosophy towards the management of people. The aim of selection is to differentiate between the candidates and to predict as far as possible their future performance at work, to ensure the right people are chosen for the job. Decisions are not necessarily based on the qualifications of a person but on the person's attitude and approach to the job. The person specification (as outlined above) can help to see if people have the right attributes for the role. There are several selection methods a company can choose from, and depending on the job different people are involved in assessing potential candidates (see Table 3.2)

Table 3.2. Selection methods and interviews.

Potential selection methods	Staff involved at interviews
(Un)structured interviews	Line Manager and HR staff
Intelligence and personality testing	Line Manager, Senior Manager and HR
Work sampling	Line Manager and Senior Manager
Assessment centres (e.g. team-working exercises)	Line Manager, Functional Manager and HR
	Recruitment Consultant and Line Manager
Desk exercise (letter writing, calculations)	Recruitment Consultant, Line Manager and HR
	Recruitment Consultant, Line Manager and Functional Manager
Presentations	
Group interviews	

Questions

1. Which one of these methods have you experienced? What would you consider to be the advantages and disadvantages of each?
2. What skills are being tested with each of these methods?

HR departments usually offer training for anyone involved in recruitment. Most organizations require each interview to be documented to ensure equal opportunities have been adhered to.

Some of the most competitive interview processes within the travel industry exist within airlines and overseas tour operators, both of which receive tens of thousands of applications each year. The type of person likely to be able to thrive as either an air stewardess or holiday representative will be quite specific as these are some of the most demanding customer-facing roles in any industry. Subsequently, the interview process is designed to identify those with potential while putting off time wasters.

Group interviews normally involve between 20 and 50 interviewees all being scrutinized at the same time. They will be graded on their appearance, personality, how they interact with the rest of the group as well as by their performance in predetermined tasks such as public speaking, selling and sometimes entertainment. It is normal that group interview lasts anything from 3 to 6 hours with those interviewees not impressing early on being asked to leave midway through the session.

CASE STUDY: SC TOUR OPERATOR RECRUITMENT PROCESS

SC Tour Operator is based in the West Midlands and its operation involves all-inclusive holidays in the Mediterranean region. The organization employs 35 full-time members of staff and 80 part-time staff – this includes office and administration staff as well as tour representatives in the destinations.

Last year a number of changes where introduced to aid recruitment. This was to ensure that the right people were selected and to reduce the turnover of staff. It started with the creation of an internal and external web site that advertised available positions as well as giving access to role profiles and online application. Initial

Continued

S. Heitmann and C. Roberts

competencies are tested on the system through an online questionnaire and real-life scenarios before an application is submitted to the correct person. This online system tests, for example, general interest, educational qualifications and problem-solving skills.

For external applicants, the test is followed up with an initial telephone screening. Here personality and communication skills are assessed as well as motivation and the ability to deal with difficult situations with customers and staff. If successful, all candidates will then be called into the head office for a one-to-one interview. In this interview identical questions will be asked to all people applying for the same position; this will ensure consistency across all candidates. It also ensures that all interviews can be reviewed in a fair way.

As the process is intense, it enables the recruiting manager to make the right decision. There is also the opportunity to give good-quality feedback to all applicants, as well as being the initial stage of a training and development programme for the successful candidate going forward. It has also aided the reduction of staff turnover.

Looking good, sounding right

Recently, the concepts of 'aesthetic labour' and 'emotional labour' have been added to the issues surrounding recruitment and selection. While aesthetic labour is concerned with the way an employee represents him/herself, emotional labour involves the requirement of displaying certain emotions as part of their job. There is an apparent trend among recruiters to select staff who display abilities to present themselves in a way that 'looks good' or 'sounds right' to the customers, with less emphasis being placed on experience and technical skills. These skills that are sought by companies with a high customer service focus include body language, dress sense, style and grooming as well as voice and accent and can be classified as 'soft skills'.

CASE STUDY: EMOTIONAL AND AESTHETIC LABOUR

Anne: Aesthetic labour – that is exactly what the tourism/hospitality industry is all about and I agree with the points that were made. If an organization has a particular corporate image then the employees on the front line should reflect that image. I don't necessarily think that this is based on looks alone, I think that it is more to do with personal presentation and personality. If you are promoting a product you are in essence selling yourself. If people do not warm to you they will not buy the product or will not return. For example, when I was a resort manager overseas, if I had a hotel that had predominantly young single groups of men then I would put my best looking, liveliest female rep in there. Some people may see that as discrimination towards the other reps but that is the nature of the business I'm afraid and ensured that I hit my sales targets. It was also expected by the guests who had bought into the brand image that the company was projecting at the point of sale. Similarly, managing a team of cabin crew, I expect them to look and behave a certain way. If one of my crew members turns up for work with ladders in her tights, no make up

Continued

---

and her hair all over the place she will be sent home. I absolutely agree that employees should be expected to look and act a certain way when dealing with members of the paying public.

Mary: I think in the travel industry emotional skills are really important as staff must have the ability to communicate and build rapport with the customer. They also need to be able to adapt their style of communication depending on the customer and the situation.

I do think it is also important to take people with academic skills as particularly now the industry is more competitive so there is a need for staff to be educated and knowledgeable on their trade.

I personally feel it's important to get a balance between the both as things like personal appearance are important, however these can be worked on. Also the company plays a part in developing the individual's skills to build on their knowledge. However the individual must be passionate about the job and this is also down to their personality.

Amanda: Whilst I think it is totally wrong to recruit on the grounds of how a person looks or sounds, I think it is important in any customer facing industry to employ people with 'emotional skills'. Social and interpersonal skills are essential for those dealing with customers.

Remembering back to a few years ago, I had the impression that all travel agents, reps and cabin crew were tall, blonde, young, pretty women. I think that this may have been the case many, many years ago and the impression stuck with me

Fig. 3.4. Tour representative.

Continued

S. Heitmann and C. Roberts

even though in reality it had changed. I also recall a manager talking about a member of staff not being suited to a 'well off/well travelled' shop as she was not 'posh enough'.

Today, although the aesthetics of our front line staff are still important, i.e. smartly dressed, neat and tidy appearance and use of appropriate language, it is far more important to be responsive to customers and be able to get on their level, be courteous and understand their needs. Personality and presence is very important for front line staff in any industry and therefore I don't believe it is wrong to employ people on that basis so long as skills are also taken into account.

Finally, I find Anne's strategy of using the looks of a person over their ability to do a job quite scary and wonder how I would feel if I were the person that was never chosen because I'm not pretty enough.

Questions

1. Reading the above passage, who do you agree with most and why – Anne, Mary or Amanda?

2. Looking at the picture above (Fig. 3.4), what visual messages is it conveying?

3. How important do you consider the aspects of emotional and aesthetic labour with regard to a tour representative, tour guide, travel agency staff, air hostess, manager, taxi/bus driver, administrator or a training provider?

4. In the advertisement above, how many aspects can you identify that match the idea of emotional and aesthetic labour?

5. What issues regarding potential discrimination may occur?

Following from the recruitment and selection process (Fig. 3.3), the HR manager should now be able to match the right candidate to the job. Once an employee is selected, the induction process begins. Ideally, the appointee stays with the company. If a new vacancy arises, the cycle/process starts again.

Motivation

Motivation studies are essentially concerned with answering questions such as the following:

- Why do people do what they do?
- Why do people choose a particular course of action in preference to others?
- Why do they continue with a chosen action, over a long period, and in the face of difficulties and problems?

Motivation is thus not only concerned with that which energizes human behaviour, but also with what directs and channels such behaviour and how this behaviour can be maintained over a longer period of time. The underlying concept of motivation is the internal driving force within individuals, which encourages them to strive to achieve certain goals in order to satisfy their needs and/or expectations (Mullins, 2007). Many studies have investigated motivation within the workplace, but whether considering work-related studies on motivation or examples from the original field of psychology, the study of motivation requires the same general characteristics to be taken into account.

Theories of motivation

Motivation is typified as an individual phenomenon (every person is unique), but most theories allow for this uniqueness to be demonstrated. Motivation is described as intentional, goal-directed behaviour that is assumed to be under the worker's control; behaviours that are influenced by motivation are seen as choices of action. Furthermore, motivation is multifaceted, as two factors are important: first, that which gets people activated (arousal); and second, the force of an individual to engage in a desired behaviour (direction or choice of behaviour). Despite some apparent difficulties with the concept of motivation, the main purpose of motivational theories is to predict behaviour, as motivation is not the behaviour itself, and is not performance; motivation concerns action, and the internal and external forces which influence a person's choice of action.

A simple threefold division of motivators is between extrinsic, intrinsic and social factors. Economic rewards, or tangible rewards, are the instrumental orientation to work (pay, fringe benefits, pension rights, material goods, security). As more intangible rewards, intrinsic rewards are the personal orientation (derived from nature of work itself, interest in job, personal growth and development) and social relationships are the relational orientation (through friendships, group working, desire for affiliation, status, dependency) to work.

More advanced theories on motivation within academic research can be divided into two sets of theories: content theories explain specific things that actually motivate an individual at work. These theories are concerned with identifying people's needs and their relative strengths, and the goals they pursue in order to satisfy those needs. Content theories place emphasis on the nature of needs and what motivates people. Process theories in turn attempt to identify the relationship among the dynamic variables which impact motivation. These theories are concerned more with how behaviour is initiated, directed and sustained. Process theories place emphasis on the actual process of motivation. However, for the purpose of this chapter we are going to cover the content theories in more detail as these are most commonly referred to.

Maslow's hierarchy of needs

One of the most prominent motivational theories is Maslow's hierarchy of needs (Fig. 3.5). His theory is based on the belief that people are 'wanting beings' who want more, and what they want depends on what they already have. From this basis he established a pyramid or the hierarchy of needs including five stages.

At the bottom are the physiological needs that have to be met (food, water, air, sleep, shelter, sex). The second stage includes safety needs (security, stability, protection from danger/deprivation, need for predictability and orderliness). Third, social needs such as love, affection and belongingness have to be met. The fourth stage includes esteem needs (self-esteem, self-respect, prestige, status), while the final, fifth stage is concerned with meeting self-actualization needs (growth, advancement, creativity). Maslow's hierarchy of needs assumes that once a lower-order need is satisfied, individuals strive to satisfy a higher-order need, i.e. physiological needs have to be met first before an individual strives to meet safety or social needs, or only once physiological, safety and social needs are met can a person aim to get self-esteem or self-actualization. Of course, the hierarchy has been criticized for

S. Heitmann and C. Roberts

Fig. 3.5. Maslow's hierarchy of needs. (Adapted from Mullins, 2007.)

being too simplified as there is not necessarily a fixed order and that lower level need not necessarily be fully satisfied before subsequent need arises. To some individuals, self-esteem can be more important than love, while creative people may lack satisfaction of more basic needs (think of the 'starving artist'). In turn, higher-level needs might be lost to some people who are satisfied with lower-level needs (e.g. chronic unemployment).

Question		
How could an organization assure the fulfilment of needs at the workplace according to Maslow's hierarchy of needs?		
Needs levels	General rewards	Organizational factors
1. Physiological	Food, water, sleep, etc.	
2. Safety	Safety, security, stability, protection	
3. Social	Love, affection, belongingness	
4. Esteem	Self-esteem, self-respect, prestige, status	
5. Self-actualization	Growth, advancement, creativity	

Herzberg's two-factor theory

Another widely recognized motivation theory is Herzberg's two-factor theory. Through his research Herzberg identified several factors which have an impact on the motivation of workers, which he divided into two different categories – 'Hygiene' (also known as maintenance) factors and 'Motivators' (or growth factors). Hygiene factors (or preventive, environmental factors) are related to job context and job environment – these are extrinsic to the job itself and serve to prevent dissatisfaction. If hygiene factors are absent, job dissatisfaction may occur. 'Motivators' in turn are related to job content of the work itself. If present, these factors cause job satisfaction (see Fig. 3.6).

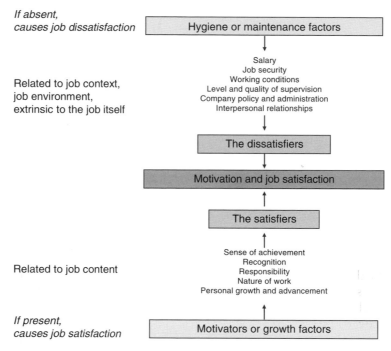

Fig. 3.6. Herzberg two-factor model. (Adapted from Buchanan and Huczynski, 2007.)

Question

Cast your mind to a time when you felt exceptionally good about what you were doing. Examine the experience carefully. Ask yourself:

- Why you enjoyed the job?
- When did it happen?
- What was it about the job or the circumstances that made you feel enthusiastic about it?

Try to make brief notes about your work experience at that time when work seemed to be interesting and rewarding.

Cast your mind to a time in your life when you were most dissatisfied with your work situation. Ask yourself why you were uninterested in your job. Try to write down those things which undermined your morale.

Ask your peers to do the same and compare notes in groups. Agree on those factors which could be described as job-satisfying. Try to rank them in their order of importance to you, bearing in mind the time when you were most enthusiastic about the job you were doing. When you have agreed a list of potentially job-satisfying factors consider the job-dissatisfying factors in the same way. Try to record a short list, in rank order, of those aspects of the job which brought about feelings of despair and low morale.

Compare your two lists to Herzberg's two-factor theory.

S. Heitmann and C. Roberts

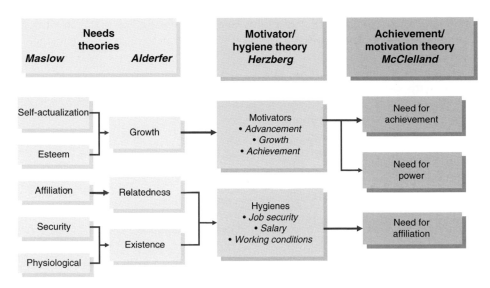

Fig. 3.7. Content theories on motivation.

Two further prominent theories are those proposed by Alderfer and McClelland (see Mullins, 2007). Aldefer identified three categories of human needs that influence an employee's behaviour – existence, relatedness and growth. Existence covers the basic needs such as hunger, thirst, safety and security. Relatedness is mainly concerned with social or external esteem through the belonging to a group (family or co-workers). Growth is about internal esteem and personal development. McClelland in turn identified three motivational needs: achievement motivation, authority or power motivation and affiliation motivation. Depending on the individual's needs, an employee might have a high need for achievement but less so for affiliation (meaning that it is more important to the employee to be successful than to belong to a group). Another employee might have a high need for affiliation but is not concerned about authority, meaning that it is more important to get on well with colleagues than to try to dominate them through a higher status. As you can see from the theories outlined above, there are significant overlaps, as depicted in Fig. 3.7.

The following factors are commonly seen as demotivators within the travel industry:

- delayering;
- low pay and a lack of other rewards and benefits;
- unsocial working hours;
- seasonality of employment;
- high staff turnover;
- extra hours often required, sometimes without compensation – or only paid at the basic rate;
- need to rely on tips to supplement low pay;
- some staff contracts lack any guaranteed minimum number of hours' work or pay;

- ethnic minority staff are often given low-paid menial jobs;
- inadequate breaks during peak seasons;
- low levels of job satisfaction;
- low upper age limits for certain types of staff;
- inadequate staff training and development;
- low levels of respect often shown by customers to staff;
- often poor, and sometimes unqualified, management;
- authoritarian and remote management cultures; and
- key staff are often imported from outside, rather than recruited from the pre-existing workforce.

Question

Discuss how these demotivators apply to the above models of motivation.

Lucy: Twelve months ago, I found myself lacking job satisfaction. Motivation was low, with key factors – both extrinsic and intrinsic – missing. I felt my salary hadn't developed at the same rate as my role. I saw little room for promotion, with a newly appointed manager meaning progression was unlikely. On a psychological, or intrinsic, level, I felt I wasn't maximising my full ability, there was no sense of challenge and positive recognition was lacking. Eventually, I had an honest discussion with my manager whose response was inspiring. Not only did he communicate the value I brought to the team, he made dramatic changes to my job role, assigning me key managerial responsibilities and setting me clear goals to achieve. He outlined a development path, highlighting the potential of a new management level – a level which I could aspire to. He also awarded me a pay rise in recognition of the additional experience I brought to the team. A year later, I have just been promoted into the new, higher role. I feel challenged, appreciated and extremely well motivated.

Question

Using the theories on motivation, which motivation factors can you identify in Lucy's report?

Although motivation theories have been subject to criticism, they can be useful tools for managers. Identifying the needs of individual employees can be matched with appropriate rewarding techniques. For example, in order to cater for those with a high need for achievement (coinciding with Maslow's higher levels, Alderfers' growth need, McClelland's need for achievement and Herzberg's motivators) high expectations, approval, praise and recognition from the manager will encourage and motivate the employee for a sustained good performance. Providing foundations for trust, respect and loyalty will motivate those employees with a high desire for social interaction (corresponding with Maslow's third-level, Herzberg's motivators, Alderfer's relatedness, McClelland's need for affiliation). These theories can further give a better understanding of what organizational barriers stand in the way of individual and group performance (smooth business processes, systems, methods and resources).

S. Heitmann and C. Roberts

Questions

What we have omitted in our discussion is the role of money:

1. To what extent do you consider money a motivating force for employees? Consider the theory discussed and your own experiences.
2. Does the importance of money change as you ascend the corporate ladder?
3. To what extent are tips motivators?

Appraisal and Performance Review

Another important aspect of HRM is performance management which is seen as a strategic and integrated approach to delivering sustained success to organizations. This is done by establishing what goals and targets are to be achieved, and by improving the performance of individuals and teams in order to establish how and when these goals and targets are met. The performance review or appraisal is the process whereby current individual's performance in a job is observed and discussed for the purpose of adding to that level of performance. The aim of an appraisal is to facilitate development, motivate and improve performance. It is a two-way discussion of past and present experiences and achievements at work, which can be used as the basis for agreeing future training and development to the benefit of the organization and the employee. This could include the identification, discussion and resolution of difficulties or obstacles to effectiveness. An appraisal can also be a formal opportunity to recognize achievements and celebrate successes, an opportunity to strengthen working relationships, improve teamwork and clarify roles and responsibilities. The purpose of a performance review is a form of management control, to link pay to performance, to identify potential, to solve any potential problems, for succession planning, and to comply to regulations imposed by quality standards such as Investors in People (if the organization is a member; Nickson, 2007).

Techniques for performance appraisal can include written essay, critical incident reports, graphic rating scales, behaviourally anchored scales, and multi-person comparison through group-order ranking, individual ranking and paired comparison. There are different approaches to performance appraisal – the usual one is the top-down approach whereby the management appraises the employee. Most commonly, the direct line manager carries out appraisals and evaluation, as it is generally they who are responsible for the employee's shorts falls. Ninety-five per cent of all appraisals at lower to middle staff level are conducted by the immediate senior of the employee. However, there are alternative approaches. Self-appraisals are very popular among employees. They tend to lessen employee defensiveness regarding the whole process and therefore can be more revealing. This in turn creates an excellent environment for stimulating job discussions between the two sides. Peer appraisal is not widely used within the tourism industry, although it is considered as one of the most reliable sources of appraisal data. Peers are close to the action; daily interaction provides them with a comprehensive view of an employee's job performance. Using peers results in a number of independent judgements, which when combined, often proves to be more accurate than the sole judgement of the immediate superior. Upward appraisal by immediate subordinates is a further source of opinion. As with peer approach, the value of this method revolves around the subordinates having frequent contact with the employee being appraised. Subsequently, this can be a valuable source of accurate and detailed information. Customer appraisal is carried through customer surveys or mystery shoppers. Three-hundred-and-sixty degree appraisal indicates feedback from a full circle of sources and that is exactly what it is. This method has become popular over the last decade. Here feedback is gained from the appraisee's line manager, subordinates and peers.

However, when carrying out an appraisal, there are some issues that have to be taken into account:

- Depending on the relationship between managers and employees, it can be difficult to remain objective when appraising. Your appraisal depends on your relationship with the supervisor. If you are liked, or socialize with him you are more likely to get a good review.
- Prejudice can influence the process, and in some cases sex or race discrimination might become clear which of course should be avoided.
- Managers might be uncomfortable when they are in the position of 'playing God' (Nickson, 2007).
- The criteria for performance measurement have to be established clearly – is it the context of work or should performance be compared to others? Appraising can often go wrong if there is too much focus on irrelevant features.
- External factors have to be taken into account (such as market conditions and the economic climate which might affect the organization's performance).
- An appraisal can only be effective if the appraiser has the right skills, but also the appraisee needs the right skills (e.g. communication and interpersonal skills).
- Quite often taking the time to carry out the appraisal as well as filling in all the necessary paperwork (bureaucracy) can get into the way of an appraisal.
- An appraisal can have an immense impact on employee motivation, both in a positive and a negative way. When one person begins to make a judgement on another, unless that judgement is favourable, reaction and resistance might begin to set in. Furthermore, the appraisal can have an impact on the team.
- If dealing with employees from different backgrounds, the cultural dimension comes into play.
- Once the performance review has been carried out, outcomes of the appraisal might be ignored which is a vital mistake.
- When carrying out peer appraisals, co-workers might be unwilling to evaluate each other.
- Friendships and/or animosity between workers could cause biases.
- With regard to self-appraisals there is the danger of overinflated opinions or self-serving biases by the employee.

Appraisals in a travel context

The seasonality of many travel-related roles can have a negative impact on the completion of staff appraisals. Some managers feel that there is no benefit in carrying out an appraisal for a member of staff who may only be working for a couple of months during peak season. This is also the period when work load is at its heaviest, so the added burden of carrying out an appraisal is often one that is swept under the carpet. Furthermore, carrying out an effective appraisal is not a 20-minute exercise. An example for carrying out an overseas representative's appraisal is outlined below:

- A letter is sent out to the representative inviting them to come for an appraisal interview. The letter would include the time, date and venue for the appraisal.
- The letter would be accompanied by a blank appraisal sheet which listed all the headings that the representative was to be graded on. The representative would be invited to grade themselves prior to the appraisal interview which would generally be with the resort manager or resort supervisor.
- The appraisal form would then be completed by the relevant line manager who would give a grade for each area of work and then back up that grade with comments on past performances and possible areas for improvement.

CASE STUDY: EXAMPLE OF PERSONAL DEVELOPMENT REVIEW

Sarah, travel agent: I had been in my current position for nearly 18 months and hadn't received any form of appraisal from my line manager. Within our organization every employee is supposed to have a Personal Development Review (PDR) every six months. This meeting is an opportunity to discuss my performance over the last six months and to set clear objectives for the future. It also gives staff the opportunity to receive recognition for good performance and this is also the time that my manager should give me ratings that will count towards my annual salary increase. Ratings are given for several areas including; making decisions and accountability, communication and influencing, and skills and knowledge, ratings arc given from not achieved through to outstanding performance over and above requirements. The results of your ratings will influence the director's decision on your salary increase. Due to my manager's lack of organizational skills I didn't receive a PDR so my director had to give not only myself but also everyone within our department a flat rate salary increase. This affected staff morale within the department as some staff work harder than others but everyone received the same pay rise. Some staff then took the attitude to just do the bare minimum work duties and not their usual 'above and beyond' approach. Staff motivation was also very low.

Questions

Imagine you are Sarah:

1. How would you approach the line manager and convince him of the importance of the appraisal?
2. What recommendations would you make to the line manager?

Training and Development

The training and development of HR adds to the effectiveness and responsiveness of the organization to a constantly changing and dynamic external environment. Training can be provided in order to develop generic, vocational and job-specific skills. Most training is focused on hard skills (e.g. health and safety, ICT and work methods) but soft skills are deemed more important, such as customer care, communication, problem solving, business awareness, team working. In a more global industry with a diverse workforce, additional training is provided for cultural diversity.

The justification for employee training and development is endless. New members of staff need to be properly inducted in order to become part of the organization. Additionally, recently promoted staff must also undergo effective induction training in order to adapt to their new roles. If the organization undergoes changes, training can act as a response to any resulting differences in staff needs, customer expectation, technologies, legislation or company goals. Quality standards have to be communicated and may give rise for further training. The development of staff can contribute significantly to job satisfaction and motivation as well as the confidence and success within individuals and the organization as a whole. Effective training and development can increase the flexibility of staff and overall productivity. Last but not least, training is also more practical in terms of health and safety issues within the organization.

There are training approaches evident at all different levels – this can range from national/governmental policies down to the individual requirements. Table 3.3 provides a useful overview for the key activities at the different levels and how these can inform each other.

Table 3.3. Level of training approaches. (Adapted from Nickson, 2007.)

Level	Organizations involved/activities
National/ governmental level	Government policy (e.g. UK government) seeking a more proactive approach to encourage training in organizations Training initiatives, such as Investors in People (IiP) and apprenticeships, creation of NVQs
Industry level	National training organizations (NTOs), e.g. People First, which is the Sector Skills Council (SSC) for areas such as hospitality, tourism, travel and leisure Industry-level initiatives, such as Excellence Through People, Welcome Host
Company level	Creation of an overall view of the company's approach to training, e.g. seeking IiP accreditation, being involved in Welcome Host and Excellence Through People Matching departments' units-training strategies with organizations' overall strategy, ensuring implementation
Unit level	Implementing on- and off-the-job training (e.g. quality training, customer service training) Monitoring individuals' training, performance and development Succession planning and development
Team level	Motivation and performance Team building
Individual level	Improvement in skills, knowledge, attitude, discipline and behaviour Sustaining employability Enhancing motivation and performance Career progression

S. Heitmann and C. Roberts

Apprenticeships are schemes that are funded by the government and primarily aimed at 16–24-year-olds with benefits of not only attracting people into the tourism industry but also offering young people on-the-job training and work-based learning as opposed to more traditional methods of learning (e.g. attending college). Thus, apprentices have an opportunity to learn specific occupational skills (such as communication, numeracy, literacy and team working) while earning money. The usual duration of an apprenticeship is 2 years, at the end of which the apprentice will achieve a National Vocational Qualification (NVQ) Level two, which can then be further enhanced by the completion of an NVQ Level three. Companies that have been part of this scheme are, for example, De Vere, Yates' and TUI Travel plc.

Training can be delivered internally or externally in the organization. Internal training includes on-the-job training, which is the most common form of training. On-the-job training involves learning through watching or observing a colleague/line manager as well as participating (learning by doing). Advantages include that it is inexpensive and cost-effective, whereby the learner actively engages in real-life situations. Trainees get immediate feedback and can give feedback to future trainees. A further advantage is the social aspect and development of team integration. Disadvantages can arise if existing employees are not adequately trained, if training is not properly planned and if trainees pick up bad routines which are more difficult to eliminate later on. A variation of on-the-job training is mentoring or coaching, which is an ongoing, one-to-one process whereby a more senior employee develops a relationship with the trainee, offering counselling and advice when needed. Again, this has to be well planned in order to be successful. This is not necessarily a one-way process as it can benefit the senior staff to reflect on processes and procedures. Finally, another on-the-job training technique is job rotation. This involves the trainee being allocated to different jobs in order to acquire a wider range skills and understanding of the wider picture.

Off-the-job training in turn involves training being delivered from specialized training departments outside the workplace of the trainee, such as lectures, seminars, workshops, case studies, role plays, simulation and e-learning. This is common practice in the tourism and hospitality industries. The advantages are that new knowledge and an external point of view are introduced into the department, which are potentially being overlooked internally. Bringing together people from different departments can also encourage wider socialization and networking. However, it can be more generic and thus not specific or relevant enough. Furthermore, the more passive approach to learning can jeopardize motivation and concentration. Finally, the quality is dependent on the deliverer and beyond the control of the department.

CASE STUDY: EXAMPLE OF EMPLOYEE INDUCTION

Tim: When the department expanded and new staff were employed, I had to train a new starter while trying to perform my usual duties. While the company and department professional trainers provided a basic induction it was left to regular non-managerial staff like myself to teach and train the new starters their day-to-day job. I didn't feel this was very professional, as the new starters were starting at our busiest time of year. While I found the training straightforward and rewarding, my day-to-day work started to suffer as I was spending the majority of my time away

Continued

from my desk. I informed my line manager of the situation and it was decided that all members of staff in the department would train the new starters, although this was helping me with my workload I didn't feel it was the best way to train new staff by them being passed around the office.

Questions

1. How could this situation have been avoided? In your answer, consider also aspects of motivation and HRP.
2. Propose a training plan that could have been implemented beforehand
3. Looking back at the discussion surrounding emotional and aesthetic labour (Section 'Case Study: Emotional and Aesthetic Labour'), do you think that soft skills can be trained and developed? How would you design a training session to ensure employees learn how to sound and look right?

Grievance and Discipline

A case of grievance happens when an individual employee formally expresses dissatisfaction because policies and processes are ignored or not properly implemented. The employee may also pledge grievance in situations that cause him/her to be severely distressed. In the case of an individual concern, we tend to speak of a case of grievance, but if dealing with collective aspects (such as dissatisfaction expressed by a large group of employees) it can lead to an employment dispute.

Dissatisfaction includes anything that disturbs an employee, whether or not the unrest is expressed in words. A complaint in turn is a spoken or written dissatisfaction brought to the attention of the supervisor/shop steward. If the complaint has been formally presented to a management representative or to a union official, we speak of a grievance. Dissatisfaction can arise because of an environmental conflict (such as working conditions or the nature of work), a social substantive (inequity/inequality and disagreements with the management) or social relational (between individuals and groups, for instance, personality conflicts, racism, sexism, and so forth; Nickson, 2007) conflict.

The grievance procedure

The grievance procedure provides a formal way to handle concerns, problems or complaints from employees. It operates in exactly the same way as the disciplinary procedure.

Disciplinary procedure

1. Notify the employee: The employee should be notified of the problem and invite them to a meeting to discuss the problem. They should be given 72 hours' notice of the meeting and be informed of their right to be accompanied by a colleague or a trade union representative.

S. Heitmann and C. Roberts

2. Hold the meeting: Set out clearly the complaint against the employee. The employee should be given the chance to explain his/her version of events, call witnesses and present evidence.

3. Decide on the outcome: This may mean disciplinary action. Consideration should be given to the employee's overall record, outcomes of similar cases within the organization (if there are any – remember this outcome could set precedence for consistency going forward).

4. Notify the employee of the outcome: This is usually by letter. If disciplinary action is taken then the employee's right to appeal the decision and guidance on how to go about this should be included.

5. Hold the appeal meeting: If the reason for the appeal is because the employee thinks the finding or penalty is unfair, new evidence has come to light. The appeal meeting may also be held if the employee thinks the disciplinary procedure was not used correctly. Not agreeing with the decision is not reason enough to appeal.

6. Notify the employee of the appeal outcome: The employee should be notified of the appeal outcome.

The grievance must be made in writing. Recent case law has highlighted that any complaint in writing is likely to amount to a grievance without the need for the person to state that they are actually raising a formal grievance. This means that a letter from a solicitor or a formal resignation letter may also constitute a grievance. Failing to recognize a grievance and implement the grievance procedure could increase compensation in a tribunal claim by 50%. This is particularly important in small firms where there may be a more informal culture. Often grievances are raised as a result of a disciplinary procedure, where an employee feels that they have not been treated fairly. In some cases, such as those that could form the basis of a claim to a tribunal (e.g. constructive dismissal), the lodging of an appeal in a disciplinary procedure will amount to raising a grievance and should therefore, bring the grievance process into play. The ambiguity as to whether an appeal constitutes a grievance means it can be difficult to formulate an all-encompassing policy, as each case is likely to be different.

Discipline

While the employee brings grievance forward, there are also cases of discipline in which case the management takes formal steps because an individual or a group of employees has broken the rules. Discipline is initiated if an employee is guilty of misconduct such as: theft or fraud; physical violence; bullying; deliberate and serious damage to property; serious misuse of an organization's property or name; misuse of the Internet; serious insubordination; unlawful discrimination or harassment; alcohol/ drugs; breach of health and safety rules; and breach of confidence. The disciplinary procedure is outlined below and follows similar steps as the grievance procedure.

The seven deadly sins of discipline

Employment law specialist Kate Russell believes that 'seven deadly sins' exist that are a sure way to poor staff relations and standards, dismissals backfiring and even compensation claims totalling tens of thousands of pounds:

1. **Leap frogging:** Employers often skip stages of the disciplinary process when their frustration with an employee leads them to make a snap decision to sack them. But by disregarding the correct procedure, bosses could find themselves in an employment tribunal, facing claims of unfair dismissal.

2. **Burying your head in the sand:** Sometimes known as the 'Ostrich Manoeuvre', and common in cases of misconduct or poor performance, employers frequently choose to bury their head in the sand and do nothing. This approach means the employee is often unaware of the problem. However, the onus and legal responsibility is on the employer to ensure staff are aware of acceptable standards and disciplinary procedures.

3. **'Where angels fear to tread':** Employers often fail to know the difference between acting promptly when a problem occurs and dashing in 'all guns blazing where angels fear to tread'. Bosses must gather the facts of a case before proceeding with any action, even if an employee has been caught 'red-handed'.

4. **Failure to keep proper records:** Employers commonly ignore the importance of collecting data regarding a disciplinary incident as soon as possible after it happens. Witness statements, records and the testimony of the 'accused' are all vital, particularly if the matter goes any further.

5. **Making assumptions about employees:** Bosses need to be fair and, more importantly, be seen to be fair. They must ensure they investigate all the facts of a case, including the employee's account of the incident, and be as objective as possible. Relevant personal details, such as work experience, length of service and any current warnings against the employee, must all be considered.

6. **Inconsistency:** Unless employers can prove that staff in disciplinary situations had all been taken through the same procedures and framework, they risk being accused of unfair dismissal unless there are mitigating circumstances that clearly distinguish between different cases.

7. **'The Sausage Machine':** While it is important to be consistent, it is crucial that employers realize that their disciplinary procedure is not simply a sausage machine churning out set outcomes. Each case must be considered on its own merits and the personal details of the employee in question, such as length of service, past disciplinary history and any current warnings, should be considered relevant. Any decision to discipline an employee must be reasonable, and must not discriminate on grounds of race, gender, disability, religious belief or sexual orientation (Russell, 2004).

Welfare Within the Workplace

In this section, we are going to outline the wider issues that fall under health, safety and work-related stress and how companies can address any problems through proper welfare policies.

There are many factors at the workplace that can result in work-related stress and affect the health and safety of employees. Stress can derive from different stressors:

- demand (workload: too much or not enough to do, long working hours, emotional labour);
- environment (physical conditions difficult, demanding customers, smoking);
- control (how much the employee can control his/her work, i.e. pace of work, which skills to use, when to have a break, absenteeism by colleagues leading to higher workload);

- support (poor management/supervision, no access to necessary resources or information);
- relationships (bullying or harassment, discrimination, office politics);
- role (no clear understanding of role and responsibilities, conflicting roles within department/organization); and
- change (poor management and communication of small or large changes, uncertainty of employee's or organization's future).

Companies can adopt welfare policies for various reasons: driven by legislation, whereby an organization sees it as something that has to be complied with; because of corporate conscience, adopting a strong welfare orientation; or because of company paternalism, whereby the company is adopting a fatherly manner with a strong sense of commitment towards its employees and concern not only about work issues but also about life outside work. Finally, and which is nowadays taken as the key argument for companies adopting an efficient approach towards welfare policies, it is for the simple reason of reducing absence and improving performance which will lead to sustained higher level of productivity. Ignoring any of the stressors above can have immense impacts on the organization in terms of absenteeism, labour turnover, decreased performance, accidents, customer complaints and so on – everything a company should avoid. This clearly provides another example how HRM contributes to the overall business performance – having effective welfare and health and safety policies in place adds to the overall productivity.

With regard to welfare policies, legislation and employment law plays an important role. Table 3.4 provides an overview of some laws to be considered by the human resource department and organization as a whole.

Question

Which areas do these legislations affect most – recruitment and selection, training and development, appraisal or grievance and discipline?

Table 3.4. Legislation affecting human resources.

Legislation	What it is about
Sex Discrimination Act (1975)	Prevents discrimination on the grounds of gender
Equal Pay Act (1970)	Equal treatment and equal pay for men and women in same employment
Race Relations Act (1976)	Prevents discrimination on grounds of race
Employment Equality (Age) Regulations (2006)	Prevents discrimination on grounds of age
Disability Discrimination Act (1995)	Prevents discrimination on grounds of disability; employer to cater for disabled person's needs
Rehabilitation of Offenders Act (1974)	Prevents discrimination on grounds of a spent conviction
Health and Safety at Work etc. Act (1974)	Assures occupational health and safety – places duties on the employer, employee and customers
EU Directive on Working Time Regulations (1998)	Limits average working time to 48 hours per week as well as covering breaks, rest and holiday

Labour Turnover and Retention

Having discussed the key areas of HRM, it is now worth paying some attention to the issues that are crucial to the tourism and travel industry. Given the very dynamic and flexible nature, one characteristic of the industry is its high levels of labour turnover and low levels of retention.

Labour turnover entails the number of staff leaving and being replaced, while retention indicates the number of staff staying. Labour turnover includes retirement, dismissal and resignation. Turnover is the number of employees leaving their jobs within a certain period of time expressed as a proportion of the number of workers in that establishment at the start of the period.

Turnover (along with the corresponding 'withdrawals' through absenteeism, sickness and burnout) has long been perceived as a fact of life, and has thus been ignored to a great extent which is ironic considering that the travel industry is so orientated to satisfaction of people's needs, but does not extend this philosophy to core of production – their staff. Labour turnover is an important issue in the industry as it is expensive to the company, reduces morale among employees, lowers quality/productivity and presents advantages to the competition. However, labour turnover is not always negative as it is necessary where work is seasonal and also results in poor performers leaving and allowing 'fresh blood' into the organization. Nevertheless, economic costs for separation, replacement and training, productivity losses, impaired service quality, lost business opportunities, increased administrative burden and demoralization of stayers are enough evidence that labour turnover has to be tackled by the organization. It prevents continuing relationships between employers and employees which in turn inhibits growth of mutual responsibility.

Useful sources for information on reasons for high labour turnover rates are employee opinion surveys or exit interviews. Reasons for leaving need to be analysed with variables such as position, length of service, background, performance and potential and it can also be useful to recognize any correlation between turnover and lateness/absenteeism in order to prevent high labour turnover.

Strategies in order to avoid labour turnover are wide and varied. It is ultimately a complex issue with differing responses; however, labour turnover can be prevented through intervention at each stage of the HR cycle. A retention culture of communication, participation, empowerment, supportive relationships, teamwork, recognition and other variables associated with job satisfaction can significantly lower labour turnover rates.

Mullins (2007) suggests both short-term prescriptions (identifying the nature and character of an organization, finding out why staff leave or stay, asking staff what they want from their jobs, providing opportunities to voice opinions, and developing recruitment, selection and induction procedures) and long-term prescriptions (establish effective socialization, training and development programmes, adoption of quality circles, develop profit-sharing and incentive schemes, establish child care facilities, maintain competitive pay scales). Similarly, Go *et al.* (1996) suggest to offer attractive rewards and benefits, provide promotion opportunities, maintain positive and supportive working environments, create flexible working conditions, reduce stress through appropriate job design, provide family, welfare and social support systems, implement effective communication and interpersonal interaction systems and develop effective conflict resolution processes. The Chartered Institute for Personnel and Development (CIPD) offers the

S. Heitmann and C. Roberts

following: give future employees a realistic job preview, make line managers accountable for staff turnover in their teams, reward managers with good retention record, train line managers in effective supervision, maximize opportunities for promotion, ensure that employees have a 'voice', consultative bodies, regular appraisals, attitude surveys and grievance systems, and accommodate for flexible working hours and provide as much job security as possible.

Challenges and Future Trends of Human Resources Management in the Travel Industry

Having discussed the status quo of HRM, we have to consider future implications on travel companies and working within the industry. One major issue, labour turnover, has been discussed in the previous section, and the following paragraphs will focus on some of the wider issues.

Working practices and patterns have already changed over the past decades and are continuing to transform. The impact of technology beckons the question as to 'whether we need people?' This trend has already been observed in other industries, such as manufacturing, but also within the travel industry, computers have replaced human beings. A good example of this is the airline industry, where low-cost airlines are relying on the Internet for ticket issuing, but also the traditional carriers have now installed check-in kiosks at airports in place of staff. While this has obvious economical advantages to the companies, it has a major impact on employment as well as customer service. A further issue related to work is the trend towards flexible working conditions; the industry has always been characterized by seasonal and part-time workers, but societal changes have increased the demand for home working (supported by technological developments) and also for work–life balance (which is about people having more control over when, how and where they work).

Given the international orientation of the industry, diversity is another key issue that has to be taken into account. Diversity can manifest itself in terms of gender, age, race and culture. An increasingly diverse workforce requires different measures from any human resource department, particularly in order to avoid any cases of potential conflicts and discrimination. However, apart from the legal aspects, cultural diversity within the workforce can add to customer service as a diverse cultural make-up can provide a wider variety of skills needed for international customers.

The industry has recently been criticized for the promotion of deskilling, often referred to as McDonaldization, which creates a standardized approach to service and low-paid labour. At the same time more and more courses are becoming available within further and higher education, indicating a trend of professionalization within the travel industry. The apparent paradox creates confusion over the level of skills needed for workers.

Further external factors include globalization as travel companies have to compete on a global level which requires globally orientated workers and managers. Particularly in large companies, HRM has to work on an international level with a range of employees from different countries working in different countries. This requires different approaches towards recruitment, training, motivation and compliance with international laws. It further requires employees to be increasingly mobile and culturally sensitive. Within globalization, technological developments lead to employees having to learn new skills to adopt to these developments (Baum, 2006).

Finally, changes in consumer demands affect organizations. First, today's tourists are more experienced and more demanding. Combined with more access to information and choice of service, employees have to cater for these increasingly sophisticated demands. Particularly the move away from mass tourism products to more individually tailored niche products requires a new set of skills and knowledge from employees within the travel industry. Second, consumers have become more critical towards industrial practices and more conscious about environment and social issues. Sustainability, ethics and corporate social responsibility have become part of many companies' agenda – whether this might be for marketing purposes or for true concerns.

Summary

This chapter has stressed the importance of people within the travel industry. The high orientation towards customer service requires the effective management of HR in order to cater for the demands of customers and to assure the smooth running of the organization. Competing within a global context requires the best possible deployment of people, thus influencing every single aspect of the HRM cycle. The planning of HR provides a first step in order to assure the effective command of an organization with help of its people. This is supported by proper recruitment and selection practices, which have to be designed in such a way that the organization is able to attract and detect suitable candidates. Once the employee is attracted, training and motivation techniques should be implemented, as these are instrumental to retaining a competitive workforce and reducing labour turnover. The different aspects that have been discussed in the chapter (planning, recruitment and selection, appraisal, training and development and grievance) should not be seen in isolation but as a holistic picture. Furthermore, the aspect of HRM should not be seen in isolation but as a part of the wider organization and its strategy. However, given the variety of businesses within the travel industry, an organization has to assure that it has an individual 'best fit' approach towards HRM instead of relying on generically accepted practices.

Acknowledgement

Stefanie Renz.

Further Research

Nickson, D. (2007) *Human Resource Management for Hospitality and Tourism Industries*, Butterworth-Heinemann, Oxford.

S. Heitmann and C. Roberts

Web Sites

Chartered Institute for Personnel and Development (CIPD): www.cipd.co.uk
Advisory, Conciliation and Arbitration Service (ACAS): www.acas.org.uk
Human Resource Management Guide: www.hrmguide.net
Personnel Today: www.personneltoday.com
Sector Skills Council People 1st: www.people1st.co.uk
Investors in People: www.investorsinpeople.co.uk
Excellence Through People: www.etp.org.uk

Review Questions

1. Your company is experiencing problems of high labour turnover and low staff morale. As part of you HR strategy you have the options of: (i) external recruitment; (ii) internal training and development; and (iii) introduction of flexible working. Discuss the advantages and disadvantages of each option.

2. A HR manager in a hotel tells you that he discriminates against applicants with supervisory or management qualifications who apply for operative-level jobs. Do you agree with this approach? What are the arguments against it?

3. You are the manager of a hotel restaurant in the USA where tips are an important component of staff pay. You discover that European guests are not treated as well as American guests because they are not seen as being good tippers. What do you do?

References

Armstrong, M. (2003) *A Handbook of Human Resource Management Practice*. Kogan Page, London.

Baum, T. (2006) *Human Resource Management for Tourism, Hospitality and Leisure*. Thomson Learning, London.

Buchanan, D. and Huczynski, A. (2007) *Organisational Behaviour – An Introductory Text*. Prentice-Hall, Harlow, UK.

Go, F., Monachello, M. and Baum, T. (1996) *Human Resource Management in the Hospitality Industry*. Wiley, New York.

Mullins, L.J. (2007) *Management & Organizational Behaviour*, 8th edn. Pearson Education, Harlow, UK.

Nickson, D. (2007) *Human Resource Management for Hospitality and Tourism Industries*. Butterworth-Heinemann, Oxford.

Rahman, A. and Eldridge, D. (1998) Reconceptualising human resource planning in response to institutional change. *International Journal of Manpower* 19, 343–357.

Russell, K. (2004) *Can I Sack the B****d?* Authors OnLine Ltd, Sandy.

4 Operations Management

PETER ROBINSON AND STEVE GELDER

Objectives of the Chapter

This chapter provides an understanding of the nature of travel operations within the dynamic and wide-ranging travel services sector. It examines the resulting design of operations within the workplace, arising from the relationship between operations and the organization's strategic intentions, the supply chain and the customer. A central theme involves the role of individual employees in operations and how they can contribute to the overall success of the organization in meeting its operational objectives. In addition, the chapter gives consideration to the service concept and the management of customers, and establishes clear synergies between operations management, human resources, finance and marketing.

The chapter will provide an appreciation of the interrelationship existing between operations, finance and marketing in the delivery of service products by:

- providing an understanding of the implications of the service process mix on the organization's stakeholders in the context of achieving organizational objectives;
- applying operational management forecasting and planning techniques to achieve business targets and manage capacity; and
- reflecting upon, and collating, reasoned deductions and conclusions about the management of service operations.

Introduction

Operations management is a concept that is understood in all business sectors and finds its theoretical origins in the secondary industries of manufacturing and production, where the concepts discussed apply very clearly to the development and manufacture of an item or good. In adapting these concepts to the service sector, clear definitions are required. One of these definitions is offered by Needle (2000, p. 296), who demonstrates that:

> operations is concerned with the transformation of a variety of inputs such as information, people, material, finance and methods into a variety of outputs such as goods, services, profit, customer and employee satisfaction...the centrality of the function means that operations has a significant influence on costs and revenue as well as organizational structure.

Of key importance in this quote is the notion that operations management is manifest in every aspect of the business, providing tools to understand how the business

©CAB International 2009. *Operations Management in the Travel Industry* (ed. P. Robinson)

works and performs. The models and frameworks discussed in this chapter provide information to inform managers about business performance and are, therefore, closely linked with strategic management, discussed in Chapter 6 (this volume).

Swarbrooke (2002, p. 239) provides a very useful set of definitions to explain the nature of operations management and the interdependencies of different areas of the business within operational practice:

> It is about marshalling the attractions resources, notably the staff and physical equipment such as machinery, to provide a satisfactory service for the customer, and an acceptable rate of return on the use of these resources... the goal... is the smooth and efficient operation of the site.

Of particular note here is the idea that operations management involves everybody in the business, something that becomes clear in considering customer service management later in this section.

Other definitions are suggested by Certo (2000, p. 450): '[O]perations management is the systematic direction and control of operations processes that transform resources into finished goods and services' and Wright (2001, p. 7): '[O]perations management is the ongoing activities of designing, reviewing and using the operating system, to achieve service outputs is determined by the organization for customers.' Furthermore, according to Russell and Taylor (2009) companies today have to compete in a global market place where new trade agreements, innovations in information technology and improvements in transport and shipping have combined to demand effectiveness in the operational elements that influence business success.

Some Definitions

There are many terms which will be used frequently through the next pages as principal aspects of operations management. These include the following.

Facilities: Within travel operations, the facilities that exist are numerous and the operational detail is discussed in a later part of the chapter, where consideration is given to design, legislative requirements and management. In summary, facilities within the sector include airports, railway stations, freight terminals, docks, cruise ships, coach and bus stations, resorts, car parking, offices, maintenance facilities and supply infrastructure.

Processing: To understand the operational process there are a range of tools available, and new ideas and approaches can be tested on an operational network chart where outsourcing, new systems and processes such as outsourcing can be modelled and tested to assess their impact on the business. These are commonly referred to as service blueprints and offer problem-solving solutions, identifying issues and allowing modelling of different solutions to remedy these issues before implementation.

Capacity: This is the ability of the organization to manage or produce a service or good. Often in this industry it is related to the seating capacity of an aircraft or a train, the maximum number of rooms available at resort hotels or the number of aircraft which can be serviced at an airport, but it could also refer to internal capacities, such as budgets, technology, staffing levels or operational performance. It may also be discussed in environmental terms, where it is concerned with the maximum number of people that a particular site or destination is able to cope with at any one time. This is also known as *carrying capacity* and is discussed in further detail in Chapter 9 (this volume).

Quality and standards: Quality management is covered in detail in Chapter 5 (this volume) and is an essential aspect of operations management as the delivery of products and services must adhere to certain standards which may include benchmarks and quality schemes which allow managers to monitor quality and deliver effective quality management. They may be a code of conduct, or a voluntary agreement, although they could also be part of legislative requirements.

Scheduling: This refers to the process of internal work planning and the management of timetabling and capacity through the effective use of physical and human resource. Most businesses in the sector will aim to achieve maximum productivity through effective scheduling, within the constraints of health and safety and capacity management.

Inventory: The inventory of a business traditionally refers to the organization's stock levels which are managed through databases to meet customer demand while avoiding overstocking. This is common practice in the manufacturing industries where Just-In-Time systems use inventory management systems to order stock on demand. In car manufacturing, this means the correct number of seats, engines, tyres and wheels arrive at the factory just as the vehicle body is ready for the parts to be fitted. But it is not just manufacturing where this happens. Imagine an aeroplane requiring refuelling before the next passengers board. Fuel has to be ordered, delivered, stored and dispatched to aircraft when refuelling is required. Food has to be ordered and delivered regularly to aeroplane kitchens to ensure food is fresh and supply can meet customer expectations. Similarly, airline and train operators need to be able to order spare parts for maintenance to minimize the down time of equipment by ensuring parts are received and fitted quickly.

Control: If operations are to be effectively managed there have to be controls in place. This is achieved through understanding and maximizing efficiency throughout the business, supported by the concept of operating controlling.

Operating controlling: Businesses have to remain competitive. This may mean investing in new technologies or updating equipment, which could be large capital investments or loans from banks. Research is ongoing to manage competitiveness and to ensure that technology and equipment offers best value for money and increased financial productivity. Certo (2000, p. 451) describes this as operating controlling, the setting of 'production levels and scheduling production and workforce, managing inventory and overseeing quality assurance programmes'.

The operational process model

To contextualize the many aspects of operations management for the sector, the operational process model presented here will identify how all the different aspects of operations management fit together. This model (Fig. 4.1) explains the service process model as it applies to the travel industry.

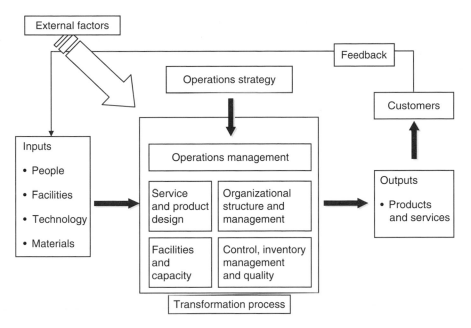

Fig. 4.1. Open-systems view of operations processes in the travel industry.

Facilities Management

Facilities management incorporates many disparate and connected activities. They range from the need to understand implement and review the processes and procedures that help the organization to achieve its business objectives. Slack (2001) suggests that the service package incorporates the core product, the supporting goods and services and the facilitating goods and services. An airport, for example, would see the flights in and out of the venue as the core product; the facilitating goods and services would incorporate check-in areas, passport control and a holding space prior to embarkation. In this example, where the consumption of the core product is not simultaneous, the provision of the 'supporting goods and services' is of primary importance, particularly when there are numerous unforeseen circumstances that can delay departure such as planes delayed through maintenance issues or problems in take-off from other countries.

Airports will need to process customers in the most efficient way through a series of designated areas. In an airport these will include:

- arrival;
- check-in;
- passport control;
- departure space;
- embarkation.

Potentially all of these areas can encounter any number of problems that can delay the 'process' and cause anger and frustration leading to customer dissatisfaction.

While an airport would represent a larger facility and thus a more complex range of operational systems, the operations function in its simplest terms:

transforming inputs into outputs of greater value is necessary in all transport-related venues of varying scale and scope. A railway station, for example, would involve similar priorities of processing passengers from an arrival point on to a train in the most efficient manner possible. Within this period, the customer may wish to experience service in a number of formats which may include retail/shop services, food and beverage or welfare facilities such as left luggage, restroom provision or information points. The facility manager will need to ensure that these areas along the supply chain each have effective policies and practices that not only provide service quality in its broadest sense (see Chapter 5, this volume) but, primarily, that avoid delays in processing travellers to their ultimate destination. It should also be noted that many of the ancillary services provided, such as food and retail, link to yield management and opportunities to generate additional secondary spend from a relatively captive audience.

Resorts provide another example of how the travel industry works on a short-term strategy of customer processing. Peak-season loading in resorts is even more reliant on efficient management of people through the visitor experience.

- **Dependent demand:** This is viewed as demand for one item (resort meals) as dependent on demand for another item (confirmed holiday bookings) because this serves to 'prepare the ground' as the number of visitors is predetermined. This allows the resort manger to confirm, for example, staffing levels and food requirements.
- **Independent demand:** This presents far more problems for travel facility managers as it is typically beyond the control of the venue and is influenced heavily by external market forces.

CASE STUDY

The example of Pittsburgh International Airport (Fig. 4.2) with its innovative 'X' design facilitates a significant increase in airspace with approaches from any direction which increases the airports ability to cope with demand.

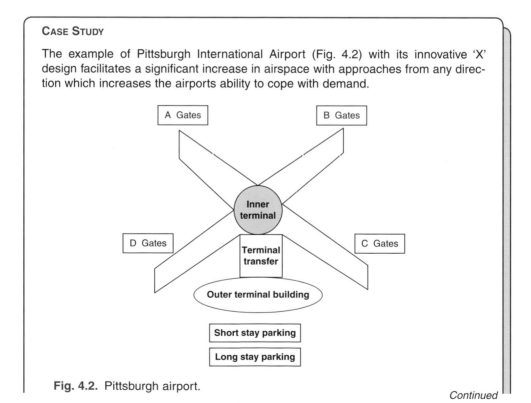

Fig. 4.2. Pittsburgh airport.

Continued

Operational Strategy

Most aspects of operations management are monitored through targets, achievement of service standards and overall business performance. In order for operations to be managed effectively throughout a business an operational strategy is required, which may be business-wide or specific to certain departments. The likelihood is that there will be an overall long-term strategy which will translate into an operational strategy at department level, and then into individual and team objectives through the appraisal and performance monitoring system, ensuring that everyone in the organization is aware of business objectives and how these translate into roles and responsibilities (Fig. 4.3). Each strategy may look at a whole range of factors and information will need to be provided on these. They may include 'capacity, location, product, process layout and human resources' (Certo, 2000, p. 451).

A strategy may be developed from two perspectives. The first is the creation of a strategy which focuses on specific areas for the business, such as product development, quality or cost. The second is department-specific.

As an example, within a human relations department at organizational level, it is likely that there is a long-term strategy for recruitment and training, which will translate within the department into the systems for delivery of the training and tools to measure the impact of the training on the business. Although it may seem like a paperwork exercise at first glance, the reality is that in businesses with hundreds or thousands of staff it is essential that there is a plan for training which can be disseminated through the business and realistically delivered to the relevant staff.

Fig. 4.3. Organizational relationship to operationalizing strategy.

Some other examples of strategies include the following:

- **Product development:** This encompasses development of new and existing goods and services to improve market share, service levels or competitiveness.
- **Financial management:** This considers financial performance of the organization, putting systems in place for revenue and yield management.
- **Service management:** This describes the development of customer service enhancement, training and management.
- **Risk management:** This type of strategy is particularly effective in an uncertain marketplace where the business can cope with changing demand.

The design of the operational strategy is not dissimilar to that of a longer-term business strategy, although the level of detail required will be less. It may be that in some cases the operational plan is actually a business plan (see Chapter 8, this volume), especially if it is focused on product development. An example of the format and structure of an operational strategy is presented here.

Structure of a strategy

A mission or vision for the business: A single paragraph, or even just a sentence identifying where the business wants to be in the future. This will be linked to the strategic vision, but will have a more specific focus.

An example of a mission statement is given here from Andaman Discoveries (www.andamandiscoveries.com):

> Our mission is to support community-led development by acting as bridge to respectful visitors and volunteers through sponsorship of education, conservation, and cultural empowerment.

Aims and objectives: To achieve the mission, or vision, a set of objectives are essential. These should be based upon the accepted SMART principle that the objectives are:

> Specific – clear and concise targets that are
> Measurable through targets that are
> Achievable and
> Realistic to ensure that targets can be met, and these need to be
> Time-limited so that there are realistic systems to monitor progress.

For each aim there should be a number of objectives, which together achieve the aim.

Development of strategy to achieve the aims and objectives

This section is about gathering information, understanding internal and external influences and identifying what will need to be done to achieve the organizational objectives. Much of this information can be collated through environmental scanning tools, such as Strengths, Weaknesses, Opportunities and Threats (SWOT) and Political, Economic, Social and Technological analysis (PEST), which will be discussed in the next section.

P. Robinson and S. Gelder

Implementation plan: A system of implementation which is governed by effective resource management is needed to activate the strategy, particularly focusing on the who, how and when aspects.

Monitoring and review: Feedback systems monitor and review progress. These will inform future strategy and product development. Referring back to the earlier model that was presented, this feedback becomes one of the inputs and an integral part of the transformation process.

Internal and External Influences on Operations Management

To fully understand the factors which affect operations management within the organization, a range of tools can be used. It is essential that managers are able to look inside and outside the business. There are environmental scanning tools available to support this activity. The most commonly used are SWOT (see Chapter 7, this volume, for full details) and PEST. The simplest PEST analysis considers political, economic, sociocultural and technological issues, although more complex versions are becoming increasingly popular to promote a wider view of the business climate. These include Political, Economic, Social, Technical, Environmental and Legislative (PESTEL), which adds in environmental and legal considerations, and DEPICTS, which considers PEST factors plus Demographics, Infrastructure and Competition and is more likely to be used in a marketing strategy.

Each factor can be further expanded with other tools, such as resource analysis or competitor analysis. In operational terms the most useful method to apply is PESTEL (Fig. 4.4) and a generic example is given here to identify some of the external influences which may impact upon the business.

Political

- Planning regulations
- Building regulations

Economic

- Key indicators such as Interest rate, average incomes, inflation, tax generation
- Profitability of the business
- State of financial reserves for the business
- Access to investment
- World markets
- Cost of overheads

Sociocultural

- Increased environmental concerns
- National economy
- Understanding of demographics, current trends and fashions, popular destinations
- Quality management (ISO 9000)
- Customer expectations

Technological

- Interpretation and information
- Presentation of information and services

- Access to services and type of, and access to, support
- Ticketing systems
- Booking systems
- Retain systems
- Business modelling and financial forecasting
- Health and safety
- Security
- Use of the Internet

Environmental

- Environmental concerns
- Impacts of business on the environment
- 'Green' initiatives

Legal

- Licensing regulations
- Planning regulations
- Health and Safety at Work Act
- Disability Discrimination Act
- Race Equality Amendment Act
- Equal opportunities
- Industry regulation (voluntary and compulsory)

Fig. 4.4. PESTEL analysis for operations management.

Product Design and Development

All businesses need to innovate to remain competitive. Innovation may be small and with incremental changes with new ideas and services, or radical new products or entering new market places. This strategy is designed to increase business and enhance profitability. In reality, many new ideas fail early in the design process, so other developments and products have to cover the cost of the failed ideas. As Slack *et al.* (2004, p. 94) identify, it is 'the process by which some functional requirement of people is satisfied through the shaping or configuration of the resources and/or activities that comprise a product, or a service or the transformation process that creates them'. There are two reasons to innovate. One has been identified as the need to gain competitive advantage or to compete in new markets thereby diversifying the product. The other may be in response to customer feedback. This can be seen easily in the operational model proposed at the start of this chapter (Fig. 4.1). This diagram also allows managers to identify the systems and processes taking place within the business. These can be expanded into flow chart models for individual products, or to understand better the supply chain, which is discussed in further detail in Chapter 5 (this volume).

All products are susceptible to the product life cycle model (Fig. 4.5), which shows how a new product goes through stages of growth stagnation and decline.

Decline can be avoided through innovation at the correct time. It is simply a case of identifying the reason for decline and responding appropriately. Some suggested responses are provided in Table 4.1.

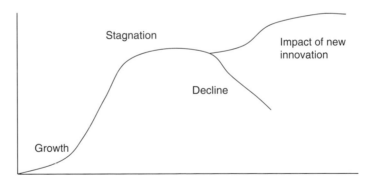

Fig. 4.5. Product life cycle.

Table 4.1. Responses to operational issues.

Issue	Response
Less money in the economy	Reduce prices or offer lower-cost products
Losing market share	Need to innovate to create new products to regain competitive advantage
New fashions or trends	Development of new products or services
Crisis (war or terrorism for example) in destination country	New destinations needed

IT and Innovation in Operations Management

In terms of product development, the most notable impact over recent years has been the growth of e-commerce, which has created three clearly different product markets in addition to providing an online shop front for traditional operators. These include last-minute booking agencies and groups of businesses belonging to a single organization and selling products through a single portal. Figure 4.6 illustrates the advantages and disadvantages of the Internet for travel retail.

Strategic planning and capacity management

Strategic planning is seen as the initial process of preparing a direction and a broad programme of activity for the organization (Veal, 2002). Greasley (2006) views planning and control as the matching of customer demand to the operations capacity.

Advantages for the business	Disadvantages for the business
Opens up new markets to businesses	Need high-quality 24 hour technical support and customer support
May improve customer service in some instances	Back-office services need to be managed
Reduced marketing and printing costs	Web sites quickly become outdated
Reduced operating costs because the Internet can in many instances replace the need for shops, and many back-office systems can be automated	Redundancy, although cost saving in the longer term, requires final payment offers and may damage the businesses image
Direct business rather than middlemen is advantageous for some suppliers especially as agencies do not have to be paid commission	The impact of competition forces prices to a level so low that operators fail to make more than a 5% profit, and in some cases rely on additional sales, such as car hire or insurance to generate profits
Advantages for the customer	**Disadvantages for the customer**
Lower prices	May receive no professional advice about legal or medical requirements such as visas or injections
Greater independence and flexibility in product design	Not all customers have Internet access or would want to buy on line, but choice in the high street has decreased
Customers are better informed and the Internet offers a wider range of specialist operators	

Fig. 4.6. Advantages and disadvantages of IT to the travel sector.

Capacity in turn is viewed by Russell and Taylor (2008, p. 663) as 'the maximum capability to produce – measured as units of output, dollars of output, hours of work, or number of customers processed over a specified period of time'.

In an ideal world the demand for products or services is stable over time, which allows the operations manager to acquire the necessary resources for a stated production period. Minor variations in demand can, in this instance, be handled through manpower planning via the usage of 'overtime and under time' working. There are advantages and disadvantages to this approach.

Advantages:

- Expensive recruitment costs are avoided.
- No need for induction or mandatory training.
- No need for investment in new resources.
- Regular staff who are familiar with company policy, processes and practice are needed.

Disadvantages:

- Overtime enhances costs.
- Pressure on staff potentially leads to elevated stress levels.
- Alternatives are restricted if increased demand continues.

Strategies to adjust capacity

Level capacity planning, chase demand planning and demand management are three traditional methods for handling capacity (Veal, 2002; McMahon-Beattie and Yeoman, 2004; Russell and Taylor, 2008).

Level capacity planning: This is where capacity is fixed at a rate estimated to meet 'average' demand. Throughout a given period of time, this approach is most appropriate for operations where the surpluses generated between capacity and demand are able to be stored. In this model, managers can plan ahead to acquire the resources (manpower, equipment, materials, etc.) necessary to meet the fixed capacity.

The chase demand approach: This works in opposite to the principles of level capacity planning. It attempts to adjust 'rapidly' to the changing conditions that influence demand. During periods of low demand the organization responds by cutting back on the workforce and in times of high demand the recruitment process provides additional workers to meet the demand. Clearly a prerequisite for this strategy is to have an effective and 'legal' employment system compliant with contract law. It also assumes that the labour market is freely available and that the skills necessary within the organization are not in short supply. Many sections of the travel industry utilize low-skilled workers where high staff turnover is a common factor and thus this approach becomes a valid option.

Demand management: This recognizes that service industry organizations exist in an environment of uncertainty and that demand for products and services is at best 'an educated guess'.

As with many other organizations within the broader leisure industry, predicting demand in the travel sector is difficult and influenced by many variables at both the macro and micro level. External influences such as changes in legislation or economic downturns combine with internal issues such as strategic management policy or practice or changes in local market conditions to create huge challenges for operations managers. There is a need to implement effective capacity management strategies/ techniques to address this uncertainty. Two types exist generally: first, the smoothing of demand as viewed by McMahon-Beattie and Yeoman (2004); secondly, attempting to influence demand with techniques such as price incentives. There are some of the strategies that exist in an attempt to influence demand and thus to predict capacity:

- **Membership incentives:** In the travel industry airports have developed member lounges where regular flyers can relax prior to departure. Knowing numbers in advance helps to organize and control capacity around the area.
- **Frequent user discounts:** This offers discounted products or services at specific times that help to spread demand. For example, the growth of the 'out of season' holiday-maker particularly for the retired market has helped to spread demand, a demand that has developed as a product of demographic factors around increases in age profiles and technological factors around low-cost travel.
- **Peak load premium pricing:** This is grounded in basic economic theory around 'exploitation, willingness, or ability to pay' premium rates. Ethical issues abound here where extreme pricing policies are implemented. McMahon-Beattie and Yeoman (2004) suggest that more incentives for customers to utilize 'off-peak' periods is a more sensible approach to achieve capacity levelling. Examples include the saver schemes frequently utilized by road and rail travel companies.

Question

Think of an occasion when you have utilized one of these capacity management techniques. Was the experience satisfactory, did you detect any 'lowering' of standards/expectations of service quality?

Managing Customer Care

Customers can be internal and external to the organization. While the external customers may be evident, it is perhaps less clear who the internal customers are. They are the internal departments, which service other departments. All staff will be customers of the human relations department for example. Johnston and Clarke (2005) suggest that customers in the service sectors are buying concepts rather than products or a set of components that create a product. Translate this into a package holiday and it is the holiday concept that is purchased, not the set of components that create the holiday. This requires the provider and the customer to have a shared understanding of the product. Johnston and Clarke (2005) propose a service concept to identify the customer service vision for the business. An adapted example is presented in Fig. 4.7.

Service concept
High-quality cruise holidays

Service experience	Service outcome
• Relaxing	• Good-value, good-quality holiday
• Lots of on-board activities	• Enjoyed by the whole family
• Opportunities for excursions	• Exhausting or relaxing to meet different needs
Service operation	**Service value**
• Good-quality facilities	• Expensive ticket but great value
• Extensive range of activities	• Only a few on-board extras to pay for
• Well-trained and exceptionally helpful crew	• Fairly priced bars
	• Overall excellent value for money

Fig. 4.7. The service concept. (Adapted from Johnston and Clarke, 2005.)

Meeting Customer Needs

The industry is characterized by standardization and individualization (customization).

Standardization: One service fits all, or a set of services (first and economy) are tailored slightly to meet customer needs.

Individualization: The entire experience can be tailored to individual needs.

While low-cost airline operators and local rail travel providers offer a single price service where all customers have the same experience, there are services where there are distinctly different service levels. This is demonstrated through first-class ticket purchases, where the additional cost includes free food, waitress service, connections for laptops and business equipment, making the services popular with business users, and through the completely individualized services offered at resorts where customers can enjoy a range of additional services, which means the product offering is tailored specifically to the needs of individual customers.

Johnston and Clarke (2005) also proposed a service process model, which acknowledges the simple concept that the more a product is individualized, the more work is required to create the product and, therefore, the higher the cost. This work is considered to be the process, and is often paired with the volume. A high-process product is likely to be low volume (high-end cabin in cruise ships) while the simpler process, which will also be cheaper, is higher volume (economy cabins on a ferry).

Management of the service encounter

The service encounter describes the point, or moment, when the customer comes into contact with the service of an organization or the people providing the service. This is usually referred to as a 'moment of truth'. In the case of travel operations management, this is manifest in the booking halls and shops of airports, ticket office and cafes of railway stations, the drivers and tour guides on coaches and the crew aboard their cruise liners. This emphasizes the fact that everybody in the business is key to delivering effective customer service, which impacts upon the likelihood of repeat business.

The need to provide a high-level service is highlighted by Shackley (2001, p. 21) who recognizes that:

> [o]nce the visitor has arrived at the site of his or her choice the nature of the experience is also affected by the availability of suitable visitor services, which may include interpretation, transport, parking, accommodation, catering, signage, guiding and merchandising, as well as by the attitude of site staff and manager.

As has been seen before, travel operations borrow heavily from tourism theory but while this quote may be satisfactory in the context of a resort it does not touch upon the needs of the myriad other services in this tourism sub-sector. In this instance, a better definition may be:

> The experience of the visitor throughout the service experience, from making the decision to purchase, to arriving at the point of travel, and through the travel experience and tourism activities that succeed it to the return journey and the feelings of satisfaction or dissatisfaction that remains post trip.

Question

What, where and when are the moments of truth in your department or organization?

Understanding the customer and their interaction with the business requires a basic understanding of some of the underpinning sociological theory. In essence every customer will have a different comprehension of his or her experiences because each customer is different. There are some generalizations that can be made and these are based upon the society in which the person has lived. In the UK, for example, the star rating system used for hotels is universally understood, but a visitor from a different cultural background would have a different understanding of the quality inferred by the star rating. There is a degree of individuality within the decision-making process as well, often referred to as push-pull factors, and most often apparent when people view marketing materials and are making a decision to purchase.

This is described in expectancy-disconfirmation theory (Johns, 2003), which suggests that the visitor's experience is measured by the disconfirmation of customer expectations, so when they experience a flight or a visit to an airport they make their judgement based on the way in which the experience has disproved what they expected. If it is better than expected, customers are likely to be satisfied; by contrast, if the experience is not as good as that which was expected, they are likely to be dissatisfied.

These experiences can be mapped through the moments of truth and the customer flow patterns using the visitor journey framework, which highlights the different stages of a consumer's experience. Examples of the application of the visitor journey are given in Table 4.2.

Although many aspects of the experience of services are described as intangible, because the customer never owns the equipment, the actual equipment still plays a crucial role in the delivery of a good service. Some considerations, which impact upon the successful delivery of the service, encountered through the visitor journey are also included, and tend to be factors which contribute to the intangible 'quality' of the experience:

- comfortable, safe and secure spaces (in airports, facilities, toilets, hotels, cruise ships);
- overall visitor satisfaction;
- quality of accommodation;
- quality of food;
- value for money; and
- level of customer service.

Table 4.2. Application of the visitor journey.

Stages of the visitor journey	Example of resort	Example of single flight
Pre-trip	Research to inform decision making, influenced by marketing materials	Research to inform decision making, influenced by marketing materials
Reception	Greeting on arrival at the airport and at the resort	Greeting on arrival at the airport
Consumption of core, secondary and ancillary components	All aspects of the airline flight, the resort and any excursion. Also includes use of any resort facilities and additional services	The flight, together with any extra items purchased (such as refreshments)
Departure	Getting to the airport and leaving the airport	Leaving the airport
Follow-up	Thoughts, memories and levels of satisfaction afterwards	Scheduling, quality and satisfaction in retrospect

CASE STUDY: A COMPARISON OF SERVICE STANDARDS

Longer-distance train services offer two distinct levels of service: first class and standard class.

Standard-class passengers purchase a ticket that offers seating in a row of four with an aisle down the middle. Some seats have tables, others have a fold-up 'picnic' table mounted on the back of the seat in front. Some companies offer plugs for laptops and mobile phones and some services also have radio broadcast facilities. There is a shop on board where passengers can purchase refreshments, magazines and other items.

By contrast, first-class passengers are offered greater legroom in seating rows of three (two on one side, one on the other side of the aisle) and all seats have tables. In addition, there is often a waiter/waitress service and passengers are offered complimentary food. First-class tickets are a higher price so these additional benefits are considered to be the added value.

On quieter services, train operators will offer cheaper tickets for all classes and cheap first-class upgrades to standard-class passengers. This is a yield management technique designed to increase income on services that may be running at a

Continued

P. Robinson and S. Gelder

loss, and to reduce any loss of stock that is kept for first-class passengers, such as food. In addition, some companies run travel clubs which offer free train travel on quiet services, designed to encourage passengers to spend money once on board and to develop customer loyalty. Often these schemes require passengers to purchase a specified number of tickets over a given period of time, and so encourages use of the railway during busier times when ticket prices are much higher.

Rail operators are regularly criticized for higher ticket prices at peak times, but often this is the only way for operators to cover the costs of quieter services during the daytime and at weekends. While this can be a disincentive for people to commute by train, regular customers are offered season passes and discounts which reward this greater commitment with lower prices.

(Sources: various)

Question

What else could train companies do to encourage passengers to spend extra money while on board?

Managing health and safety

'The risks that scare us and the risks that kill us are two different things' (Levitt and Dubner, 2006, p. 136) This statement prepares us immediately for the hysteria and 'misinformation' that underpins risk management within a travel operations context. The processes for risk management remain the same for all industries and within the EU are bound by the Health and Safety at Work Regulations 1992.

This mandatory requirement (for businesses with over five employees) addresses the hazards that are evident in all industries and identifies the control measures to remove or reduce the associated risk to an acceptable level. A legal duty of care further endorses the need for contemporary businesses to consider not only the moral importance of maintaining customer safety but also to recognize the growth in 'business risk management' as a strategic necessity for the economic well-being of the organization. While this is not included in this chapter, it nevertheless needs to be considered within a holistic assessment of the risk management process.

Risk assessment process

The process for managing risks in any industry is *not* standardized and while mandatory compliance to the legislation is required, the way in which this is achieved varies considerably from industry to industry and company to company. In the UK, the Health and Safety Executive (HSE), in the event of a major incident or accident, will need to see a range of documentation to assess that the identified risks have been effectively managed. The key document will be the risk assessment form, but other documents may include training logs, equipment maintenance logs, company induction programmes or accident records to see if 'near misses' or specific trends have emerged in a certain area. Briefly, the risk assessment process should require the employer to first understand the following key terms.

Hazards: These are anything that has the potential to cause harm.
Risks: These are the likelihood that that harm will become realized.

The process requires employers to:

- identify significant hazards and remove them if possible;
- evaluate risks;
- control the risks, or reduce them to insignificant levels; and
- record and review the risk assessments. (Chartered Institute of Environmental Health, 1994)

A travel industry example at the macro level would be the occasions where the Federation of Tour Operators has suspended departures to countries in the midst of turmoil. Examples would include: suspension of visits to Kenya due to election unrest; or advice not to travel to Middle Eastern countries during military conflict or to countries where natural disasters have compromised the infrastructure of the area.

Codes of practice

Many industries produce their own code of practice often developed through governing body expertise. The Institute for Sport and Recreation Management initiated the Safety in Swimming Pools guidelines from which lifeguard training and effective pool management techniques have emerged. Again the Federation of Tour Operators has produced preferred codes of practice tools for resort venue suppliers. Key areas for attention include:

- fire safety;
- food hygiene;
- children's clubs;
- beach safety;
- pool safety; and
- *Legionella* management.

Examples of best practice continue in the field and ABTA, in partnership with the Parabis group, has compiled a new health and safety database – the ABTA Resort check or 'ARC'. The online database is anticipated to grow to include up to 30,000 properties in the UK and abroad.

The travel industry will, by nature of its day-to-day operations, include specific types of risks that are unique to its business (Fig. 4.8).

The events of 9/11 have arguably affected the travel industry more than any other; the increases in security alone have had a profound effect on the operation of the industry where the supply chain has had to include 'additional links' to ensure that the 'perception' of safety is maintained. The sign depicted in Fig. 4.9 considers the key areas of travel – travel risks are multidisciplinary and need to be proactively managed.

It is appropriate to consider the demand placed on a travel venue and the capacity that the venue will be exposed to, and readjust accordingly. For example, in a busy train station at a peak period (either regular peaks or induced peaks generated through effective demand management techniques) exposure to risks around crowd management becomes more prominent. More people in a confined space increases the

Security	Medical
Risk assessments	Health insurance
Emergency evacuation plans	Health planning
Emergency action plans	Accident procedures
Emergency contacts	Qualified staff
Staff training/vigilance	

Risk management: facility-specific examples of risks

Airports' prime risks:	security, crowd management
Cruise ships:	outbreak of illness
Resorts' prime risks:	outbreak of disease, alcohol-induced disorder
Coach companies:	driver fatigue

Fig. 4.8. Key areas for managing travel risks.

Fig. 4.9. Managing risk requires more than signage! (Courtesy of Grace Gelder, 2008.)

risk of accidents that fall into the category of slips, trips and falls (responsible for around 40% of all accidents (HSE, 2007)). Petty theft and competing claims for limited space leading to conflict are other examples of the types of incidents common in travel venues.

The industry does have its own 'monitoring' organizations that serve to oversee the best interests of the industry. Briefly these include: the Association of British Travel Agents (ABTA), who offer a code of conduct with benefits beyond the minimum requirements of the law; the Federation of Tour Operators (FTO), who monitor policy for the tour operators sector; and the Association of Independent Tour Operators (AITO), who represent small- and medium-sized operators. The Travel Trust Association (TTA) and the Confederation of Passenger Travel (CPT) are other smaller agencies that will consider the issues of health and safety as part of their terms of reference.

Forecasting and Demand Trend Analysis

Aligned to risk management is the 'capacity' of any organization. The closer to maximum capacity, the more risks this presents. Forecasting therefore plays a major role in travel businesses; accurate forecasting for example of international tourism demand can play a major role in the policy formulation of both central and local government, and strategic planning for the tourism sectors: public, private and voluntary. Forecasting falls into two main categories: quantitative and qualitative methods. This section will highlight some of the examples from each category recognizing that the numerous models that exist are beyond the scope of this chapter. The emphasis will be placed on the distinction between the two techniques.

Quantitative methods

Quantitative methods take past information about a phenomenon and organize them by mathematical rules, taking advantage of underlying patterns of interest in the data. Veal (2002) suggests that time-series analysis, also known as extrapolative methods, is the most common form of tourism forecasting, with causal methods being a further subcategory of quantitative methods.

Extrapolative techniques, in which predictions of the future is based on past or current trends, require a fundamental prerequisite that the historical data are available over a long time period. Examples of extrapolative forecasting methods are: naive, single moving average, single exponential smoothing, double exponential smoothing, classical decomposition, auto regression or box Jenkins approach (adapted from Frechtling, 2001). There are normally five data patterns to look for, which are illustrated in Fig. 4.10.

Times-series analyses are the most popular among practitioners as they are simple to use; furthermore, they are inexpensive as they only require a data series and a computer spreadsheet program.

The central objective of the causal method approach is to determine the causal (or explanatory) variables that affect the forecast variable and the appropriate mathematical expression of this relationship (Frechtling, 2001). The explicit portrayal of cause-and-effect relationships presents an advantage over time-series methods, but is more costly, time-consuming and often considerably less accurate. Causal methods include regression analysis or structural econometric models.

As mentioned above, these techniques have become very sophisticated in recent years and now involve many complex mathematical formulae utilizing the latest computer software packages.

P. Robinson and S. Gelder

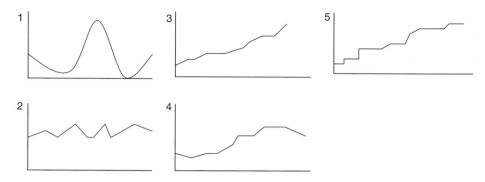

NB: *Time is measured along the x-axis, and customer numbers along the y-axis*

   1. Seasonality: patterns appear at particular times of year and recur annually
   2. Stationary: customer numbers fluctuate evenly around a horizontal level
   3. Linear trend: numbers rise or fall consistently
   4. Non-linear trend: no clear pattern but variable numbers
   5. Stepped series: there is a saturation point which may vary

Fig. 4.10. Time series for patterns.

Qualitative methods

Qualitative methods are also referred to as 'judgemental models', as experts organize past information using their experience and expertise in the industry and make judgements on future scenarios rather than the mathematical rules that underpin quantitative methods. They are often chosen over quantitative models when there is a lack of historical data from which to base predictions or the macro environment is changing rapidly. Examples of these methods include executive consensus, subjective probability assessment, Delphi method, consumer intentions survey or scenario setting (Bull, 1995; Frechtling, 2001; Veal, 2002). The Delphi technique (from the Delphic Oracle of ancient Greece), for example, involves asking a panel of experts their opinions or views on the future of an industry and predicting the state of that industry in, for example, 20, 50 or 100 years' time. Experts typically will have collective knowledge in areas of politics, economics, sociology and climatology to compliment specific industry expertise.

The advantages of qualitative methods are that they are relatively inexpensive and do not require a high level of statistical knowledge. Furthermore, they are considered less rigorous. Their disadvantages are more obvious in that errors can arise through lack of 'expertise' or bias of chosen judges. The risk associated with the human tendency to confuse desires for the future with forecasts of it is not free from subjectivity (Frechtling, 2001).

In travel and tourism, forecasting demand is essential to the overall planning process. Demand for travel and tourism can be measured in a number of ways, these include participation rates, trip volume and expenditure (Veal, 2002). It is also far from an exact science. It is still helpful for planners to attempt to measure the potential change. Veal (2002) suggests that industry forecasters should utilize a range of techniques rather than relying on one method alone, as this eliminates any anomalies relating to a single approach.

Revenue and Yield Management

Revenue management: This pays particular attention to income generation for the organization. It suggests charges should be based around:

- time of use;
- length of use;
- category of user;
- availability of spare capacity;
- impact on resources;
- scope to develop additional income streams; and
- scope to increase secondary spend.

Yield management: Businesses must be able to forecast demand, manage pricing strategies and increase both customer numbers and sales income. This is often characterized in the travel sector by the overbooking of capacity, such as airline seats, and development of different packages and/or pricing strategies. This can be achieved because it forces companies to assess visitor flow patterns (such as dwell time, seasonality and arrival times) and identifies overhead costs.

Pricing Strategies

Development of yield management into pricing strategies relies upon the premises suggested by Kimes (2000) that the ideal environment for successful implementation meets the four requirements identified and explained here.

Fixed capacity but variable demand: An example of this may be a train service which runs at maximum capacity or overcapacity while commuters are using the service. Prices are kept high because there is a captive audience and many fares, especially first class, are paid for by businesses. By contrast, during quieter times prices are much lower to incentivize train travel. This may also include cheap first-class upgrades and discounts for advance booking.

Easy market segmentation: The coach industry provides a clear example of an effective pricing strategy for different market segments. The coach industry has access to six potentially lucrative markets, explained in Table 4.3.

Perishable products that can be sold in advance of consumption: Taking a resort event or excursions as an example, tickets are perishable. They are of no use beyond the date of the activity. They can, however, be sold in the time leading up to an event, which means that if sales are not going well the purchase price can be discounted to increase income and numbers. Although ideally this needs to generate a profit, it is possible that breaking even on ticket sales will lead to profit generation through secondary spend based on higher attendance.

Marginal cost of sales is low: This allows the vendor to vary the price to meet market demand and to maximize opportunities presented through seasonal variations

---

P. Robinson and S. Gelder

Table 4.3. Maximizing appeal to enhance profitability through diversification.

Market segment	Advantage to the operator	Risk to the operator
Schools contracts	• Well-paid regular work • Older vehicles can be used • Will develop additional school trip business	• Priority service so impacts on the business if there are driver shortages
Commercial and conference work	• Well-paid 1–5-day hire for conference delegates	• Usually require luxury vehicles and work is often not guaranteed
Private hire	• Builds up a loyal customer base from the traditional coach tour market for group travel for trips organized by groups	• Highly competitive market place means hire rates and therefore profits are kept low
UK and European travel	• Can be lucrative	• Market is dominated by key players • Business has to invest in pre-booking rooms, planning trips and organizing tours • Customer expectations are increasing
Shuttle and transfer services	• Airport and event transfers provide well-paid regular work	• Market is dominated by repeat business and major players
National contracts	• Working on behalf of national carriers, reasonably secure work and brings in good income levels	• Work may be limited and service reduction may impact upon contractors

and regular peaks and troughs through flexible pricing strategies, because the cost of the sale is low enough to withstand this strategy.

Productivity and Performance Management

High productivity is good, while low productivity suggests that a business is struggling for one or a number of reasons. The larger the organization, the more complex the systems and procedures are and the more difficult it becomes to understand the overall progress that the business is making. Lashley and Lee-Ross (2003) comment that it is essential for a performance to be measured from the perspectives of stakeholders, customers, employees and the community. Some of these are discussed below.

Profitability: Financial performance can be measured on the profitability of the business using any combination of net profit, working capital and gearing rations, all of which are explained in further detail in the finance chapter (Chapter 8, this volume). Many managers will not need to understand or carry out these calculations, but will instead rely upon specialist departments to provide this in useable, understandable format. This would be part of a Management Information System (MIS).

Market performance: This can be measured using various data sets that can also be used to benchmark business performance against competitors. While it is hard to persuade competitors to reveal financial data outside of published annual reports, these data are much easier to access. Useful information includes: customer numbers, repeat visits, customer feedback and secondary spend.

Resource utilization: This assesses the effectiveness with which recourses are managed and ensures fair and equitable distribution of existing and new resources. Financial pressures usually make it difficult to acquire all the equipment that each department would ideally require. Often this is resolved by offering each department the opportunity to bid for assets that they need. The financial aspects of resource management focus upon return on investment (ROI), depreciation and long-term cost savings of using new facilities, or the ability to meet demand more effectively, providing a higher level of customer service.

People performance: This can be measured in part through the appraisal system and is designed to quantify mistakes, absences, target achievement, complaints (which are all hard measures) and friendliness and empathy of staff (soft measures).

The balanced scorecard approach: The concept of the scorecard is to offer managers an opportunity to measure performance relative to specific work tasks or staff teams. This is discussed in greater detail in Chapter 8 (this volume).

Statistical process control (SPC): SPC allows managers to look at the outputs of the operations process and compare them to a standard. This makes perfect sense in manufacturing, but in the service industry is more difficult to apply unless the SPC uses measures such as customer satisfaction or timekeeping. The process involves defining requirements and levels of acceptability within the variation – minimum and maximum. There then needs to be a system in place to actually measure the process and its outputs.

Benchmarking: Benchmarks define good practice or performance standards. A production benchmark could be used to compare production levels in several factories producing similar goods. In the travel sector, benchmarking could be used to assess timekeeping, customer service or other performance standards, and these can be compared to an industry standard or to different organizations or within the business between different departments or different operating businesses.

If there is low productivity a cause must be identified for this. A simple process needs to be followed to identify and rectify the issue:

- problem identification;
- focus on key issues;
- dialogue;
- goal setting;
- plan implementation; and
- monitoring and evaluation.

Performance management provides a good indicator of business health. There is an argument that productivity provides a more useful tool for measurement than profitability because it underlines factors which contribute to that productivity and is, therefore, a more useful management tool, as discussed by Heap in Leask and Yeoman (1999).

There is a proviso for the use of productivity as a tool for monitoring performance, because it requires benchmarking against competitors or previous productivity to understand what the data means. It is also important to highlight that productivity will always be low when setting up a new business and when equipment is nearing the end of its workable life or when there is insufficient equipment or facilities to meet demand.

Summary

The chapter has considered the role that operations plays in the achievement of organizational objectives. It has considered the responsibility that the individual employee has in almost every area of the business and how each element of operations is intrinsically linked to overall business success. These inputs can be identified as the human resource, the financial resource or the physical resource, and it is the transformation of these components which leads to the customer experience.

Acknowledgements

Kelly May, Andaman Discoveries; Grace Gelder.

Further Research

Slack, N., Chambers, S. and Johnson, R. (2007) *Operations Management*, 5th edn. Pearson Education, Edinburgh, UK.

Web Sites

www.iomnet.co.uk

Review Questions

1. Using the frameworks in this chapter as a basis, create a diagrammatic representation of the service process for an organization within the sector. How is your diagram different from the generic one included here?
2. Using relevant examples explain how operations management impacts upon customer care.
3. Consider three factors that may impact on demand for travel services.
4. Give two examples, one quantitative and one qualitative, of forecasting techniques utilized within the travel industry.
5. How often should risk assessments be reviewed? What systems exist in your workplace to manage risk? Are these systems sufficient or can you recommend improvements?

References

Bull, A. (1995) *The Economics of Travel and Tourism*. Longman, Melbourne.
Certo, S. (2000) *Modern Management: Diversity, Quality, Ethics and the Global Environment*, 8th edn. Prentice-Hall, Upper Saddle River, New Jersey.
CIEH (1994) Chartered Institute of Environmental Health. Available at: www.cieh.org
Frechtling, D. (2001) *Forecasting Tourism Demand – Methods and Strategies*. Butterworth-Heinemann, Oxford.
Greasley, A. (2006) *Operations Management*. Wiley, Chichester, UK.
HSE (2007) Health and Safety Executive. Available at: www.hse.gov.uk/statistics
Johns, T. (2003) *Perfect Customer Care: All You Need to Get it Right First Time*. Random House Business Books, London.

Johnston, R. and Clark, G. (2005) *Service Operations Management*, 2nd edn. Financial Times/Prentice-Hall, Harlow, UK.

Kimes, S. (2000) A strategic approach to yield management. In: Ingold, A., McMahon-Beattie, U. and Yeoman, I. (eds) *Yield Management*, 2nd edition. Continuum, London.

Lashley, C. and Lee-Ross, D. (2003) *Organization Behaviour for Leisure Services*. Butterworth-Heinemann, Oxford.

Leask, A. and Yeoman, I. (1999) *Heritage Visitor Attractions: An Operations Management Perspective*. Thomson Learning, London.

Levitt, S. and Dubner, S. (2006) *Freakonomics: A Rogue Economist Explores the Hidden Side of Everything*. Penguin, London.

McMahon-Beattie, U. and Yeoman, I. (2004) *Sport and Leisure Operations Management*. Thomson Learning, London.

Needle, D. (2000) *Business in Context*, 3rd edn. Thomson Learning, London.

Russell, R.S. and Taylor, B.W. (2009) *Operations, Management Along the Supply Chain*. Wiley Asia, Singapore.

Shackley, M. (2001) *Managing Sacred Sites*. Continuum, London.

Slack, N., Chambers, S. and Johnston, R. (2004) *Operations Management*, 4th edn. Pearson Education Ltd, Harlow, UK.

Swarbrooke, J. (2002) *The Development and Management of Visitor Attractions*, 2nd edn. Butterworth-Heinemann, Oxford.

Veal, A.J. (2002) *Leisure and Tourism Policy and Planning*, 2nd edn. CAB International, Wallingford, UK.

Wright, J.N. (2001) *The Management of Service Operations*. Continuum, London.

5 Logistics and Supply Chain Management in Travel Operations

ADE ORIADE

Objectives of the Chapter

This chapter aims to equip students with an understanding of the organization of operations, based on creation of responsive and effective systems. The chapter explores the organization of operations in terms of flow of information, services and resources. In particular, it analyses the effective planning and management of facilities and processes, involving operational issues such as location, information handling and supply of materials. Additionally the chapter appraises quality and inventory management and acknowledges the increasingly uncertain environment in which operational decisions are made and their implementation controlled. The chapter will:

- explain the nature of logistics activities and supply chain management; and
- demonstrate the relationship between these activities and how they can be managed within travel operations.

Introduction

Logistics and supply chain management are closely linked concepts which cannot be discussed in isolation. However, there is a clear distinction between the two. To avoid confusion it is useful to define each concept at this stage.

Christopher (2005, p. 4) defines *logistics management* as:

> [t]he process of strategically managing the procurement, movement and storage of materials, parts and finished inventory (and the related information flows) through the organization and its marketing channels in such a way that current and future profitability are maximised through the cost-effective fulfilment of orders.

People are usually conversant with the word logistics and they use it when talking about moving materials, but then dissociate it from its conceptual aims, which are to provide a tool to enable businesses to be responsive in providing services that meet and possibly exceed the expectations of their customers. Gourdin (2006) refers to logistics as a systematic management of a range of activities which are necessary to transfer benefits from their point of production to the customer. Based on this definition, logistics places the customer at the nucleus of its focus. However, as straightforward as this may seem, managing logistics could be daunting,

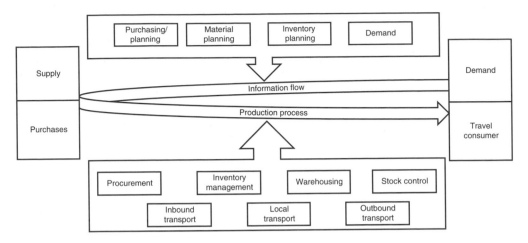

Fig. 5.1. The logistics process. (Adapted from Page, 1999, p. 185)

particularly in travel operations, and it is not uncommon for managers to face challenging and problematic issues in achieving agile and lean logistics processes. These complexities stem from increased competition, increased customer demand, improved technology, continued business expansion, increased demand on organizational resources and a host of other factors. Figure 5.1 outlines the logistics process for the travel industry, demonstrating the importance not just of physical resources but also information.

Christopher (2005) describes *supply chain management* as a wider concept, which builds upon the 'single-plan' framework of logistics which explains the flow of products and information through a business (Fig. 5.2). In this sense, supply chain management aims to achieve coordination and linkage between operations and the business processes that take place between an organization, its suppliers and customers. The concept may be regarded simply as the integration of key

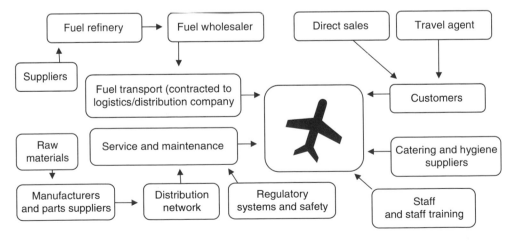

Fig. 5.2. Example of a supply chain for an airline operator.

A. Oriade

business processes among industry partners with the view to adding value for customers. It closely links numerous successive elements of the industry value chain, from upstream suppliers, through sub-assembly manufacturers, final manufacturers, distributors and retailers to the end-customers. For instance in travel operations, one linkage may be from catering suppliers to individual cruise ships moored in dock to individual customers. Any changes which take place within this relationship may be based upon cost savings, quality enhancement or ideally both. The main aim is to have a commercial and competitive advantage over rival organizations by making the process more cost-effective, more efficient and the products more differentiated (Richard and Wisner, 2005).

As tourism involves movement of people from the tourism-generating zone to the tourism-destination zone, it is inevitable that, with the exception of the industry's largest organizations, a number of service providers will be involved who are unlikely to belong to the same organization (Fig. 5.3). Even where they are part of a business it is likely they will be managed as separate business units; therefore the need to create a seamless system becomes imperative. Such seamless operations must strive to deliver quality service that:

● results in delighted customers;
● maintains a relationship that nurtures dependable service suppliers;
● provides an environment that encourages high standards of customer care; and
● focuses on total quality management.

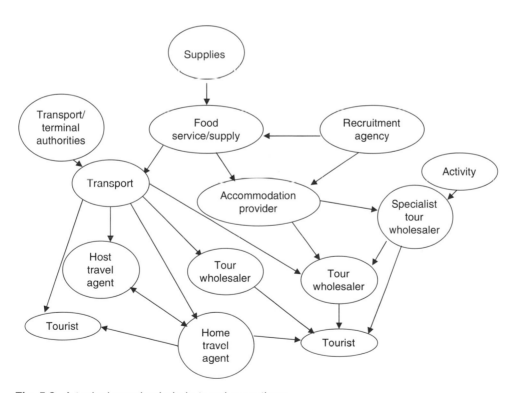

Fig. 5.3. A typical supply chain in travel operations.

Supply chain management and logistics activities in travel and tourism may range from ground handling, to delivery of catering products, to information systems management and compliance with health and safety regulations.

Question

Based on a business or business unit of your choice create your own supply chain diagram to demonstrate the complex relationships which exist in service delivery.

Context and Concepts

There is no doubt that times are changing due to advancements in technology, increased customer expectations and intense competition, especially as the world is fast becoming a more compact global village. The travel and tourism industry is multi-sectoral with numerous organizations contributing to the 'production' of one, or a bundle of products. Even though there is a tendency for vertical integration in the industry, there still exists a need for collaboration and partnership. For an organization to survive in these changing times, there has to be a flexibility and adaptability allowing the business to be innovative in its strategic vision.

Added Value and Competitive Advantage

The two most commonly used concepts in logistics and supply chain management are added value and competitive advantage. Some writers refer to these as cost and value advantages. Organizations that aim to have a competitive advantage by delivering added value to their customers must understand how that value is generated and lost. Both these ideas are best captured by Porter's (1990) value chain model. An adapted model of the value chain is illustrated in Fig. 5.4. This divides the main functions into

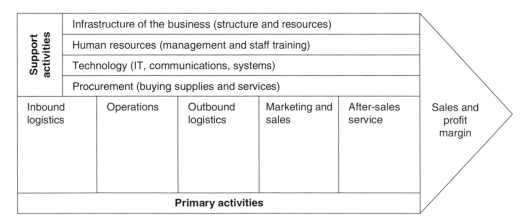

Fig. 5.4. The value chain. (Adapted from Porter, 1990.)

---

two categories: primary activities and support activities. The primary activities depict functions that are performed to deliver a service or create a product while the support activities enhance the effectiveness of the primary activities. In Porter's (1990) model the primary activities comprise inbound logistics, operations, outbound logistics, marketing and sales and service, while the support activities include organization infrastructure, technology development, human resource management and procurement.

An organization must perform these in order to provide benefits to its customers. The cost of these activities and their corresponding value determines whether or not the best value products or services are developed (Johnson *et al.*, 2008). While the value chain can be used to chart the general strategic course of an organization, its use in determining the cost-effectiveness and value effectiveness of an organization's logistics system cannot be overemphasized. As identified previously, the travel industry is multi-sectoral with a number of organizations co-producing one 'product' (e.g. a package holiday may comprise flights to a destination, hotel accommodation, visits to attractions and car rental). The effectiveness of both inbound and outbound logistics needs to be understood and managed in relation to suppliers and customers. In this case, the logistics activities of an organization and its suppliers must be understood in the context of delivering a final product or service to customers from a value network perspective (Johnson *et al.*, 2008).

Business Functions in Logistics System in Travel Operations

Logistics systems are made up of many business functions, some of which are linked or identical to the activities mentioned in the value chain model; however, unlike the value chain the functions are likely to differ from industry to industry and from one type of operation to another. Some of the major components of the logistics system identified by Page (1999) include purchasing, technical expertise, production planning, storage and materials handling, transport, inventory management, warehousing, planning, marketing and customer service.

In travel operations, some of the business functions are more prominent than others, so this chapter discusses the key elements of information processing, inventory management, transport, storage, material handling and quality, including consideration of the role of quality in customer care (which is also discussed in Chapter 4, this volume). Quality management captures precisely the art of planning, controlling and improving service delivery (Juran, 1989).

Quality management

As discussed, customers derive a sense of satisfaction in the service they are provided with and this should be the goal of every aspect of logistics management. This is made more challenging by the notion that travel and tourism products are mainly intangible and experiential, which highlights the importance of each individual customer's judgement on the service they receive. Experience is an indistinct concept that is difficult to define and measure because of its multiple elements and individualized, personal nature (Knutson and Beck, 2003). Consumer experience in travel relies on three

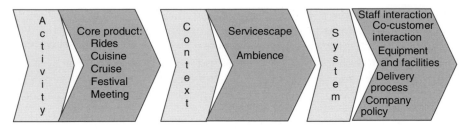

Fig. 5.5. Determinants of customer experience.

principal components, which are explained in greater detail in Fig. 5.5: the main activity, the context and the service delivery systems. The latter comprises the customer interaction with an organization's facilities, staff and co-consumers in the delivery process. The total customer experience is premised on efficient utilization of an organization's resources to provide services that meet or exceed the expectations of the traveller.

Evidence abounds that identifies quality as one of the most significant elements that determines the satisfaction of a traveller's experience. Quality, like experience, is hard to define but people know when it is absent in a product. A surprising number of businesses only pay lip-service to the provision of quality service and quality management systems.

There are two approaches employed to define quality. These are the manufacturing industry approach and the service industry approach.

In defining quality using the manufacturing approach the focus is on 'the totality of features and characteristics of a product or service that bears on its ability to meet a stated or implied need' (ISO, 1994). To this end, quality gurus like Crosby (1979) defined quality as conformance to requirements. Juran (1988) also defined quality simply as fitness for use.

On the other hand, quality in the service industry focuses on the customer experience and based on this, Engel *et al.* (1986) view quality as a function of the customer's experiences and the personal values which govern their expectations.

Although this section is focused upon quality management within a service context, the manufacturing approach is mentioned because the majority of concepts and theories of service quality are developed from quality management in manufacturing. However, it has been argued and widely accepted that quality in the service sector cannot be managed in the same manner as manufacturing because of the nature of service, a fact that has been widely documented. The most commonly cited characteristics include variability, inseparability, intangibility and perishability. However, Grönroos (2001) argues that the most important characteristic is probably the fact that services are processes, which may include simultaneous activities of co-production and consumption at the site of production. So here people's experiences are being managed and it is the quality of the service they receive that will determine whether they are satisfied or not. In managing quality in the service sector, it is recommended that managers are conversant with two things; the way in which customers evaluate quality and how to manage quality in a systematic manner.

In addition to these two vital points, Williams and Buswell (2003) submit that service design and process management could most likely be the first stage of managing service quality in leisure and tourism. The concept of service design, when properly examined, has some implications for logistics as a framework. According to Gummesson (1994), service design covers hands-on activities employed in describing and detailing a service, the service system and the service delivery process.

In the process of quality evaluation, customer's expectations play a major role in the way the characteristics of service are perceived. Expectations of a service may be built on past experience, recommendations from friends and relatives and organizational communication to the customer (promotion, shops or web sites); these inform the basis of customers' judgements of the service which, most often, are based on rational evaluation and reflection. At other times, there is ample opportunity for the customer to judge quality without conscious evaluation, so it can be said that customers judge service from both subjective and objective perspectives. In addition to these perspectives, customers evaluate quality from a number of dimensions which have been researched and identified to differ between different industries and industrial sectors. The more intangible the dimensions, the harder it becomes to understand how customers evaluate them and for service operators to measure and manage them.

Dimensions of service quality have been presented by a range of authors. These are demonstrated in Table 5.1.

Question

Using one of these sets of dimensions of quality, describe how quality is managed in an organization of your choice.

The management of quality is said to have gone through four stages; while Dale (1999) sees this as a progressive route to Total Quality Management (TQM), Garvin (1988) considers it to be a chronological evolution of quality management where new organizations join at the later stages. These two views have been found to be true of tourism and hospitality organizations. Again the lesson from quality evolution is that quality management has moved away from being predominantly internally oriented to employing and combining different methods and standards of external verification such as Visitor Attraction Quality Assurance Service (VAQAS), ISO 9000 family of standards,

Table 5.1. Proposed dimensions of quality.

Grönroos (2000) Two service quality dimensions	Parasuraman et al. (1990) Five dimensions of service quality	Otto and Ritchie (1995) Six dimensions of experience quality
Functional (process-related)	Tangibles	Hedonic
	Reliability	Safety
Technical (outcome)	Responsiveness	Comfort
	Assurance	Novelty
	Empathy	Interactive
		Stimulation

Investors in People (IIP) and the European Foundation for Quality Management (EFQM). Again the notion of quality evolution indicates the departure of quality management from being the responsibility of one department to being an organization-wide affair with particular emphasis on systems, teams, tools, communication, commitment and culture. These are what Oakland and Morris (1998) called the elements of TQM.

Transportation

Transportation has been described as the pivot around which economic activities revolve. In manufacturing, transport is mainly concerned with the physical movement of goods from the point of production to the point of consumption or storage. In travel operations, the movement of people and materials is involved. Page (1999) submits that transport is an important element in moving visitors closer to the products of tourism. This distribution calls for the introduction of different approaches to transport. Transport of people is inextricably linked to the development of modes of transport. The train first facilitated this in the 1840s, a direct result of technological developments from the industrial revolution. The aeroplane and the motor coach evolved through the 20th century and, in the case of the aeroplane, early passengers were happy to arrive without incident! Today's tourist expects a certain level of comfort, safety and reliability.

However, the consumer does not have much input into how his or her personal goods are carried. The customers' expectation is to arrive at a destination, to be reunited with their luggage and for it to have sustained no damage. The passenger may not have any idea how it has been transported and may not set his or her eyes on the luggage from check-in at the airport until reaching the baggage reclaim point at the destination.

Transport of goods also relates to the effective movement of food and equipment for trains and planes. Cook–chill food will have to be transported and stored at the right temperature with specialized equipment. Quantities and variety of food needs to be considered for each flight, and decisions taken about the level of preparation that is acceptable while on board.

Other transport considerations include the supply of spare equipment and parts for aircraft and trains, which need to be stored in central locations for distribution for service and maintenance, but with the flexibility for quick delivery to minimize disruption due to unexpected breakdowns.

The final consideration with transport is the supporting infrastructure which operators rarely have any control over. Although the operator may have no responsibility for delays caused by infrastructural failure, they will most likely have to accept the complaints from their customers. This complex situation is explained in greater depth in the case study on p. 101.

Cooper *et al.* (2005) pointed out that the following factors are likely to be considered when making a choice of transportation:

- distance and time;
- status and comfort;
- safety and utility;
- comparative price;
- geographical position and location;
- range of services offered; and
- level of competition between services.

A. Oriade

The purpose of rail travel is twofold: the movement of people and the movement of goods. In the UK rail infrastructure, which includes tracks, bridges, level crossings, tunnels, electric cabling, signals and 2500 stations, are all owned by Network Rail, whose mission is to 'create a railway for the 21st century'. This places with them responsibility for the maintenance and development of railway infrastructure, delivered through major engineering contractors. Risk management and health and safety are crucial aspects of the business. As a result most engineering works require track closures or slow-running, which creates obvious issues for train-operating companies trying to deliver a timetabled service but unable to influence works which may be causing delays. An added complication is that some operators require track upgrades to allow for faster-running trains, which includes Virgins' tilting Pendolino units on the West Coast Mainline.

The majority of train operating companies (TOCs) on the network deliver services because they have won franchises from the Government. These are generally large travel-related businesses such as Virgin, National Express and Stagecoach. A small number of operators work on an 'open access' model, which allows access to the rail network for smaller enterprises usually running a small number of very specific routes. Decisions about this cheaper form of access to the network are, like Network Rail itself, managed by the Office of Rail Regulation.

A further logistical complication is the fact that most of the rolling stock is not owned directly by the operator but by rolling stock operating companies (ROSCOs), which are owned by UK banks, who lease the equipment to the TOCs. This reduces the financial risk to the business and increases flexibility. It ironically makes it much easier to transfer equipment between operators when franchises are won and lost. There are also additional spot-hire companies who provide rail equipment at short notice to train operators. Some of these are also owned by banks.

The other market sector which deserves mention here is the heritage railway business because there are some organizations in this sector running excursions and trips along main-line routes. They are restricted by the need to have suitably qualified steam train drivers and these are a dying breed in one of the most lucrative parts of the heritage railway sector.

The key message then, in this brief resumé of the structure of UK railways, is to highlight the complexity within which operators work while striving to deliver high-quality customer care, weighted against a whole raft of legislative and operational issues, in a commercially driven environment.

(Sources: various)

Question

What alternative structures would work better? It may be useful to research the management of railways in other countries, or to reflect on the history of British Rail and its privatized predecessors to try to understand some of the challenges and advantages that were presented by the management structures of the past.

When travelling a tourist may not necessarily be able to put all these into consideration; the last two are likely to enable the customer to form their perception of the quality of service received from a particular operator and subsequently make a decision about whether or not to use that operator again. It can be argued that with the increase in budget choices, such as low-cost airlines, people are not concerned with a range of services, preferring instead the lower cost. However, customers still expect a basic level of care and have the opportunity to judge the range of services offered between different providers. According to Cooper *et al.* (2005) the basic elements that constitute a typical transportation system include:

- the way;
- the terminal;
- the carrying unit; and
- the motive power.

While the operator has little influence on the quality of the road or the quality of the terminal, a travel operator must put into consideration the carrying unit giving consideration to safety, functionality and social responsibility issues. Table 5.2 illustrates this in more depth.

One major factor that has contributed immensely to tourism development in relation to transport is the deregulation of air transport. Liberation started in the USA in 1979 and was introduced in Europe in 1997. This has many implications in terms of increased competition, strategic alliances, development of budget airline operations and management within the air transport industry. Tactical partnerships developed after deregulation in line with growth in global distribution systems (GDS). Among numerous benefits to partners are reduced costs of marketing and reservation, joint loyalty programmes and code sharing. In the future, the role of transport is likely to become broader and environmental issues have already taken centre stage in the transport debate, with many businesses looking to negate their carbon footprints to avoid the likely impacts of otherwise enforced legislation.

Storage and materials handling

The majority of operators in the travel trade hold very little stock, and much of what is held is only temporary, for example, food waiting to be taken on to planes or travel brochures waiting to be put on shelves. There are exceptions to this, though. Airline operators have to store planes, maintenance equipment and parts. Airports have to store vehicles and equipment. Train companies have to store rolling stock. Any physical asset which is owned by a business becomes part of the inventory of the company, no matter how small. There are, of course, values linked to this inventory, which is discussed in greater detail in Chapter 8 (this volume). What is important here is how that inventory is managed, where it is stored and ultimately how it is moved to where it needs to be in the most cost-efficient manner.

There is, for example, no point flying a plane to one destination then bringing it back empty if it could be used for a return flight. Similarly, it is a waste of resources to fly planes around the world just to bring them back to a specific location for

A. Oriade

Table 5.2. Delivering quality transport.

Factor	Trains	Planes	Coaches and buses	Cruise ships and ferries
The way	Railways: operations management of infrastructure and operators is a key factor for success	Air: limited only by flight paths and airport capacities	Road: as with any road travel, traffic jams and accidents are a logistical risk	Sea: some ships limited by berthing size in docks
The terminal	Railway stations: some are manned and some are not. Safety may be an issue. Some TOCs run first-class lounges at stations. Major terminals may need revamps	Airports: range of facilities of varying ages. Most fit for purpose. Design for function is important. Security risks are increasing	Door to door services for charter and private hire and bus stations for scheduled journeys	Facilities at docks very variable; depends if passengers are on foot or travelling by car (ferries)
The carrying unit	Safety: improving but some notable accidents in recent years	Safety: considered to be very safe although there is a risk of terrorism and low survival rate from major accidents	Safety: very variable; other road users at risk from large vehicles. Some accidents relating to driver fatigue in recent years	Safety: very few accidents
	Functionality: UK trains notoriously late. European trains and Japanese trains very reliable. On-board radio, laptop plugs and shops for all passengers. Additional benefits for first-class travel	Functionality: extremely versatile depending on type and length of flight; range of tickets offer a range of services from basic seat to massage and champagne	Functionality: local transport tends to be functional. Travel trade tends to use vehicles with toilets, kitchens, television, air conditioning and reclining seats. Some full leather luxury coaches	Functionality: range of services and onboard facilities determined by ticket price and type of use (ferry or cruise)
	Social responsibility: some trains generate electricity under braking. All TOCs trying to reduce their environmental impacts	Social responsibility: plenty of debate in recent years and difficult issues to address because this is a global industry with shared regulations	Social responsibility: local bus companies investing in alternative technologies; reduced emissions from newer diesel engines	Social responsibility: operators are keen to reduce impacts
	Added value: different ticket levels, complimentary food, refunds and compensation for major issues	Added value: depends on the ticket	Added value: discounts on repeat business. Reduced admission to tourist sites	Added value: repeat discounts, discounts linked to other operators (hotel discounts, for example)
The motive power	Diesel or electric	Propeller or jet engines	Diesel, gas and biofuels	Ship fuel
Examples	The Orient Express West Coast Mainline Vintage Trains	Concorde (now defunct) Airbus A380 Boeing 737, 747, 767	Wallace Arnold National Express Arriva	Queen Mary 2 Sheraton Nile Cruises P&O Isle of Wight Ferries

maintenance checks. It is also fruitless to have broken and faulty equipment out of use, as this in business terms is a cost, so parts for repairs need to be able to be transported to where they are needed as quickly as possible. Similarly, travellers on long-haul flights will need breakfast, lunch and dinner. Preparing, cooking and packing food to serve 555 passengers on board an airbus A380 from London to Cape Town is impossible and businesses specialized in preparing and packing food will be a key part of the supply chain. By contrast, many train companies now have chefs on board and provide a range of light meals and dinners which can be cooked in onboard kitchens. This model is increasingly replacing the traditional onboard buffet car and food is distributed through the same network that supplies the hotel and catering trade.

Of course this supply chain can fail and there are plenty of tales of flights where there was insufficient water for everybody on board. At some other time, some operators will have to deal with handling of travellers' belongings. Management of the supply chain to minimize these risks relies on those businesses in the chain having their own contingency plans and for the operators to also have alternative options. This becomes increasingly challenging as more people have different dietary requirements and demand is not always easy to predict.

Inventory management

The principle of effective inventory management is based upon the production of only the quantity of stock required for immediate demand. The aim is not to hold excess stock, as this brings with it storage costs, so a minimal level of inventory must be maintained based on demand management tools (Chapter 4, this volume) and in this sense the need to balance the costs of holding and not holding inventory is a key factor. The cost of holding stock may be in the form of storage, insurance, handling and risk of loss through perishability. On the other hand, the cost of not holding stock can be manifest as lost revenue through the unavailability of items and potentially the resulting negative image that may accompany such an incident if a number of customers are affected and are consequently dissatisfied with the level of service. From both perspectives, inventory is more focused on cost reductions even though it has not been seen in that light in the past. However, times are changing and the high cost of inventory has encouraged organizations to concentrate on efficient supply chain and quality management (Russell and Taylor, 2009).

Types of inventory

It is essential to understand the various forms that inventory can take. The list of six types of inventory below is based on the work of Gourdin (2006):

- **Normal:** These stock levels meet regular levels of demand and are predictably replenished, such as airline food and travel brochures.
- **Safety:** Stock is held as insurance to meet uncertainty in demand.
- **Transit:** Stock is held en route between two or more locations.
- **Speculative:** Stock is held in anticipation of meeting future demand. This type of inventory is common in the travel trade. Stock may be held or released depending on what an operator or a number of operators envisage the future could be. Examples include selling of flight or hotel room at a discounted rate.

A. Oriade

- **Seasonal:** This is applicable to the travel trade where stocks are held and accumulated in readiness for a certain season. Ski resorts, for example, will buy in new hire equipment in preparation for the start of the season, but are likely to sell it cheaply at the end of the season.
- **Dead:** Stock is not sold within a given time. Dead stock translates into lost revenue.

Inventory management usually relies on supply chain models such as just-in-time (JIT), where stock arrives just as it is needed with orders processed along a computer-based distribution network. Other models include material requirement planning and distribution resource planning, but these methods evolved in the manufacturing sector and the nature of travel products does not suit these philosophies. The principal approach within the service sector is yield management (Chapters 4 and 8, this volume). Yield management is a revenue management method that provides tools to forecast and sell products at prices which maximize profit and minimize loss.

Information processing

This is one significant activity which links all other components of the logistics system; it is the key to success in supply chain management. Whereas historically the travel business relied much on intermediaries to distribute products and maintain relationships with travellers, with the growth of the Internet, organizations have been able to reduce distribution costs and have gained access to, and increased control over, their actual and potential customers. From a logistics perspective, the major benefit has been the shortened length of time required to reach suppliers and end-users directly and quickly. Information systems enable organizations to match demand with supply, particularly where a number of co-producers and distribution channels are involved in product delivery. Information processing cannot be overemphasized if travel organizations are to deliver total tourist experience, and these data are often shared over a global distribution system. There are, however, problems here related to the number of small and medium enterprises (SMEs) who do not engage with the technology. This means the traveller or travel agent trying to book a holiday cottage in Italy is likely to have to phone up to get prices and availability. There are of course some small businesses that can see the benefits of these systems, and the investment made by the bigger businesses often reduces the costs for the smaller operators. This gives SMEs the opportunity to link their databases and spreadsheets with those of their suppliers and clients (Gourdin, 2006).

No doubt this has allowed for greater versatility in the way in which organizations manage data to improve responsiveness to customers' needs. With organizations including those in the travel industry now able to generate, accumulate and process vast amounts of information concerning their suppliers and customers, they are more able to perform their planning, coordination, control and customer service functions. See Fig. 5.6 for an illustration of the functions of a logistics information system of a typical tour operator. It must be noted that each and every one of these functions has a direct or indirect influence on customer satisfaction and, subsequently, an effect on the organizations' aims and vision.

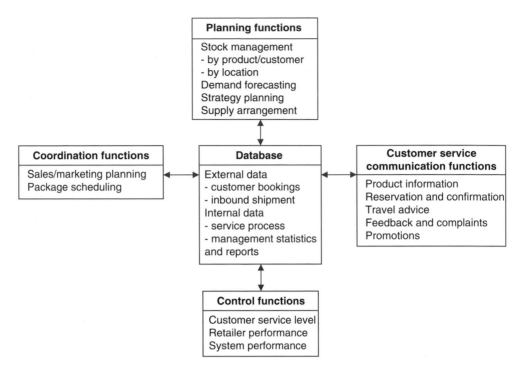

Fig. 5.6. Functions of a logistics information system of a typical travel firm. (Adapted from Christopher, 2005.)

Question

What are the benefits of models such as this to illustrate how information flows work within a business?

In Nilsson's (2006) study of experienced logisticians, it was found that customer demands on logistics had both increased in scale and in scope and involved several factors such as customized order bookings and customized labelling among other. According to Buhalis (1998, p. 411):

> Increasingly, new, experienced, sophisticated, demanding travellers seek information about more exotic destinations and authentic experiences, as well the requirement to interact with suppliers in order to satisfy their specific needs and wishes.

Only organizations that can effectively identify and satisfy these specific needs through their information systems are likely to succeed in the competitive travel market. Traveller satisfaction is said to depend highly on whether information provided by the operator on the accessibility, facilities, activities and attractions at a destination are accurate and comprehensive (Fesenmaier *et al.*, 1992 in Buhalis, 1998).

Location

Traditionally, organizations locate their facilities either close to the market or the source of raw materials. In travel and tourism, the location of facilities can be operation-, market- or product-led. Of course in some instances there is no choice. Railway stations have to be alongside the railway and new railways and trams are limited by their infrastructural requirements, but some facilities have more flexibility in their location. In fact in some instances, it is the presence of airports, docks and train stations which are the catalyst for the development of other travel businesses (hotels, restaurants, entertainment) and for the development of distribution hubs for their suppliers. East Midlands Airport (EMA) in Derbyshire has made a significant impact on the local economy not only because it draws in crowds of tourists (most depart at EMA for European holidays), but because it is an affordable location for freight and is surrounded by dedicated distribution depots for leading freight and courier businesses, many of whom have their own planes. Some of the factors which influence the choice of location are discussed below.

- **Government policy:** Irrespective of the type of facility, it will be subject to policy on town planning, and to justification on the basis of economic and environmental impact assessments. There may be incentive schemes to encourage investment.
- **Risk:** The perception has grown over recent years due to terrorist attacks, political instability and natural disasters. In locating facilities, this factor needs careful consideration to ensure the supply chain is not truncated.
- **Proximity to market:** Facilities located close to their market benefit from reduced transport costs and maintain close links with their customers. Although customers may have to travel to get to their destination, the services they need from travel operators can be brought closer to them. Technology has also made it possible for customers to assess operators' facilities without leaving the comfort of their home.
- **Competition:** It is not uncommon to find operators locate their facilities close to their competitors. This is in part to maintain their visibility in the market place and to offer customers a greater choice. This is particularly pertinent for high-street retail, but can be just as applicable when businesses are advertising on the Internet.
- **Complimentarity:** The location of suppliers may be influenced by the location of the businesses that they supply, reducing transport costs. There may be commercial benefits in sharing the same facilities, or leasing facilities back to suppliers.
- **Accessibility:** Facilities need to be supported by safe and secure infrastructural support.

These factors cannot be considered an exhaustive list, but they do point to the fact that the location of facilities needs careful consideration.

Planning

Christopher (2005) sees production planning in the manufacturing sector as the centre of the entire logistics process; this is equally true in the travel sector, but unlike the manufacturing industry, process planning in the service sector focuses on the customers. The design and delivery of service is based on the relationship between people (customer, employees, distributors and suppliers), equipment, facilities and the physical environment in providing products that will meet the expectations of the customer. Generally, planning is a process that comprises objective formulation, assessment of the current situation and identification of issues. Others include data gathering and analysis, actions and responsibilities, and monitoring and modification of variance where necessary. More specifically, process planning in travel operations involves establishing who the customers are and what their needs are to develop products and services that satisfy customers' needs.

The identification of customer types, behaviours and needs is discussed in greater detail in Chapter 7 (this volume), but the process of forecasting is a logistics tool and Archer (1980 in Gunn, 2002) defines it as the art of predicting the occurrence of events before they take place. Forecasting is used by managers and marketers alike to study the feasibility of a project, determine its operational requirements, set marketing goals, explore the potential market and ensure adequate capacity is provided (for detail coverage of forecasting see Chapter 4, this volume). The role of logistics in terms of gathering and processing information cannot be overemphasized in carrying out these activities.

Organizations deploy different methods in transferring plans to the operating team; mostly manuals or service blueprints are used. Service blueprints are a valuable tool for operations and logistics managers as they illustrate all the elements that comprise a service or process. Some diagrams have already been illustrated in earlier sections of this chapter but these can be developed further to create a flowchart of service delivery. A simplified flowchart is demonstrated in Fig. 5.7 with failure points illustrated by the letter F. This could be presented with additional information to assess costs and relationships between staff and resources.

Question

Can you design a service blueprint for a travel product or service?

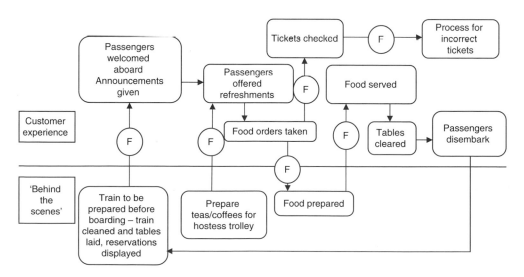

Fig. 5.7. Service blueprint for first-class train carriages.

A. Oriade

When new processes are designed, organizations naturally take steps to familiarize their employees with new systems and equipment. Often training courses are organized, tests run and simulations carried out. Failure in process planning is most likely to affect customers' experience of a service negatively, so the more planning that can be carried out at a test stage, the better.

Any negative experiences of a new product, service or facility are likely to result in bad publicity and possible refunds or compensation. There is a real need for adequate preparation before a major change in operations and the option to switch back to the older method should be retained if possible, at least during an interim phase, or an alternative contingency plan put in place.

CASE STUDY: PROCESS PLANNING AT HEATHROW

An example of the importance of process planning was illustrated by the Heathrow Terminal 5 (T5) saga. This shows how failure in one logistics activity can have a major impact on an organization's and its partners' activities. The two principal operators at the centre of the T5 incident were airline operator British Airways (BA) and British Aviation Authority (BAA) as the airport operator. Both organizations are market leaders in the industry, with a wealth of experience and a reputation for quality service. This incident is a one-off teething problem which had huge consequences.

The construction of T5 started in September 2002 and it officially opened in March 2008. The terminal was funded by BAA at the cost of £4.5 billion and it was envisaged that the expansion would benefit passengers and create a world-class airport. It was constructed with the capacity to process 12,000 bags per hour, with 96 self-service check-in kiosks, 56 standard check-in desks and 20 security lanes.

Despite the magnitude of preparation, the operation was far from smooth. The main problem started early on the first day of operation. In the first instance, both staff and passengers had trouble locating the car park. This resulted in staff turning up late, by which time queues had started building at the check-in desks and arrival passengers had to wait for their bags. This completely clogged the system.

By lunchtime, the problem had escalated and the airline was forced to cancel 20 flights. By the end of the first day of operation a total of 34 flights had been cancelled. In addition there was a backlog of around 15,000 bags. In the end 400 extra staff were drafted in and distribution of lost and left baggage had begun, but the impact of poor publicity will leave people with a somewhat disappointing memory of T5.

(Sources: various)

Questions

1. How do you think this incident might have been prevented from happening?
2. What are the logistics functions involved here?
3. What are the consequences of this incident?

Summary

This chapter has considered a range of aspects of logistics management within the travel industry, but key to operationalizing this is the fact that the logistics efforts should explore and take advantage of the relationship of all the different functions rather than concentrating on individual components or treating them in isolation. There is, therefore, a need for an integrative approach, so that the underlying principles of logistics are deployed in planning and coordinating operational management.

With efficient logistics and supply chain management, travel products and services are moved in the supply chain from one stage to another in a system of regular communication between the travellers and the service providers, so that the right quality and quantity of products are delivered to the end-user at the right time through a well-designed delivery process, based on careful consideration of the relationships between the organization's resources.

Loyal customers are the most important asset that a successful business can have. How well it can retain its customers and win new ones will go a long way towards determining its success. Christopher (2005) states that it no longer holds true that good products will sell themselves or that the success of a company today will carry forward into tomorrow. What really counts is standing out among competitors and the only two ways this can happen are for an organization to continually perform its functions and produce its products at a competitive cost or by being seen as adding value to the benefits received by its customers. Even then, an organization needs to identify which of these two directions to take and formulate strategies that will enable its logistics efforts to help to achieve its aims.

To succeed in this increasingly uncertain environment, organizations must respond to changing customer profiles and needs, and understanding the way logistics is managed will help to determine the success that can be achieved. Effective management of logistics and the supply chain must be geared towards the achievement of commercial and competitive advantage.

Review Questions

1. What is the relationship between logistics and supply chain management? Support your answer with examples.
2. How can managing logistics help an organization to achieve competitive advantage?
3. Explain how failure in one logistics activity can have a spiralling effect on the activities of an organization and its partners.

References

Buhalis, D. (1998) Strategic use of information technology in the tourism industry. *Tourism Management* 19(5), 409–421.

Christopher, M. (2005) *Logistics and Supply Chain Management: Creating Value-Adding Networks*, 3rd edn. Prentice-Hall, Harlow, UK.

Crosby, P.B. (1979) *Quality is Free: The Art of Making Quality Certain*. McGraw-Hill, New York.

A. Oriade

Cooper, C., Fletcher, J., Gilbert, D., Fyall, A. and Wanhill, S. (2005) *Tourism Principles and Practice*, 3rd edn. Longman, Harlow, UK.

Dale, B.G. (1999) *Managing Quality*, 3rd edn. Blackwell, Oxford.

Engel, J.F., Blackwell, R.D. and Miniard, P.W. (1986) *Consumer Behaviour*. Dryden Press, New York.

Gourdin, K.N. (2006) *Global Logistics Management: A Competitive Advantage for the 21st Century*, 2nd edn. Blackwell Publishing, Oxford.

Grönroos, C. (2000) *Service Management and Marketing*, 2nd edn. John Wiley & Sons, Chichester, UK.

Grönroos, C. (2001) The perceived service quality concept – a mistake? *Managing Service Quality* 11(3), 150–152.

Gummesson, E. (1994) Service management: an evaluation and the future. *International Journal of Service Industry Management* 5, 77–96.

Gunn, C. (2002) *Tourism Planning*, 4th edn. Routledge, London.

ISO (1994) *ISO 9000: 1994 Quality Management Standard*. International Organization for Standardization, Geneva, Switzerland.

Johnson, G., Scholes, K. and Whittington, R. (2008) *Exploring Corporate Strategy*, 8th edn. Prentice-Hall, London.

Juran, J.M. (1988) *Juran on Planning for Quality*. The Free Press, New York.

Juran, J.M. (1989) *Juran on Leadership for Quality: An Executive Handbook*. The Free Press, New York.

Knutson, B.J. and Beck, J.A. (2003) Identifying the dimensions of the experience construct: development of the model. *Journal of Quality Assurance in Hospitality and Tourism* 4(3/4), 23–35.

Nilsson, F. (2006) Logistics management in practice – towards theories of complex logistics. *The International Journal of Logistics Management* 17(1), 38–54.

Oakland, J. and Morris, P. (1998) *Pocket Guide to TQM: A Pictorial Guide for Managers*. Butterworth-Heinemann, Oxford.

Otto, J.E. and Ritchie, J.R.B. (1995) Exploring the quality of the service experience: a theoretical and empirical analysis. *Advances in Services Marketing and Management* 4, 37–61.

Page, S.J. (1999) *Transport and Tourism*. Addison-Wesley Longman, Essex, UK.

Parasuraman, A., Zeithaml, V. and Berry, L. (1990) *Delivering Quality Service*. Free Press, New York.

Porter, M.E. (1990) *The Competitive Advantage of Nations*. Free Press, New York.

Richard, J. and Wisner, J. (2005) Small business and supply chain management: is there a fit? *Journal of Business Venturing* 20(3), 403–436.

Russell, R.S. and Taylor, B.W. (2009) *Operations Management. Along the Supply Chain*, 6th edn. Wiley, Hoboken, New Jersey.

Williams, C. and Buswell, J. (2003) *Service Quality in Leisure and Tourism*. CAB International, Wallingford, UK.

6 Business Planning and Strategy

CRISPIN DALE

Objectives of the Chapter

This chapter aims to introduce those aspects of strategic management which impact upon the operations of the organization. The impact of operational management on the overall strategic direction of the firm will also be considered. The chapter will initially discuss what is understood by strategy before explaining each element of the strategic management process. This will include an analysis of the travel businesses' strategic environment, the basis upon which competitive advantage can be sought and those factors that need to be considered when implementing strategies. The discussion is supported by a range of questions and case studies that demonstrate the application of the key concepts and theories. The objectives of the chapter are to:

- explore the elements of the strategic management process that impact upon the operations of the travel business;
- analyse the dynamics of operations management on the strategic direction of the firm; and
- discuss strategic issues that influence the management of operations within travel businesses.

Introduction

Strategy is important from an operations management perspective, as the strategic direction of the firm will have a significant impact upon the operations of the firm. Indeed, the operations of the organization itself can have a major influence over the strategy of the travel business. As will be explained, the organization's operations can also be a source of competitive advantage for the organization. It is important to initially define what is understood by strategic management before going on to consider the impact of strategic management upon the operations of a travel business. A number of definitions of strategy exist, some of which are illustrated below:

- Strategy is the direction and scope of an organization over the long term which achieves advantage in a changing environment through its configuration of resources and competences with the aim of fulfilling stakeholder expectations (Johnson *et al.*, 2008).
- Corporate strategy can be described as the identification of the purpose of the organization and the plans and actions to achieve this purpose (Lynch, 2005).
- The means by which organizations achieve, and seek to achieve, their objectives and purposes; there can be a strategy for each product and service, and for the organization as a whole (Thompson, 2001).

Strategic management should not be a static process and needs to consider factors that occur from within the external environment that may impact upon the operations of the travel business. The travel business needs to be receptive to these factors and be able to react quickly to those that are influencing the direction of the firm. In this respect, strategy can be analysed from two different perspectives, *deliberate* or *emergent*. Deliberate strategy is an intended strategic direction that an organization wishes to pursue. This strategy will have been through a systematic process of analysing external factors which the organization may need to respond to, to meet future challenges. An emergent strategy considers the organization as operating in a complex and dynamic context and can be driven by the actions of those from within. The organization, therefore, needs to be flexible to change so that it is able to embed strategies that may emerge from within the organization. The *realized* strategy occurs as a result of deliberate or emergent strategies. This process is illustrated in Fig. 6.1.

Drivers of Strategy

From the context of operations management, Johnston and Clark (2005) identify three different drivers of strategy. These drivers influence the development of an organizations strategy and include operations-led strategy, externally driven strategy and corporate-led strategy. Operations-led strategy occurs when new developments emerge within the organization and it requires strategies for the effective marketing or financing of these technologies. For the travel business this may include new reservation and booking systems which require a strategy that is able

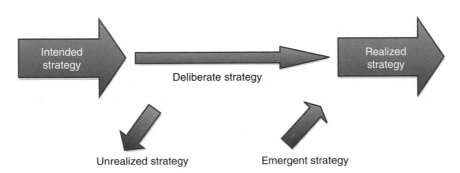

Fig. 6.1. Deliberate and emergent strategy. (Adapted from Mintzberg and Waters, 1985.)

to effectively resource the systems, in addition to a strategy that involves the management of change to operate the systems effectively. Externally driven strategy is based upon external factors such as new competitors, changing customer demands and so on. These factors will be explored further in the next section of the chapter. Corporate-led strategy is top-down and led by the directors of the organization. It takes a holistic view and is driven by the needs and expectations of key stakeholders.

Strategic Management Process

The strategic management process enables the organization to go through a number of logical steps in putting together a strategic plan for the organization. This process can be illustrated as a number of different stages (see Fig. 6.2).

Strategic analysis considers the external environment of the travel business. This encompasses both the micro environment and macro environment. This stage enables the travel business to consider those factors which may have an impact upon the operations of the travel business. An understanding of the organization's competitors and their strategies enables the travel business to exploit opportunities and circumvent threats. Strategic analysis also entails the review of the internal activities of the travel business. The travel business can then have an understanding of its strengths and weaknesses. In this respect, a review of its internal resources and competences can enable the business to determine its future strategic direction. Following this, the process of strategy formulation enables the travel business to consider its strategic options and sources of competitive advantage that it may be able to exploit from operational aspects of the business. These strategies then have to be successfully implemented and may involve the process of change to be managed effectively. It is acknowledged that parts of the strategic management process have more of a bearing upon the operations of a travel business than others. Therefore, operations managers need to be aware of this and must consider the impact this may have on their day-to-day activities. The remainder of the chapter will consider each of these stages in more detail and draw out those aspects which have an impact upon the operations of the travel business. The first stage of this process is strategic analysis.

Fig. 6.2. The strategic management process. (Adapted from Henry, 2008.)

C. Dale

Strategic Analysis

The strategies of travel businesses have to be flexible enough to adapt to a changing and dynamic external environment. The travel business needs to be able to understand those factors that can have an impact upon its operational functions and consider how it is positioned to be able to react to changing environmental forces and competitive activities.

The external environment can be analysed from two perspectives: the macro environment and the micro environment. The macro environment is the far environment within which the organization operates and over which it has little control. The micro environment is the near or competitive environment and is made up of competitors, markets and industries. Figure 6.3 illustrates the external environment in diagrammatic form.

The macro environment

A number of models can be used to analyse the external environment of a business. The most common of these is the PESTEL analysis. This is an acronym that stands for political, economic, social, technological, environmental and legal factors. This model can be used to understand those factors which may have an impact upon an organization and from which it can develop strategies to counter challenges or exploit opportunities. What is important to understand is how these factors can have an impact upon the operations of a travel business. For example, political factors such

Fig. 6.3. The external environment.

as terrorism can have an influence on consumer demand for holidays in destinations where terrorist activity could occur. Operations managers therefore have to consider the strategic impact that this may have on the marketing of their services. Economic factors, such as the rising cost of oil, have had a major impact on the airline industry and have resulted in fuel surcharges being passed on to customers. This can then lead to a negative impact upon customer satisfaction due to higher flight ticket prices. Social factors such as new market trends towards long-haul and activity-based holidays mean operations managers have to think strategically about targeting new market opportunities as and when they occur. Technological factors, such as the massive growth of e-commerce activity, have meant that operations managers have had to develop strategies to adapt to direct methods of booking holidays that have simultaneously disintermediated the channel of distribution. Environmental factors such as climate change have encouraged travel businesses to consider strategies that minimize the negative impacts of their activities upon the wider environment. In terms of legal factors, travel businesses operate in a global environment and the strategies of organizations have had to reflect the differing laws and regulations that operate in different destination contexts. The aforementioned factors are just examples that can have an impact upon the operations of a travel business and there are many more that need to be considered when conducting a macro environmental analysis. It is essential that the operations manager prioritizes the factors and determines which of them may be opportunities and which may be threats against the operations of the business.

Questions: the macro environment

1. Using an environmental analysis model such as PESTEL, identify those factors which are currently impacting upon a travel business of your choice.
2. Consider how each of these factors may have an impact upon the operations of the business.
3. Identify which of these factors are opportunities and which are threats.
4. Prioritize those factors which you believe may have the greatest impact upon the operations of the business.

The micro environment

The travel business needs to understand those factors which influence competition within a given industry. Furthermore, it is important to understand how competitor activity can have an impact upon the operations of the business. For this purpose, the operations manager needs to consider who the competitors are, what are their strengths and weaknesses and also how the operations of the travel business are positioned relative to the operations of competitors. To enable a great understanding of these factors, Porter (1980) forwards his model of competitive structural analysis (see Fig. 6.4).

Porter presents five competitive forces that he argues influence competition within a given industry and it is the collective strength of these which determine the profit potential of the industry. Porter continues to argue that by determining the relative importance of each of these forces, an organization can identify where to position itself to take advantage of opportunities and overcome or circumvent threats.

C. Dale

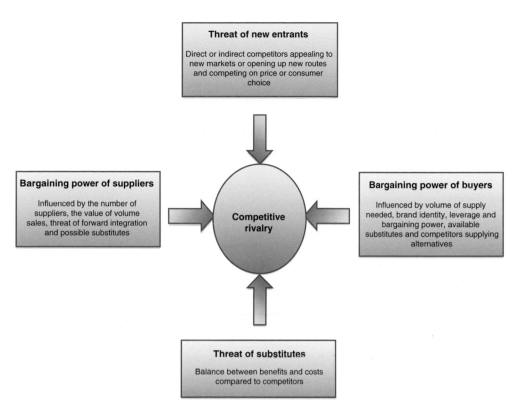

Threat of new entrants

Direct or indirect competitors appealing to new markets or opening up new routes and competing on price or consumer choice

Bargaining power of suppliers

Influenced by the number of suppliers, the value of volume sales, threat of forward integration and possible substitutes

Competitive rivalry

Bargaining power of buyers

Influenced by volume of supply needed, brand identity, leverage and bargaining power, available substitutes and competitors supplying alternatives

Threat of substitutes

Balance between benefits and costs compared to competitors

Fig. 6.4. Competitive structural analysis. (Adapted from Porter, 1980.)

First is the threat of new entrants and the barriers to entering into an industry. Barriers to entry include the ability to gain economies of scale, the accessibility of distribution channels, the amount of capital required for entry, the ability to differentiate goods and services and the extent of government regulation in the industry. Second is the bargaining power of suppliers. Suppliers have power within an industry if other suppliers and substitutes are few, the costs of switching to alternative suppliers are high, there is the threat of forward integration from suppliers or the suppliers' products are differentiated. Third is the power of buyers. Buyers have power if they are concentrated in number, they are able to switch easily between alternative sellers, there is the threat of backward integration or products are undifferentiated. Fourth is the threat of substitute goods and services that are either the same or can satisfy the same need. Substitute goods and services are threatening when the switching costs for buyers are low and there is a high propensity for the buyer to purchase substitute products. Finally, there is competitive rivalry. This forms the basis for the amount and intensity of competition and is influenced by the number, size and diversity of competitors, the rate of industry growth and the relative exit and entry barriers to an industry. Dale (2000) has applied Porter's forces model to the UK tour-operating industry and has argued that a number of alternative forces are apparent which include the threat of new entrants, the threat of customer expectations, the influence of synergistic alliances, the threat of regulation, the threat of alternatives and the influence of digital information technology and organization reinvention.

An analysis of the external environment will enable operations managers to understand the extent to which their business may be suffering from strategic drift. Strategic drift is a situation which occurs when organizations inadvertently move away from their planned strategy as they fail to adapt to changes that are occurring within the external environment. For example, demographic and social trends may occur which the business fails to recognize and so begins to encounter declining sales. It is therefore important for travel businesses to continually review the influence of the external environment so they can develop strategies accordingly.

Stakeholders

Stakeholders are individuals and groups who have an interest in the travel business and can influence its strategic direction. Stakeholders can be influential in determining the overall operational strategy of the travel business and, therefore, the identity of these stakeholders has to be determined. As illustrated in Fig. 6.5, there are many stakeholders who comprise a travel business.

It is necessary to identify the needs and expectations of each of these stakeholders to enable the travel business to operationalize strategies that meet their needs and expectations. The operations manager has to contend with balancing the needs and expectations of different stakeholders who have the potential to come into conflict as a consequence of the overall strategic direction of the travel business. For example, customers may want value for money and quality service, whereas employees may want payment of their wages and job satisfaction. However, with the threat of rising costs and the need to satisfy shareholders and their desire for a return on investment (discussed further in Chapter 8, this volume), the operations manager has to consider those stakeholders who may hold the most power and interest in determining the future direction of the travel business. Figure 6.6 outlines a model that classifies the relative power and interest of stakeholders.

Power is the extent to which the stakeholder has the ability to influence the organization, whereas interest concerns the willingness of the stakeholder to influence the organization. Key players are those stakeholders who have high power and high interest. The key players are usually those who are responsible and have the authority for determining the future direction of the organization. This may include senior managers and directors of the travel business. Stakeholders who should be kept satisfied are those who have a high level of power but a low level of interest. This may include the major shareholders who have a vested interest in the business and desire for a return on their investment. Those stakeholders who have a high level of interest but a low level of power

C. Dale

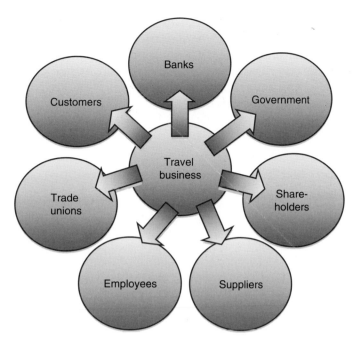

Fig. 6.5. Stakeholders for a travel business.

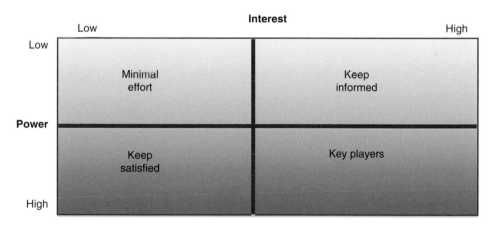

Fig. 6.6. Power and interest matrix. (Adapted from Mendelow, 1991.)

need to be kept informed. This can include employees of the organization, who individually have a low level of power in governing the overall strategic direction of the business but will be interested in ensuring that they are paid for working. Stakeholders who have a low level of interest and power require only a minimal effort. It should be noted that stakeholders are not static and can reposition themselves depending upon the situation and the level of power and interest they hold. For example, in the early 1990s, the major shareholders of one of the leading hospitality enterprises, Forte, exerted their power and influence by ultimately deciding that the business should be bought by the media and leisure company Granada. Even though this was counter to the wishes of the then chief executive, Rocco Forte, it led to the break up of the company and illustrated the growing influence and power of key stakeholders. Similarly, employees can unionize themselves to form a powerful opposition to the company if it is perceived that the future direction is counter to their interests. The same can be said when environmental groups can form to protest at the development of airports and runways. These groups can very quickly have an impact upon the future direction and operations of travel businesses and their level of power and influence should not be underestimated. The following case study discusses a situation where stakeholder power and interest had an operational impact.

CASE STUDY: GATE GOURMET AND STAKEHOLDER POWER AND INFLUENCE

Gate Gourmet supplies in-flight meals to airline carriers including British Airways (BA), American Airlines and Continental Airlines. In August 2005, Gate Gourmet made 350 employees based at Heathrow Airport redundant. It was explained that this was due to 'outdated working practices' and the need to cut costs in light of declining revenues from the airlines that had been impacted upon by rising fuel prices and aggressive competitor strategies. The redundancies resulted in unofficial industrial action, not only by employees of Gate Gourmet, but also by baggage handlers and ground staff working for BA. Flights at Heathrow Airport were grounded for around 24 hours and had the logistical knock-on effect of having pilots and cabin crew out of position around the world. In addition, stranded passengers had to be accommodated in hotels and provided with food and drink at the expense of BA.

Questions

1. Who are the stakeholders of Gate Gourmet and identify their needs and expectations?
2. Using the power/interest matrix, identify which stakeholders had the most influence and power.
3. How and why did this event have such an impact upon the operations of BA?

The vision and mission of the organization (see also Chapter 4, this volume) needs to be communicated to all stakeholders. This is so that the aspirations and overall purpose of the organization are fully understood. Obviously, this requires operational managers to consider strategies for both internally and externally communicating this information to stakeholders. Furthermore, the mission should reflect the needs and expectations of the key players who have the greatest influence over the direction of the organization.

Strategic Formulation

The travel business needs to decide what strategy to select in pursuit of a particular strategic direction. Once the organization has conducted a strategic analysis of its current situation, it will then know how well positioned the travel business is relative to its competitors and the extent to which it is meeting the opportunities and threats that are apparent in the external environment. If the travel business is suffering from strategic drift, then a strategy needs to be implemented that steers the business in the

C. Dale

appropriate direction. The travel business also needs to consider how it can gain competitive advantage in a fiercely competitive environment.

Competitive advantage

When two or more firms compete within the same market, one firm possesses a competitive advantage over its rivals when it earns (or has the potential to earn) a persistently higher profit (Grant, 2008).

Competitive advantage involves the way in which a company makes its products or services better or cheaper than those offered by its competitors (Capon, 2008). It depends on the ability of an organization to add more value for its customers than its rivals, and thus attain a position of relative advantage. The challenge is to sustain any advantage once achieved (Thompson, 2001).

Questions

1. What are some of the common themes that emerge from these definitions?
2. From an operational perspective, suggest ways in which a travel organization can gain a competitive advantage.
3. How should a travel organization sustain a competitive advantage?

The travel business needs to consider how its operations can be utilized as a source of competitive advantage. Competitive advantage can be analysed from two perspectives: the competitive positioning school of thought and the resource-based view. The competitive positioning school of thought is centred on establishing strategies that are positioned relative to competitors in the marketplace. Porter (1985) argues that competitive advantage is based upon three generic strategies: cost, differentiation and focus. As illustrated in Fig. 6.7, Porter argues that these strategies can take either a broad or a narrow focus in scope.

Cost leadership: This strategy argues that an organization can become the lowest-cost producer in the industry and thus gain higher profits. Cost leadership can be achieved

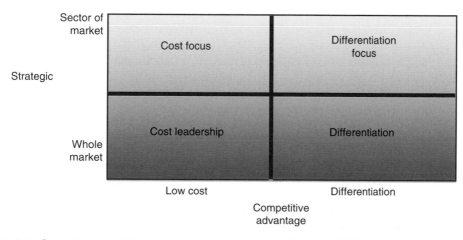

Fig. 6.7. Generic competitive strategies. (Adapted from Porter, 1985.)

through gaining economies of scale, reducing the costs of resource inputs or having more efficient distribution systems. Travel businesses have attempted to reduce their costs by, for example, Internet booking and electronic distribution of tickets and outsourcing customer enquiries to overseas call centres where wages and running costs are cheaper. Though competitors in a given industry may attempt to achieve an advantage through cost leadership, it should be noted that there can only be one true cost leader.

Differentiation strategy: This strategy is used when the travel business offers something unique and sells it a premium price. Differentiation may therefore come through better-quality service, brand reputation, better design and so on. To ensure differentiation can be achieved, the travel business will need to add value to its product and/or service range. If this added value is perceived by customers as being superior to competitors' offerings, then the travel business can command a premium price.

In the broadest sense, these two generic strategies can be targeted across the whole market. However, the travel business may wish to focus on a particular niche sector of the market based upon, for example, demographic or need variables. In this respect, the travel business can pursue a strategy of cost focus or focus differentiation.

Cost focus: This strategy is used when the business focuses on a sector of the market which may be particularly price-sensitive. Like differentiation focus, this approach is focused on allowing the business to be the market leader in one or more specific market segments.

Differentiation focus: This strategy is used when the business differentiates the product to meet the needs of a niche market. The major tour operators distinguish their holiday package brands so as to meet the needs of different markets. This is often based upon factors such as cost focus, where budget brands cater for those with limited expenditure, while the premium brands, which are targeted at those with higher disposable incomes, have better perceived product options such as, for example, inclusive spa treatments. However, these are then reflected in the premium price of the holiday package.

Porter argues that a business needs to be clear about which generic strategy it is following, otherwise it will become 'stuck in the middle' and have no clear basis upon which to gain competitive advantage. Furthermore, in pursuit of the generic strategies, the operations manager needs to consider how operational aspects of the business can be a source of cost reduction or differentiation. The following case study illustrates the generic strategies used in the budget airline sector.

CASE STUDY: GENERIC STRATEGIES AND THE BUDGET AIRLINE SECTOR

The budget airline sector is made up of a number of competitors including easyJet, Ryanair and BMIBaby to name a few. These airlines drive down costs and generate revenue by focusing upon operational aspects of the business. In terms of reducing costs, the airlines provide Internet booking, use regional hub airports that can generate faster turnaround times for the planes, provide limited customer call-centre facilities and have lower numbers of ground handling staff. The cheaper landing costs at regional airports also opened up new markets of consumers who want to travel from more local airports. The airlines generate revenue through the customer purchase of on-board meals and drinks, advertisements being placed on the planes, charges made for additional luggage and the selling of hire-car agreements to customers.

Continued

C. Dale

Once the travel business has considered the basis upon which it can gain a competitive advantage, it needs to determine its strategic direction. Ansoff's (1968) directional matrix (see Fig. 6.8) offers four different strategic directions which the business can pursue. These directions are based upon its markets and product range and include four alternatives.

Market penetration: This alternative is used where the travel business attempts to grow its market share by focusing on its existing markets and product range. So in this respect, the business wants its customers to buy more of its current products. From an operational perspective, the travel business can pursue this strategy by exploiting its existing resources. This may take the form of revising the marketing of the service offering so as to increase sales. For example, in June 2008, P&O Cruises redesigned their brochures to take a destination focus as opposed to marketing holidays based around the ships themselves. This then encourages customers to consider holidays to destinations that they may not have considered taking a cruise to. Market penetration is often pursued when there is room for further growth in the marketplace.

Market development: This alternative is used when the travel business decides to enter into new markets using its existing products. This can be based upon identifying and targeting new market segments or entering into new geographical regions where markets can be exploited. As national markets have begun to stagnate due to

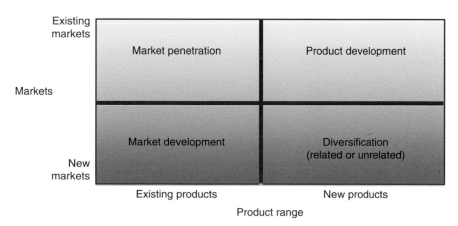

Fig. 6.8. Directional matrix. (Adapted from Ansoff, 1968.)

competitive pressures, travel businesses have attempted to pursue internalization strategies. As consumer tastes grow increasing fickle and diverse, travel businesses have to be receptive to the development of new markets as and when they occur. For example, in April 2008, Touristik Union International (TUI) entered into a joint venture with a Russian capital management group to explore the development of tourism markets in Russia and the other independent states in the Central Asian region. By acquiring the luxury tour operator Elegant Resorts in April 2008, Thomas Cook further developed markets in the luxury end of the tour operations market. The challenge for the operations manager is the diversity of strategies that have to be embedded so as to cater to a range of markets that will have different tastes and preferences. It cannot be assumed that the existing product can be easily transferred to a new market.

Product development: This alternative is used when the travel business develops new products for existing markets. This can be as a consequence of changing consumer tastes, and the travel business therefore has to tailor and update its products to meet the needs of its existing markets. For example, Disney entered into the cruise liner industry and began to sell Disney-themed cruise holidays to its existing family markets. The development of alternative meals such as salads by McDonalds was due to changing consumer tastes towards health-related products. The operations manager has to consider the implementation of these new products into the day-to-day operations of the business. This may require adjustments to the service delivery of the product so as to generate additional sales from an existing market.

Diversification: This alternative is used when the travel business enters new markets with new products. In this situation the business may embark on a strategy of 'related' or 'unrelated' diversification. Related diversification is when the travel business enters into a new market with a new product which is related to its core business activity. For example, tour operators have become vertically and horizontally integrated companies that have diversified into owning airlines, hotels and travel agencies. This means they own all parts of the channel of distribution, from the supplier to the retailer. This can be further classified as backward integration, where the tour operator acquires a supplier such as an airline, or forward integration, where the tour operator acquires the retailer such as a travel agent. Horizontal integration is where the tour operator purchases a competing tour-operating firm. Diagonal integration occurs when the travel business enters into related services such as travel insurance. Figure 6.9 outlines this process in diagrammatic form.

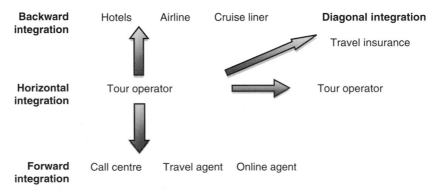

Fig. 6.9. Related diversification in the travel industry.

The other method of diversification is known as unrelated. Unrelated diversification is when the travel business enters a new market with a new product that is unrelated to the core business. Companies such as the Easy Group (www.easygroup.com) and Virgin (www.virgin.com) are good examples of organizations that are highly diversified and have extended their brands across a range of different businesses. The Easy Group initially began as easyJet but has diversified into a number of unrelated areas including cinemas, finance and Internet cafes. The travel operations manager needs to be aware of the risks that are involved in pursuing this strategy. New operational systems and structures may have to be adopted to successfully operate the business. In this respect, the business may not have the operational expertise, resources and know-how to effectively incorporate the unrelated business into the wider organization. The operations director will, therefore, have to consider carefully the implications of any strategic manoeuvres that the travel business may make into an unrelated activity. The following questions assist in understanding issues on strategic direction.

Questions: strategic directions in the travel industry

1. Go on to web sites such as Travelmole.com and etid.com. Search for information that relates to the strategic activities of travel businesses.
2. Using Ansoff's matrix, what strategies are the travel businesses pursuing? What are the reasons for them pursuing these particular strategic directions?
3. To what extent do you feel this is an appropriate strategy to follow? What will be the costs and benefits of adopting this strategy?
4. Consider how the strategy will impact upon the operations of the business. What aspects of the travel business will the operations manager need to consider when pursuing this strategic direction.

Resource-based view

An alternative approach to developing strategy is through what is widely known as the resource-based view (RBV). If we take a systems approach, an organization's resources are those inputs which it then converts to outputs and this process has been discussed in Chapter 4 (this volume). The travel business is made up of a number of both tangible and intangible resources and it can utilize these to gain a competitive advantage. Tangible resources include human, financial and physical resources, whereas intangible resources include brand reputation and image. The resources can be further classified into threshold and strategic or unique resources. Threshold resources are those which the business must have if it is to operate in a given industry. So, for example, a travel agent may need physical premises from which to operate unless it is selling directly online. It also requires human resources to discuss the travel options with customers and technological resources, such as computer facilities, are needed to process the bookings and transactions. However, strategic or unique resources are those resources which are over and above the industry standard and enable the travel business to gain an advantage over competitors. A number of criteria exist for classifying whether a resource has strategic value to the organization. These can include: the rarity of the resource and whether it is difficult for the travel business to obtain; whether the acquired resource is valuable or becomes valuable over time; and whether the resource is difficult to acquire, copy or substitute. This can occur when the culture or operating systems of the organization become difficult, if not impossible, to replicate by competitors. The Disney Corporation, with its multiple business interests in leisure, entertainments and media, is a good example of an organization that has a distinctive way of operating which makes it very difficult for competitors to copy, and is therefore able to sustain an advantage over competitors. It should be the objective of the operations manager to develop the strategic value of their resources overtime. This may be through cultivating the operational processes so that they become difficult for other competitors to imitate and substitute.

Alongside resources are the travel business's competences. Competences are the attributes that the travel business requires if it is to compete effectively in the marketplace. Competences emerge from the organization's bundle of resources and can encompass skills, knowledge and technology. The organization has to have a baseline set of competences to be able to compete effectively. For example, an airline requires competences in coordinating the distribution and marketing of its flights, the training and development of its personnel and the maintenance of its fleet of aircraft. Prahalad and Hamel (1990) note that core competences should satisfy the following criteria. First, the core competence should provide the company with access to a wide range of markets. The tour operators TUI and Thomas Cook have global coverage in a host of markets due to their competences in arranging the distribution and marketing of their product range. Second, the core competence should make a major contribution to the perceived customer benefits of the end product. For example, the tour operator Kuoni has core competences in arranging specialist vacations, which enable them to market their holidays at a premium. Third, the core competence should be difficult for competitors to copy. The budget airline Ryanair has core competences in arranging fights at the lowest possible cost. Though a plethora of other budget airlines has similar resources, it has been difficult for these competitors to replicate the exact competences of Ryanair which have been key to its sustained advantage in the marketplace. As core competences can only be developed from within the travel business, the operations manager will be integral to developing those capabilities of the business that can offer a sustained competitive advantage. Table 6.1 offers a framework for classifying an organization's strategic resources and core competences.

Table 6.1. Strategic resources and core competences.

Criteria	Strategic resources	Core competences
Rare	Established supply chains	Arranging fights at the lowest possible cost
Valuable	Brand reputation and identity	Coordinating the distribution of flights
Difficult to acquire	Skilled, qualified people	Marketing of flights
Difficult to copy	Organizational systems and business units	Arranging the distribution and marketing of a product range
Difficult to substitute	Target and achievement-driven organizational culture	Arranging specialist vacations

C. Dale

The value chain (Porter, 1985), discussed in Chapter 5 (this volume), is a framework that enables the operations manager to determine what activities the travel business can generate to add further value and thus competitive advantage. Value is based upon the difference between the cost of the resource inputs and the margin of value that is generated by the product or service. This value is further determined by the amount the customer is willing to pay for the product or service. The operations manager should consider how the activities of the business could be configured to enable further value to be generated. The operations manager also has to seek out areas of distinctiveness that can be developed within the configuration of activities. The value chain is separated into primary activities and support activities. The primary activities impact directly on the delivery of the product or service, whereas the support activities ensure that the primary activities can be supported efficiently and effectively. Via an analysis of the organization's value chain, the operations manager should break down the component parts of the travel business to determine where value can be created. The questions given below will enable you to gain a greater understanding of the issues that have been discussed.

Questions: resources, competences and adding value through operations

1. Select a travel business with which you are familiar.
2. Using Table 6.1, identify the organization's strategic resources and core competences.
3. Construct a value chain for the travel business.
4. Which operational aspects of the business could add further value?

Strategic Methods

Once the travel business has decided upon its strategic direction it will need to consider the strategic methods that should be adopted in pursuit of this direction. The selection of strategic methods offers the opportunity for the travel business to expand its portfolio of activities and further strengthen its resource base. These methods include the following:

- organic growth;
- mergers and acquisitions;
- strategic alliances; and
- franchising.

Any one of these methods has the potential to have an impact upon the operations of the business and therefore the operations manager has to consider the implications that any strategic method may have on their functions. The following will outline the different strategic methods and discuss their advantages and disadvantages while also discussing the impact they may have upon the operations of the travel business.

Organic growth

Organic growth, or internalization as it can otherwise be known, is where the travel business maximizes its existing resources to pursue a particular direction. It therefore makes the strategic decision to effectively 'go it alone'. As has been discussed previously, the travel business may have certain strategic resources and core competences that it can further exploit to its own advantage. It can utilize these resources and core competences for developing new products or entering new markets. There may be aspects of the business where value can be added and the operations manager will be key to identifying where this can occur. The advantage of pursuing a strategy of organic growth is that the travel business is able to retain total control over its expansion plans and therefore retain all the gains that may derive from the outcome of the strategy. However, counter to this are the financial risks that are involved in undertaking this strategy, so if it was to fail the travel business has to bear the brunt of any costs that may occur. When compared to the other strategic methods, organic growth can also be a slower process for achieving the strategic direction that the business wants to go in. This can present difficulties when the external environment is dynamic and fast-moving, which is often the case within the travel industry. Nevertheless, for the operations manager organic growth can offer the opportunity to capitalize upon those operational areas that have potential for enabling the travel business to gain a competitive advantage. An example of this is the Disney Corporations Parks and Resorts buying into the cruise industry.

Mergers and acquisitions

These occur when organizations combine forces to exploit resources and competences. There are differences between the process of mergers and acquisitions. A merger is when two or more organizations agree to combine forces to become one organization. On the other hand an acquisition occurs when one organization purchases another. This may be hostile in nature, where the company does not want to be taken over, or it may be consensual and the acquired business enables the utilization of strategic resources that otherwise would not occur. Examples of mergers between travel businesses include the airlines Air France and KLM and consolidation in the UK tour-operating industry between Thomas Cook with MyTravel and TUI with First Choice (see case study 'Consolidation in the tour-operating industry'). By embarking on a merger or acquisition the travel business can enter quickly into new markets and product areas that it currently does not have access to. For example, the acquisition of Hotels4U.com by Thomas Cook in February 2008 enabled the tour operator to further exploit the expanding independent holidays market.

The potential problems of mergers and acquisitions may include the failure of successfully integrating the combined companies and so the synergistic effects do not occur. The operations manager will play a crucial role in bringing together the systems of the different firms so as to ensure that added value can be generated. It should also be acknowledged that this is a difficult process due to cultural incompatibility between the travel businesses, leading to management and employee conflict. The management of change process therefore has to be dealt with effectively by the operations manager and this will be discussed in more detail in a later section. If one company acquires another it also has to be careful that it does not overextend itself financially, leading to an overstretching of resources to the detriment of the combined business. Nevertheless, mergers and acquisitions can be effective for quickly growing market share and asserting the businesses position in the marketplace.

C. Dale

Strategic alliances and joint ventures

These are formal arrangements between organizations. Alliances in the travel industry are not uncommon and enable travel businesses to build upon areas of weakness that can be capitalized upon by joining forces with another partner. These alliance partners may have been viewed as competitors but via a process of 'co-opetition' they can combine forces to become much more powerful in the marketplace (Brandenburger and Nalebuff, 1997). In the airline industry, alliances such as the Star Alliance (www.staralliance.com) and One World (www.oneworld.com) exist where the airlines code share between one another. Code sharing is when airlines jointly market the flights of other airlines that they are in an alliance with. This enables the airlines to maximize load capacities and increase efficiency for customers. Other alliances include e-tourism operators such as Opodo (www.opodo.com), which is a collaboration between a number of major airlines who distribute their services via the web site. Alliances enable partners to share resources and competences that each may be lacking. The travel business can then utilize these resources and competences to gain entry more quickly into new markets and product areas. In April 2008, the tour operator TUI formed a joint venture with the cruise operator Royal Caribbean to gain access to the growing German premium cruise market. It enabled the partner organizations to share any risks that may occur from pursuing the shared strategy.

The operations manager has to be astute to the integration of any combined operational aspects between the different travel partners. A rigorous feasibility plan should be developed to ensure that synergies can be generated as a consequence of partners forming an alliance or joint venture. Synergy occurs when the resultant effect of combining forces is greater than what can be achieved as separate companies. It is important that there is a good 'strategic fit' between the respective businesses and that they meet the 'four Cs' operational functioning criteria as forwarded by Medcof (1997): 'capability' and whether the partners are capable of effectively engaging in the alliance; 'compatibility' and the ability of the partners to operate reciprocally in an alliance relationship; 'commitment' in terms of the alliance partners having the staying power to achieve the potential benefits of the alliance; and, finally, 'control' of the alliance in determining its strategic direction and growth potential. The operations manager has to consider how any partner travel business can be incorporated into the day-to-day activities of the business. This requires careful planning so as to not cause undue internal tension within the organization. Trust between the partners also needs to be apparent, otherwise there is the potential for one organization to exploit the resources and capabilities of the other partners before leaving the alliance or joint venture completely.

CASE STUDY: CONSOLIDATION IN THE TOUR-OPERATING INDUSTRY

In 2007, the UK tour-operating industry went through a period of consolidation. Through two major mergers, the industry changed from four dominant players to just two.

Thomas Cook merged with MyTravel to become the Thomas Cook Group. The merger included Thomas Cook's 33 tour-operating brands, 2400 travel agencies, 66 aircraft and approximately 20,000 staff with MyTravel's 17 tour-operating brands, 31

Continued

---

aircraft and approximately 13,000 staff worldwide. The combined companies argued that the cost benefits of the planned merger would be at least £75 million a year.

In response, TUI Travel merged with First Choice to become Europe's largest tour operator called TUI Travel. This merger brought together 200 tour-operating brands with a combined company value of more than £3 billion. In addition to a wide travel agency network, First Choice employed more than 15,000 staff and operated 34 aircraft. TUI had a fleet of 127 aircraft and over 200 hotels. Both companies operated their headquarters in Luton and Crawley. However, to accrue the benefits of these mergers, the businesses have had to go through a period of 'operational restructuring' and 'cost synergies'.

(Sources: various)

Questions

1. What do you understand is meant by the terms 'operational restructuring' and 'cost synergies'?
2. What are the operational advantages of merging for the tour operators?
3. What operational management issues need to be considered when travel businesses decide to merge together?

Franchising

This occurs when there is a contractual arrangement between two parties, that is the franchisee and the franchisor. The franchisee trades under the franchisor's brand name and operating procedures in return for an initial fee and percentage return once trading. Franchising has become a popular strategy among many hospitality-related businesses that have sought to expand their businesses rapidly across the globe. Companies such as McDonalds and Costa Coffee are good examples where this has occurred. Although franchising is not as widespread an activity in the travel industry, the Global Travel Group is another example of a company that has used franchising as a means of developing an independent travel agency network. Franchising therefore offers the travel business an opportunity to exploit alternative markets at a relatively low cost. However, operations managers have to be aware of the need to ensure consistency in operating standards across the franchise network. This is to ensure that brand standards are maintained across the company's portfolio of businesses.

Strategic Implementation

Once the travel business has been through the process of analysing its strategic position and has formulated strategies to determine its strategic situation, it then needs to be able to successfully implement its chosen strategies. The operations manager will be required to successfully manage those internal aspects of the business which may be impacted upon as a consequence of the organization's transition towards its intended strategic position. This involves a consideration of the internal culture of the business as well as the process of the management of change.

We understand culture to be the values, norms and belief systems that the organization is predicated upon, as discussed in Chapter 1 (this volume). These values, norms

C. Dale

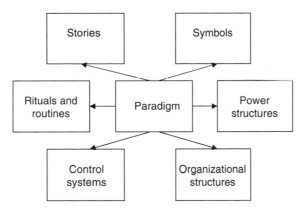

Fig. 6.10. The cultural web. (Adapted from Johnson *et al.*, 2008.)

and belief systems will be deeply embedded within the organization and will have formed as a consequence of a number of factors. The organization's culture can be highly influential in determining employee motivation and thus the productivity and quality of the end product or service. Therefore, an analysis of the organization's culture within the context of strategy is important as there may be cultural issues which are preventing the travel business from moving in a particular strategic direction.

An understanding of the organization's culture will enable the operations manager to deploy strategies for developing an organizational climate that is dynamic and flexible to strategic change. Johnson *et al.* (2008) propose a model, described as the cultural web, which can be used to analyse the cultural orientation of the firm. According to Johnson *et al.* the cultural web consists of seven different elements as illustrated in Fig. 6.10.

At the heart of the cultural web is the paradigm. The paradigm is the assumptions that bind the overall philosophy of the organization and the way in which it operates. The paradigm can emerge as a consequence of the different elements of the cultural web. Stories are told to members of the organization and include the organization's history about figures and events that shape the perceived values of the organization. Symbols of the organization's culture represent aspects of the travel business that convey some kind of meaning. For example, the logo of the business, the layout of the office or job titles can act as symbolic examples of the culture of the organization and the way it operates. Organizations are made up of many groups and power structures represent where the overall power in the organization lies. This is not necessarily hierarchically driven and can be influenced by a powerful subgroup within the organization that can impact upon the direction of the business. Organizational structures are determined by the lines of authority that are apparent within the organization. Whether the organization has a tall or flat hierarchical structure will influence the overall culture of the firm. Control systems are those which govern the overall behaviour and performance of individuals and groups in the organization. These can be linked to methods of rewarding employee for their work through, for example, bonuses, employee of the month schemes and so on. Finally, rituals and routines are those day-to-day activities that are carried out within the business. These can range from formal routines such as interviewing and training procedures through to informal rituals that include, for example, the end of month social event. The combined elements of the cultural web will represent the dominant cultural philosophy of the organization. It is upon this basis that the operations manager needs to determine the extent to which their working practices have an impact upon the strategic direction of the travel business.

Questions: the cultural web

1. Select a travel business with which you are familiar.
2. Develop a cultural web of the organization.
3. Determine to what extent the culture of the organization prevents it from moving forward strategically.
4. Suggest ways in which the operations manager can influence the repositioning of the organization's culture to enable it to pursue a particular strategic direction?

Management of Change

The dynamic nature of the external tourism environment is such that travel businesses have to be receptive to changing rapidly as and when factors may occur. However, change should not be viewed merely as a reactive process and the operations manager should be seeking ways in which the travel business can drive change in the competitive environment. This occurred when the budget airlines entered the airline industry and altered the rules of the game and the nature of competition within the industry. The implementation of any proposed strategy is likely to have an impact upon the operations of the business. However, operational staff can become resistant to change and this can be due to a number of factors including poor communication and consultation, opposition to the proposed strategy, internal politics or lack of interest or incentive to change. To overcome these barriers, the change process will need to be managed effectively by the operations manager. By and Dale (2008) identify eight critical success factors for change management within tourism small- and medium-sized enterprises (SMEs) which are outlined in Table 6.2.

The operations manager is integral to ensuring that the tourism business is able to meet these criteria and needs to be proactive in quickly adapting to change when it may be required. The following case study illustrates the opening of Terminal 5 and issues surrounding strategic implementation.

CASE STUDY: STRATEGIC IMPLEMENTATION AND TERMINAL 5

On 27 March 2008, Terminal 5 (alternatively known as T5) at Heathrow Airport opened to the public. T5 is owned by the British Aviation Authority (BAA) and cost £4.3 billion to build. BA is the sole tenant of the terminal. The terminal, which incorporates a wide range of luxury shops and restaurants, was described as a terminal which would completely change the customer experience of air travel. However, following the opening of T5 the terminal encountered a number of problems which resulted in a large number of flights being cancelled and thousands of bags being delayed. The problems were described as being due to 'staff familiarization issues' and 'problems associated with processing customers' baggage'. This

Continued

C. Dale

was in addition to staff car parking issues and security checks on the day, which delayed staff in getting to their work positions in time. It was also decided that the transfer of long-haul flights from Terminal 4 to Terminal 5 should be delayed. This prevented other airlines moving to the vacated spaces in T4 left by BA. Willie Walsh, BA's chief executive, described the situation as 'definitely not British Airways' finest hour' and turned down his annual bonus of £600,000 in light of the T5 fiasco. Shortly after these events, BA announced the departure of the director of operations and the director of customer services. The Civil Aviation Authority (CAA) also requested that both BAA and BA produce reports on the problems that occurred with the opening of T5.

(Sources: various)

Questions

1. Consider those operational factors which led to the difficulties in the T5 opening? What lessons can be learned?

2. To what extent has the T5 situation impacted strategically upon BA? What has been the impact on its competitors, shareholders and customers?

3. To what extent could the process of change have been managed better by BAA and BA? Reflect upon the critical success factors in Table 6.2 when answering this question.

4. In light of the T5 experience, and from an operations management perspective, what recommendations would you make for the opening of an airport terminal or a travel business generally?

Table 6.2. Critical success factors for change management in tourism SMEs. (Adapted from By and Dale, 2008.)

Critical success factors	Organizational features
Adaptability and flexibility	Being proactive to change as it may occur in the future. Encouraging employee autonomy and receptiveness to change
Commitment and support	Management and employee support towards the organizational, vision, aims and objectives
Communication and cooperation	Continuous communication among all stakeholders. Shared and mutual responsibility among management and employees through team meetings and briefing sessions
Continuous learning and improvement	Individual learning programmes and training and development
Formal strategies	Enabling individual and departmental ownership of the organizational strategy
Motivation and reward	Encouraging employee ownership towards change. Acceptance of risk throughout by employees
Pragmatism	Realistic allocation of time and resources for change to be implemented
The right people	Employment and retention of the right people. Need for rewards and personal development

Summary

The chapter has reviewed business planning and strategic processes and demonstrated the relationship between long-term (strategic) planning and short-term (operational) planning. This has included the different stages that the business has to go through in order to understand its current situation, the strategies it needs to select in order to pursue a particular direction and the processes it needs to consider in implementing the strategies. The chapter has considered how strategy can impact upon the operations of a travel business and how operational issues can influence the strategic management process. An understanding of strategy is important as it ensures that the operations manager is able to cope effectively with any changes that may occur in the external environment. They can then develop and implement strategies that enable the travel business to compete in a dynamic marketplace.

Further Research

Evans, N., Campbell, D. and Stonehouse, G. (2003) *Strategic Management for Travel and Tourism*. Butterworth-Heinemann, Oxford.
Henry, A. (2008) *Understanding Strategic Management*. Oxford University Press, Oxford.
Thompson, J.L. (2001) *Strategic Management*, 4th edn. Thomson Learning, London.
Tribe, J. (1997) *Corporate Strategy for Tourism*. Thomson Learning, London.

Review Questions

1. Select a travel business. Conduct a macro and micro environmental analysis of the business. What factors in the external environment may have an impact upon the operations of the business?
2. In light of the travel business's present strategic position, determine what the strategic direction of the organization should be. How can the firm establish a competitive advantage?
3. How should the travel business go about implementing these strategies? What impact will they have on the operations of the business?

References

Ansoff, I. (1968) *Corporate Strategy*. McGraw-Hill, Maidenhead, UK.
Brandenburger, A. and Nalebuff, B. (1997) *Co-opetition*. HarperCollins, London.
By, R. and Dale, C. (2008) Tourism SMEs and the successful management of organizational change. *International Journal of Tourism Research* 10, 305–313.
Capon, C. (2008) *Understanding Strategic Management*. Financial Times/Prentice-Hall, Harlow, UK.
Dale, C. (2000) The UK tour operating industry: a competitive analysis. *Journal of Vacation Marketing* 6(4), 357–367.
Grant, R.M. (2008) *Contemporary Strategy Analysis*, 6th edn. Blackwell, Oxford.
Henry, A. (2008) *Understanding Strategic Management*. Oxford University Press, Oxford.
Johnson, G., Scholes, K. and Whittington, R. (2008) *Exploring Corporate Strategy*, 8th edn. Prentice-Hall, London.

C. Dale

Johnston, R. and Clark, G. (2005) *Service Operations Management: Improving Service, Delivery*. Financial Times/Prentice-Hall, Harlow, UK.

Lynch, R. (2005) *Corporate Strategy*, 4th edn. Pitman, London.

Medcof, J.W. (1997) Why too many alliances end in divorce. *Long Range Planning* 30(5), 718–732.

Mendelow, A. (1991) *Proceedings of the Second International Conference on Information Systems*. Cambridge, Massachusetts.

Mintzberg, H. and Waters, J.A. (1985) Of strategies, deliberate or emergent. *Strategic Management Journal* 6(3), 257–272.

Porter, M.E. (1980) *Competitive Strategy: Techniques for Analyzing Industries and Competitors*. Free Press, New York.

Porter, M.E. (1985) *Competitive Advantage*. Free Press, New York.

Prahalad, C.K. and Hamel, G. (1990) The core competence of the organisation. *Harvard Business Review* 68(3), 79–91.

Thompson, J.L. (2001) *Strategic Management*, 4th edn. Thomson Learning, London.

7 Marketing

DEBRA WALE

Objectives of the Chapter

This chapter introduces the process and practice of marketing products and services for the travel operations industry. It gives an explanation of the key principles and concepts and their models. The chapter follows a logical progression through the marketing process from planning through segmentation, choice of strategy and its development using elements of the marketing mix.

At the end of the chapter, students should be able to:

- understand underlying principles, concepts and the process of marketing; and
- relate theory to practice in designing marketing activity for products and services in the travel operations industry.

Introduction to Marketing

The Chartered Institute of Marketing (CIM) defines marketing as 'the management process responsible for identifying, anticipating, and satisfying customer's requirements profitably'. This definition reflects the importance of understanding the concept of consumer behaviour, the principles of which underpin all marketing activity. Consumer behaviour is concerned with marketeers providing the external stimuli in the form of communications such as advertisements to match and stimulate the intrinsic motivators (needs, wants and desires) within the targeted customer in order to induce buying behaviour.

The travel market is characterized through its domination by global companies with portfolios consisting of a range of travel products and services that appeal to consumers in a number of market segments, either as a mass or in specialist niche segments. The challenge marketeers have is developing and getting the right product or service to the target audience, in a marketplace where there is little difference between the products and services of travel companies.

The process of marketing involves analysing the market, setting marketing objectives, developing marketing tactics to deliver objectives through a coordinated marketing campaign utilizing the marketing mix to direct products or services to a targeted consumer and meeting their needs better and faster than competitors, all at a profit!

Therefore, marketing is increasing the bottom line, through sales of a product or service, by executing a coordinated, targeted, integrated marketing plan to attract and retain loyal customers and manage their expectations better than competitors.

This chapter will take the reader through the marketing process, introducing a number of models, which make a perfect toolkit for helping marketeers to make

©CAB International 2009. *Operations Management in the Travel Industry* (ed. P. Robinson)

marketing decisions. It will focus on providing a step-by-step approach to understanding and using these models to market products and services in the travel industry effectively.

Marketing Principles

Product-orientated marketing

Product-orientated marketing stems from the production era when products were produced to serve a purpose and companies produced products they wanted to produce with little consideration of consumer needs.

Market-orientated marketing

In the 1950s, mass marketing came to the forefront with the commercial opportunities presented through rapid expansion of transportation allowing geographical distribution of products and services. Consumerism has been fuelled by selling techniques developed by marketeers to encourage buying behaviour for goods out of desire rather than to satisfy basic needs, represented by the capitalist culture of consumerism which prevails in society.

Customer-focused marketing

Service culture stemming from the Quality Movement with its roots in Japan and quickly taken up by America led to a more customer-orientated marketing approach, which is practised in organizations of this era. To compete with the competition and undifferentiating nature of products and services, companies are searching for innovative ways to reach their consumers and retain their loyalty.

Customer-focused marketing puts the consumer at the heart of all marketing activities and involves developing products or services that meet the needs of the targeted customer.

Relationship marketing

Loyalty schemes are ways in which companies build 'clubs' of consumers with similar traits and buying behaviour. They store information based on segmentation variables (see Fig. 7.2) which is collected via customer information requests that make up part of the signing-up process. These data are collated and stored on databases enabling companies to market products to the relevant user group. Customers are rewarded with priority points, offers, early notification of exclusive deals, member-only promotional events, freebies and discounts. These personalized perks are designed to keep the customer loyal. In effect, the collection of airmiles points works better for a consumer who limits the number of loyalty schemes he/she buys into.

Consumer Behaviour

Lumsdon (1997, p. 25) defines tourism consumer behaviour as 'the managerial process of anticipating and satisfying existing and potential visitor wants more effectively than competitive suppliers or destinations'. The principle of consumer behaviour is about giving the customer what he/she wants by matching the product or service to the characteristics of the target user group. Understanding the characteristics of target groups of consumers allows marketeers to direct products and services to psychological, cultural, demographic and behavioural aspects of their personality.

The key to customer-focused marketing is creating a product or service, which plays to conscious and unconscious psychological factors in the make-up of the targeted consumer group so that it achieves the desired purchase behaviour. By understanding a consumer, the right product can be produced and marketed through the appropriate marketing channel.

The marketeer's angle on consumer behaviour is making a product or service desirable to consumers, thus making sure that consumers are motivated to purchase. By understanding the process a buyer goes through when making a purchase decision (see Fig. 7.1), a marketeer can design products and services, and communicate them to match the stimuli associated with the personality traits recognized as the motivator for a group's buyer behaviour.

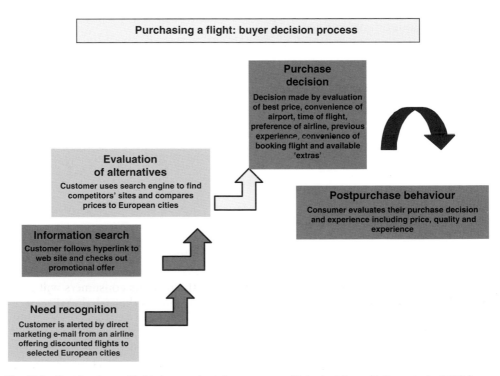

Fig. 7.1. Purchasing a flight: buyer decision process. (Adapted from Kotler *et al.*, 2006.)

D. Wale

Motivation and Marketing

The skill of the marketeer lies in understanding and responding to the behavioural motivation and psychological factors of the consumer. Motivation theorists (outlined in Chapter 3, this volume) believe that motivation is linked to variables, such as intrinsic and extrinsic factors, and these motivate specific buying behaviour. Internal motivators are a person's value system, which may motivate ethical buying behaviour, or a person's internal makeup, e.g. cultural or religious beliefs which dictate the purchase of halal meat (Muslim). Marketeers create the desire to purchase through creative advertising using stimuli that appeals to extrinsic or external motivators such as cultural norms (wanting the things that make you part of a social group).

Features and benefits

Consumers buy features and benefits rather than products and services. Marketeers need to ensure that features and benefits satisfy consumer's needs, wants and desires and stimulate purchase behaviour, e.g. in marketing a holiday a dream is being sold.

Information approach

Providing information enables the consumer to decide whether features and benefits meet the needs of the consumer better than another competitor.

Appealing to cultural values (socio-economics)

Does the product or service culturally satisfy the consumer? Does it create the right image, make the person feel good about himself/herself? Does it make them feel part of the niche market they are segmented into? Are the features and benefits capable of satisfying intrinsic needs?

Emotional marketing (psychographic)

Emotional marketing is appealing to consumers through targeting their emotional stimuli (senses). Marketing holiday destinations in developing countries can pose a problem to marketeers who want to appeal to sell the benefits consumers will get in giving back to a poorer economy without exposing them to the visual reality of the purchase behaviour. Holiday companies marketing destinations in the developing world will be careful not to expose the consumer's emotional stimuli (senses) to the reality of a situation like poverty, by providing glossy images of a destination and not the reality. The holiday will often involve holidaymakers being housed in a compound away from the actual destination experience.

Market Research

Market research is used to determine the traits of a market segment. Data used may be from in-house data collection methods (e.g. focus groups or customer care feedback surveys), may be collected from external sources (e.g. customer loyalty schemes) or may be purchased from market research specialists (e.g. customer buying behaviour, forecasts, market trends, mailing lists, detailed overview and statistics of segments of the travel market). Contracting out market research to research companies can be very effective economically. Research companies have the specialism to offer customized research and can tailor tourism intelligence data to suit the needs of their client.

Decisions on the most effective marketing communications methods will be based on market research, particularly data from previous campaigns of customer feedback (questionnaires and focus groups). Sales data are a useful indicator, but good data collection systems need to be put into place to enable evaluation, e.g. how will coupon redemption be monitored? Promotions using the Internet are easier to monitor, and search engine companies can store user behaviour data of people accessing sites via this method. Sales are not always an indicator of the success of a promotional campaign. For example, companies with product lines may advertise one product or service, but this can translate to increased sales in other products or services in the range because the promotion puts the brand into the consumers mind.

Marketing Segmentation, Targeting and Positioning

Marketing segmentation, targeting and positioning are the key to a successful marketing campaign. With finance, the main focus of an organization, marketeers need to focus marketing activities at particular markets or segments. A high-end airline will select the segment that reflects its passengers, staff, products and services and then target them through the best and most appropriate marketing channels to match their lifestyle, e.g. business passengers will be targeted directly through devices such as portable 3G mobile technology and Internet-based customer loyalty schemes such as business clubs linked to collection and redemption of rewards, e.g. business miles. The company has to look at new products and services coming into the market and position them in the right place against their competitors. A positioning map is designed for this purpose (see Fig. 7.5).

Segmentation

Segmentation involves selecting the most appropriate consumer for a product or service by looking at their attributes. Categories or groups of consumers with similar attributes are classified in a number of ways by different market research companies who collect data relating to consumer buying behaviour and sell it to companies as market intelligence to be used to target marketing spend. Large companies either collect their own data or buy marketing intelligence from market research companies to inform them of the likes and dislikes of their customers. Loyalty cards are an example of the data held by organizations. In-house loyalty schemes allow companies to

D. Wale

Demographics: age, sex, class, marital status, family, ethnicity, religion, life cycle stage

Sociocultural: occupation, income, education, social class

Lifestyle: single/married, activities, mind set, psychographics, student, professional, Internet user, technophobe, environmentalist, lesbian/gay, disabled, religion, race, sport, travel choice (Internet user groups), dietary, cultural

Behavioural/psychological: early adopter

End-user: (purpose for purchase) special occasion, business trip, gap year

Geographical: global, regional, urban/rural, type of house

Fig. 7.2. Market segmentation categories and their variables.

A Higher managerial, administrative or professional

B Intermediate managerial, administrative and professional

C1 Supervisory, clerical, junior administrative or professional

C2 Skilled manual workers

D Semi-skilled and unskilled manual workers

E State pensioners, widows, lowest-grade workers

Fig. 7.3. National readership survey.

collect their own database of customer preferences and adjust products and services according to how well they are performing with their target market.

The segmentation process may consider one (single variable) or all (multi-variable) of the categories listed when carrying out this process.

The market can be segmented by a number of methods. Segmentation includes demographics, sociocultural, lifestyle, behavioural, psychological, end-user and geographical (see Fig. 7.2) categories, and each category contains a number of variables, e.g. variables in demographics include age, sex, class, etc. Segments should be measurable, accessible, substantial, defensible, durable and competitive. Methods of segmentation include national readership survey (NRS; see Fig. 7.3) and a classification of residential neighbourhoods (ACORN).

National readership survey

The NRS method of segmentation uses the sociocultural variables social class and income.

A classification of residential neighbourhoods

ACORN utilizes geographical and demographical variables (geodemographic) for segmentation. ACORN uses statistics from the UK national census to determine characteristics of people in their habitat. It works on the premise that demographic and social factors can be correlated to where people live and allow marketeers to target geographical areas, e.g. direct mail. ACORN's classifications can be accessed at www.caci.co.uk/acorn.

Targeting

Once the target audience has been selected (using market segmentation), the targeting process can begin. A useful tool is the segmentation matrix or battle map (see Fig. 7.4). Developed by Cohen in 1986, it allows undifferentiated products and services to be mapped against a segmentation category. Gaps in the matrix indicate new possible markets. This process can be used to look at a company's portfolio in isolation from, or in comparison with, its competitors.

Positioning

A positioning strategy determines how companies want customers to think and feel about (features and benefits) a product or service.

Positioning maps (see Fig. 7.5) allow the final part of the segmentation, targeting and positioning process. Products and services are positioned against competitors' offerings to establish a good position in which to get a competitive advantage. It allows products and services to be compared and contrasted in relation to each other. Two variables are plotted against each other, i.e. quality, price, speed and market versus economy or premium. The choice of variables must reflect the mission and values of the organization and relate to the attributes a company wants its customers to feel or think about their product or service (e.g. what is the position of the product in the mind of the consumer?) – faster than the competitors, larger seats (more leg room), etc.

Holiday centres	Sandals		Butlins	
European package	Sovereign	Escapades	Aspro	Saga European Holidays
Far and away	Kuoni Weddings			Saga Long Haul Holidays
Ski	Mark Warner couples' ski	Club 18–30 Ski and Snowboarding	Neilson Ski and Snowboarding	
Cruises	Cunard Cruises	Carnival Cruises	Thomson TUI Cruises	Saga Cruises
	Couples	**Young singles**	**Families**	**Third agers**

Fig. 7.4. Segmentation matrix business battle map for the holiday industry. (Adapted from www.wrl-ne.com.)

D. Wale

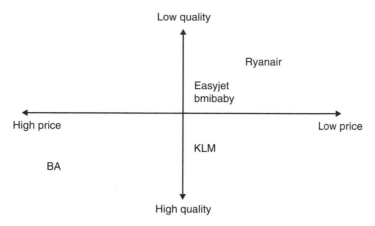

Fig. 7.5. Positioning map: airlines by quality and price.

Marketing Planning

Once the product or service has been positioned, marketing activities and campaigns can be designed, dictated through marketing objectives outlined in the marketing plan.

Marketing planning is the first stage of the marketing process. Marketing planners will construct an annual marketing plan setting out aims and objectives of the marketing department and marketing activities planned for the year.

A marketing plan is a customer-focused coordinated plan utilizing the elements of the marketing mix (explained later in this chapter) to achieve the marketing goal (aim) in line with the company's mission. It provides a framework for marketing activities over a set period of time.

Marketing planning does not work in isolation to other business activities within an organization and must satisfy the overall aims and objectives of an organization, considering other department's plans. An organization could spend billions of pounds on an elaborate marketing campaign only to be let down by operating systems, as has been thoroughly documented by the Terminal 5 launch at Heathrow airport (see Chapter 5, this volume).

Mission vision and values

The mission outlines the company's business strategy and the vision is a statement of future intent (the way it intends to achieve it). They are both customer-focused. An achievable aim spells out the activities the company will undertake to succeed in their mission and these are broken down into objectives, which provide operators with manageable and tangible activities that can be easily translated into tasks.

Therefore, in formulating marketing objectives it is essential that the activities of the marketing department fit with the company's mission. Mission statements often include the company's chosen market (e.g. budget airline) or their environmental policy (e.g. to be an environmental leader). In designing marketing campaigns, therefore, the whole marketing function must match with the mission and this determines the brand.

An example of mission and vision from the easyGroup is outlined in Fig. 7.6. See the section on *branding* for a discussion of values.

> **The easyGroup strategy**
>
> We will build on our brand values:
>
> great value;
> taking on the big boys;
> for the many not the few;
> relentless innovation;
> keep it simple;
> entrepreneurial;
> making a difference in people's lives;
> honest, open, caring and fun.
>
> We will protect our brand from internal and external threats and manage appropriately the business and other risks inherent in venturing. We will develop our people and ensure their reward is aligned to realized shareholder returns.
>
> **The easyGroup mission statement**
>
> Our mission is to manage and extend Europe's leading value brand to more products and services, while creating real wealth for all stakeholders.
>
> **The easyGroup vision**
>
> easyGroup will develop Europe's leading value brand into a global force. We will paint the world orange!

Fig. 7.6. The easyGroup mission, vision and value statement. (Available at: www.easy.com.)

Marketing Strategy

Marketing strategy, marketing plan and marketing tactics are all terms used to describe planned marketing activities. Strategic marketing is a cycle of analysis, strategic choice and implementation (see Fig. 7.7). 'Much of the work in marketing departments is concerned with drawing up, implementing and measuring the effects of action plans' (Middleton, 2001, p. 202).

Strategic marketing is the well-researched and planned execution of marketing tactics, drawn up in a strategic marketing plan. The strategic marketing process (see Fig. 7.8) involves moving the organization in a direction, which is dictated first through a situation analysis of the internal factors influencing, and the external factors affecting, the current, emerging and future marketplace. Analysis utilizes: the political, economical, social, technological, legal and environmental (PESTLE) framework; future trends analysis; competitor analysis; strengths, weaknesses, opportunities and threats (SWOT); and Porter's five forces.

A strategy is formed through the results of this analysis. Expansion is the most popular strategy and may be either into new markets or within existing ones.

Once the strategy or marketing aim has been determined, objectives can be set for achieving the strategy. These must relate directly to the companies overall mission and therefore reflect the whole ethos of the company.

D. Wale

Pre-strategic marketing analysis

Internal/external audit
Current market position: market
share, portfolio analysis (BGM)
Competitor analysis
Future trends analysis
PESTLE
SWOT
Porter's five forces

Strategy selection

Ansoff's matrix: growth strategies
Porter's generic strategies

Strategy implementation and control

Strategic application of the
marketing mix to devise tactics to
execute marketing stratgy

Market segmentation, targeting
and positioning

Auditing and evaluting the
effects of the strategic marketing
and making plans for future
activity (feeds back into analysis)

Strategic marketing plan drawn up, aims and objectives set

Fig. 7.7. Strategic marketing cycle.

The final implementation stage sees a well-planned coordinated marketing campaign utilizing marketing tactics drawn up through strategic application of the marketing mix (7 Ps) to target the chosen market and attain the desired purchasing behaviour translated into bottom-line returns. Tactics are the translation of marketing objectives into practice through application of the marketing mix.

Strategic marketing plan

Strategic marketing planning involves deciding on marketing strategies to achieve overall strategic objectives (Kotler and Armstrong, 2008).

Strategic marketing plans are the company's overall strategy for long-term survival and growth; essential as a framework for marketing activity and projected

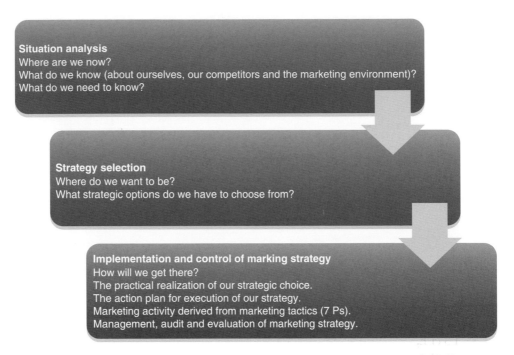

Fig. 7.8. The strategic marketing process.

expenditure and are usually set over a 12-month period to coincide with the financial year and company budgeting. It is essential that marketing planning is coordinated with, and integrated into, all business and operational processes and therefore becomes part of a company's overall business strategy. Marketing strategy relies on all departments and cannot be planned in isolation.

The marketing plan is the documented framework (action plan) for marketing activity based on the strategic marketing process. It usually spans 12 months.

Marketing Analysis

Middleton (2001) explains that the planning for strategy and tactics often utilizes the same analysis done by the same people. The important part of analysis is the continuous updating of data, particularly intelligence on competitors. Competitor analysis involves individuals plotting competitor activities through utilizing and accessing competitor products and services on an ongoing basis. Marketing analysis is necessary to avoid disastrous consequences in spend of marketing budgets. The skill in well-executed strategy is keeping abreast of the market, predicting trends and the ability to re-evaluate or pull out if necessary. The ability to do this will be facilitated by continuously updated data that can be used for re-evaluation purposes.

Through analysis, thorough market research is carried out. Tools such as PESTLE, SWOT and Porter's five forces are used to understand the factors influencing the marketing environment both internally and externally. Analysis is a way of

D. Wale

```
Political

Economic, environmental, ecological, education

Social, socio-economical

Technological

Legal

Demographics

Cultural
```

Fig. 7.9. PEST and its connotations.

evaluating the marketing position of the company in view of competitors, trends, external influences and internal resources to execute a proposed activity.

PEST

PEST, PESTLE, PESTEL, STEP, STEPE, STEEP, STEEPLE, LEPEST, DEPICT, DEPICTS: a number of acronyms exist for what is a number of versions of the same thing (Fig. 7.9). The choice really depends on what outcome is required by the company. It really is not important which model is used. (See the chapter on strategic management (Chapter 6, this volume) for further explanation of the PEST model.) In a marketing context, the PEST contained within the strategic marketing plan should clearly provide the documented evidence for the chosen marketing strategy. It is in effect a safety net or, in Dragon's Den terms, the rationale for the pitch!

SWOT analysis

A strengths, weaknesses, threats and opportunities (SWOT) analysis (see Fig. 7.10) is a way of auditing the internal marketing environment of a travel operation. As a key determiner of marketing activity, it is a useful tool for identifying the capabilities and possibilities within an organization and enables informed and appropriate allocation of resources. The opportunities and threats are influenced by the external audit, e.g. in carrying out a PESTLE analysis of the external marketing environment, a number of economic factors may have been identified that would influence marketing decisions. For example, in early 2008 the economic downturn in the USA resulted in a weak dollar against a stronger pound. For US travellers, this made the UK an expensive choice as a holiday destination. In analysing an airline's scheduling, in the threats part of the SWOT this would be a negative (US travelling to UK) and then look at ways of making it positive in the opportunities part (UK travelling to US). By carrying out a thorough audit of opportunities and threats arising out of the external audits, potential gaps in the market can be identified. The better the marketing intelligence, the more informed the SWOT will be. The strengths and weaknesses part of the SWOT is important to get a picture of the internal operational capability of the company. It will consist of auditing a product/service for strengths and weaknesses in relation to its marketing mix.

Strengths	Weaknesses
Quality staff	High staff turnover
Achievement of industry awards and leader in 'all-inclusive holidays' category	Late adopter of online sales methods has disadvantaged company in relation to competitors
Large customer base	Negative press for 'social responsibility' actions has tarnished brand
The product or range of products	Lack of 'in-house' marketing expertise
High demands for latest product in range	Undifferentiated products and service (i.e. in relation to competitors)
Catchy advertising has raised profile of brand	Business location
Opportunities	**Threats**
Potential new products	New competitors entering the 'all-inclusive' market
Increasing the market base	Price wars forcing discounting
Partnerships with other organizations (i.e. regional tourist board)	Competitor wins industry award for specialist socially responsible holiday product
Growth in Russia due to oil supplies in country	Downturn in economy, recession predicted and consumer spend on luxury items reduced
Acquisition of specialist holiday company with 'environmentally friendly' products imminent	Competitors have superior access to channels of distribution
A developing market such as the Internet	
A market vacated by an ineffective competitor	

Fig. 7.10. SWOT analysis.

Competitor analysis

Porter's five forces of competitive rivalry, substitutes, new entrants, customers and suppliers is a framework used to conduct a competitor analysis (see Chapter 6, this volume).

Strategic Choice

Strategic choice, strategy formulation and strategic direction are all terms used to describe the process directly preceding analysis. It utilizes the intelligence gained from research in determining strategic direction.

Tools such as Ansoff's growth matrix and Porter's generic strategies for competitive advantage can all be used to determine strategic direction.

Ansoff's growth matrix

There are a number of options for a company to choose from when making choices about ways to grow products and services and Ansoff's growth matrix (AGM) is the most used tool.

Ansoff's matrix is used to assess the strategic choice a company has to make to bridge the sales gap. It enables marketeers to evaluate the growth options facing the

D. Wale

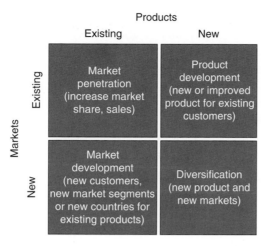

Fig. 7.11. Ansoff's growth matrix. (From Johnson and Scholes, 1999.)

company. Marketeers need to make choices about products in their existing portfolio, and new products they wish to introduce. AGM provides a useful framework to consider this choice (see Fig. 7.11).

Market extension or development

This strategy finds growth through rolling out existing products to new markets. The existing product is targeted at a new market, e.g. geographical expansion through international expansion of air routes. Companies often extend their range of products through joint marketing activities or through acquisition of intermediaries. Another way of extending existing products to new markets would be to try to appeal to more market segments, e.g. all-inclusive holidays with their mass-market appeal.

Product development

This strategy involves constant innovation and development of new products for existing markets. With this strategy, there is pressure to keep abreast of industry developments through ongoing market analysis. The key to this strategy is developing the right product before competitors do and being the first to market with it. The danger with this strategy is that competitors will copy it, e.g. current innovations include airlines' development of ranges of toiletries to comply with carrying restrictions due to security regulations at airports, which restrict the amount of liquid allowed in hand luggage to 100 ml containers.

Market penetration or concentration

This strategy aims to increase sales by selling more of the existing products to the existing market segment. The product is not altered and new customer segments are not targeted.

Growth tactics include promotional campaigns, e.g. direct mail such as short message service (SMS) texting, public relations (PR) events, relationship marketing, e.g. customer loyalty schemes such as airmiles, and targeting competitors' customers, e.g. up-selling and add-ons.

Diversification and innovation

This strategy involves creating new products for new target markets. There are four categories for diversification:

1. Vertical forward integration: This strategy involves acquisition of intermediaries that form part of the product or services supply chain, e.g. a travel operation company's own airlines, travel agents and hotel chains.

2. Horizontal diversification: This strategy involves acquisition of a competitor in the same marketplace.

3. Concentric (related) diversification: New products or services are created using an organization's key competences/related areas; extension of a company's portfolio of companies in familiar markets, e.g. holiday companies acquiring specialist holiday companies, such as activity holidays.

4. Conglomerate (unrelated) diversification: This strategy involves diversification into an unrelated area where a company expands into an unfamiliar territory, e.g. the easyGroup has a number of products unrelated to the airline industry including easyHotels and easyCinema.

Porter's generic strategies

Porter's generic strategies provide a framework for analysing industries and competitors in order to establish how to build sustainable competitive advantage and market dominance over rivals. It has three dimensions: cost leadership, differentiation and focus (or niche strategy). Strategies may be used alone or a hybrid approach to strategy formulation may be appropriate, depending on market conditions and competitors being challenged.

Cost leadership (undifferentiated)

In order to gain competitive advantage, a product or service is mass-produced at a lower cost than the competition. The product is usually an economy or no-frills product, which is cheap to produce, has low overheads and so can be distributed to a mass market at a cheaper price than its competitors. Low-cost airlines and all-inclusive holidays are examples. One company aims to have the largest market share and become or remain the market leader. Market share is defended by keeping the brand standardized, keeping ahead of trends and the competition, predicting the future market, spending money on customer loyalty and attracting new customers. Marketing tends to focus on promoting low-cost benefits.

D. Wale

Differentiation

Marketing based on differentiation of products and services focuses on matching the features and benefits of each of the sub-brands to the characteristics of different target markets. Marketing spend is distributed to all the brands on a cyclical basis, e.g. responding to the seasonality of the different markets catered for within the brand.

Currently, there are only a few major travel operation companies operating worldwide. All have strong consumer brands in a number of markets. These companies are able to offer a range of products and services from niche, e.g. special interest holidays, to mass-market experiences, e.g. all-inclusive holidays. They own the whole holiday experience (supply chain) from the aeroplane to the travel agency (marketing channel). There is little to differentiate the companies and so brand loyalty is important. Specialist holidays are easier ways to build loyalty as they create a niche with which to differentiate products and services from competitors.

Unique selling proposition

The unique selling proposition (USP) is the outstanding feature/benefit of the product or service, which differentiates it from competitors.

Niche (focus)

Companies with a number of brands focus marketing spend on brands capable of category leadership. A category is the grouping to which a brand belongs, e.g. all-inclusive holidays. Marketing spend is targeted to one brand.

Implementation of Marketing Strategy

The final stage of strategy involves the formulation of coordinated targeted marketing activities using the marketing mix.

The Marketing Mix (7 Ps)

The marker adjusts elements of the marketing mix to tactically sell products or services to a targeted group of customers. The marketing mix is made up of 7 Ps: product, price, place, promotion, people, process and physical evidence.

Product

Levels of product

There are three levels to a product: core product, real/actual product and augmented product (Fig. 7.12).

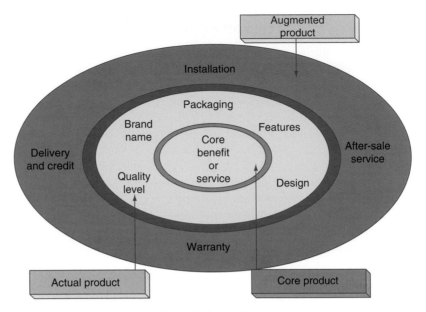

Fig. 7.12. The levels of a product. (From Kotler, 2008.)

The *core product* is the essential benefit or service the product provides for the customer, e.g. comfort, speed.

The tangible elements of a product or service make up the *actual product*, sometimes referred to as the *real product*. These are the tangible elements of the product and include: design, features, packaging, brand name and quality level (Kotler, 2008).

Service and intangible elements make up the *augmented product*, such as delivery, credit, warranty, installation and after-sales service (Kotler, 2008). The augmented product is the experience of partaking on the holiday.

The *marketing offering* is sometimes added as a fourth level or facet of a product. It represents the price and availability of the product or service.

Product line

This refers to all the products or brands in a company's portfolio. The product is one product or brand in that portfolio.

Product life cycle

The product life cycle (PLC) is a useful method for developing marketing strategy (see Fig. 7.13). It charts the stages in the life cycle of a product or service.

INTRODUCTION OF PRODUCT   New products enter the life cycle at the introductory stage. The product is heavily discounted and advertising is used to push the product to the customer. Growth is slow at this stage of the PLC.

Introduction aims: create awareness, stimulate purchase behaviour;

D. Wale

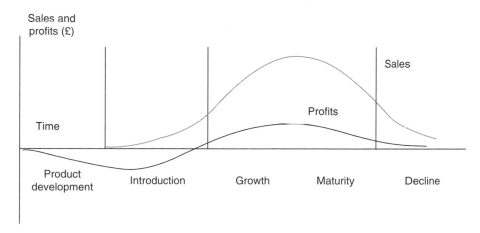

Fig. 7.13. The product life cycle.

Characteristics: low profits, high start-up costs;

Price: two pricing strategies: low price (penetration pricing) and high price (skimming);

Place: limited marketing channels;

Promotion: create awareness through high levels of marketing activity.

GROWTH   Marketing activity carried out at the product launch converts to sales as the market accepts the product or service and it enjoys rapid sales growth.

Growth aims: build consumer preference; put product/service in customer's minds;

Characteristics: rapid increase of sales; competitors emerge and challenge;

Price: starts at optimum, but reduces in response to competition;

Place: increasing number of channels;

Promotion: emphasize the benefits of the brand, build customer loyalty.

MATURITY   A product reaches maturity when sales stabilizes; often other companies enter the same market with similar products or services. It may be necessary to look at marketing activities such as promotions to improve sales of these products and to revisit marketing strategy to rejuvenate, e.g. rebrand.

Maturity aims: maintain sales and encourage repeat purchases;

Characteristics: sales stabilized, less profitable;

Price: usually need to reduce price or discount to maintain sales;

Place: wide number of channels;

Promotion: need to offer incentives, e.g. buy one get one free (BOGOF).

DECLINE   Decline occurs when sales and profits fall. As sales declines, marketeers need to decide whether to extend, rebrand or remove product. BCG and Ansoff's matrix are useful tools for decision making.

Decisions on price, place and promotion may be unnecessary if the company decides to remove the product from its portfolio.

Aims: difficult to define;

Characteristics: sales and profits falling;

Price: often rock bottom or used a loss leader;

Place: wide number of channels, including 'bucket shops';

Promotion: range of different incentives.

Branding

Branding is the key to all marketing activities. A marketing campaign can make or break a brand. In a well-documented example, Hoover ran a marketing campaign in which they offered free flights. They underestimated the high take-up and came close to going bust. In other campaigns, companies have endorsed celebrities who have the brand characteristics of their product and therefore match and add value to the brand image they are portraying, whether that is quality or value for money.

Branding immediately differentiates a company from its competitors. For many companies, the brands they own are their most valuable assets. Kotler and Armstrong (2008) define a brand as:

> A name, term, sign, symbol, design or a combination of these, which is used to identify the goods or services of one seller or group of sellers and to differentiate them from those of competitors.

Other tangible aspects that symbolize a brand include logo, font, colour scheme and sound, e.g. British Airways' adoption of the Flower Duet by Lakmé for a number of their commercials. These tangible brand attributes will be developed and updated in line with the company's overall mission to differentiate the brand from the competition, provide an expectation in the mind of consumers, deliver consistently and motivate buying behaviour.

Key concepts of branding are brand values and personality, which must match and portray the brand. Values are the core of the brand, they set out the philosophy behind everything that the company believes and aims to do and will be at the heart of everything that all stakeholders interacting with or for the company experience. Figure 7.6 gives easyGroup's values as an example.

Building a successful brand will involve ensuring that all the functions carried out by an organization reflect the brand image identity and characteristics. This includes making sure that every member of personnel is portraying the brand in everything they do; that the product or service offered by that company is standard in its production, delivery and after-service capabilities; and that the range of products or services offered within the umbrella brand portfolio (and some of these may be a sub-brand) are providing the best results in the marketplace. The Boston growth matrix (BGM) is used for this purpose.

CASE STUDY: REBRANDING LE MÉRIDIEN HOTELS

In order to compete in a rapidly expanding and competitive global marketplace where hospitality products and services are similar, individual hotels have to develop an individual identity in order to differentiate themselves successfully from the competition.

Le Méridien Hotels was founded by Air France in Paris in 1972. At this time, the brand targeted affluent travellers by positioning as sophisticated and innovative French-style hotels with a distinctive European service culture. Following a decade of changing ownership and acquisitions, the brand had acquired a faded identity, and the product had become increasingly inconsistent, with each hotel adopting its individual style.

In 2006, Le Méridien Hotels acquired Starwood Hotels and Resorts, who were a leader in branding hotel chains like Sheraton. This resulted in the rebranding of Le Méridian using a 'repositioning' marketing strategy.

To define the USP of Le Méridien Hotels, the strategy went back to the original image of its French roots. It wanted to create an emotional connection to its guests. The strategy based on the image of France as a country was defined by five columns: cuisine, lifestyle, fashion, culture and art. Le Méridien Hotels aimed to attract the creative and innovative guest with a sense for fine art and culture. The new brand positioning focused on bringing the slogan 'chic cultured discovery' alive in a credible and authentic way.

In order to create a consistent product, a corporate identity was created by introducing brand standards for interior design, service culture, staff training, in-house products and collateral material in all of their 120 hotels worldwide. To underline its commitment towards the cultural values represented by the five columns of the new strategy, strategic partnerships between the brand and a variety of public institutions, single artists and recognized experts were forged. The board of artists was named LM100 and headed by the co-founder of the Palais de Paris and Cultural Curator of Le Méridien, Jerome Sans.

LM100 has impacted on Le Méridien in a number of ways through partnerships and initiatives with members, organizations and cultural institutions.

Individual hotels have been linked with local cultural institutions, providing guests with free entrance to museums, cultural events and exhibitions. An innovative programme called 'Unlock Art' was rolled out globally in 2008 and provides guests with access to a variety of progressive and independent cultural centres like The Museum of Contemporary Art (MOCA) in Shanghai.

One of the LM100's members is US star chef Jean Georges Vongerichten. He has created a 'new breakfast', which combines international tastes in a sophisticated way. Launched in 2008, it will be the standard in all hotels by 2009. A further partnership with the French coffee maker, Andrea Illy, also a member of LM100, will introduce creative coffee breaks and intellectual reading sessions in the lobby of each Le Méridien hotel.

Strategic communication is essential to a successful rebranding strategy and several brand initiatives have supported the launch of the repositioned hotel brand. One of the marketing campaigns called 'Le Méridien One Night' involved a promotion based around each column of the strategy, such as the cultural aspect, enabling the new standard to be introduced and publicized to the international press and public.

Continued

The repositioning strategy of Le Méridien hotels has focused on the creation and delivery of a consistent hotel product, consistent and innovative brand initiatives as well as consistent communication. By serving the niche market of the creative and innovative guest, the group has differentiated itself from competitors. The success of the new strategy is already delivering results: increased revenue, numbers and repeat guests. By implementing innovative standards and communicating them effectively, Le Méridien Hotels are on their way to being recognized as a distinct brand for a certain clientele of guests.

(Case study by Martina Venus, Public Relations Manager: Starwood Hotels and Resorts, and Debra Wale, 2008)

Boston growth matrix

The Boston growth matrix (BGM), designed by the Boston Consulting Group, is a well-used marketing tool (see Fig. 7.14). A company can plot its portfolio of products in the four categories: dog, star, question mark and plough horse according to sales figures. It identifies and categorizes a company's products into either high or low market growth or high or low market share:

- High growth rate is 10%+.
- Low growth rate is below 10%.
- High market share is defined as equal to, or greater than, that of the largest competitors.

DOG Remove from portfolio: sell or abandon. Focus on a specialist segment; rebrand

STAR These are the top-selling products and marketing needs to be used to keep them prominent to protect market share.

QUESTION MARK (ALSO REFERRED TO AS PROBLEM CHILD) These are products that are on the edge of stars and dogs and could go either way. Marketing needs to be used to bring

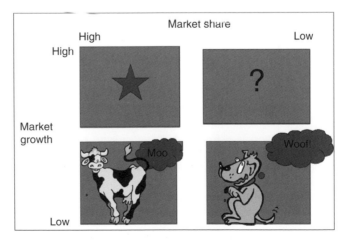

Fig. 7.14. Boston growth matrix.

D. Wale

them to prominence; however, marketing activity needs to cease should they fail. These products include fad products which tend to be snapped up by early adopters and can quickly be replicated by competitors. Exclusive deals, e.g. celebrity endorsement, may help marketeers move these products to stars.

CASH COW (ALSO REFERRED TO AS PLOUGH HORSE)   These products are the mainstay of the company's portfolio. They are safe, steady sellers, but do not bring in a big return. They can be loss leaders and are often customer's favourites. Removing them from a portfolio could seriously affect the company's overall sales.

Price

There are a number of approaches to pricing. One or many of these methods depending on the stage of the product life cycle, external market factors and the rest of the marketing mix may influence a product or service.

Seller's market

When there is little choice or competition, price premiums can be applied. They might, however, make a difference to the customer's repeat performance. Just because a product or service is purchased, it does not necessarily indicate satisfaction. An example of price premiums would be on products or services with exclusive rights (i.e. no other operator can sell). Often this will happen when companies use joint promotions.

Buyer's market

When choice is abundant and prices similar, buyers can force companies to discount, making it possible for the customer to switch companies (however, the customer may incur a charge/waiting time in switching).

Yield management

The skill of selling all plane seats and accommodation for the best possible price (squeezing as much money as possible out of the consumer) is an example of yield management.

Price sensitivity

The travel operations market is very price-sensitive due to the undifferentiated nature of products. Customers tend to be drawn to the offer rather than purchasing loyalty.

Price lining

This involves adjusting the price to reflect the product or services price within a range. Once margins have been calculated, the price of a range of products can be adjusted to reach the desired overall margin. This is also referred to as sales mix. The sales mix is the total of all the products (100%).

Psychological pricing

ODD-EVEN PRICING This refers to using a price with 9 at the end of it, e.g. £299.99. The psychological aspect of this odd-even pricing is that people perceive the rounded-up price £300 as more even though there is only a penny in it.

COMPETITIVE PRICING It is essential to research competitors. Margin pricing may be used to get a desired profit from a product, but if competitors are discounting a similar product, there is no incentive for them to purchase at a higher price. With a line of products, cost adjustments can often be made to carry less popular products. Decisions will need to be taken as to the profitability of these weaker items. BGM is a useful tool for assessing profitability within a product portfolio.

Discounts

PRICE SKIMMING This approach tends to suit niche marketing, and involves selling the product at high prices at introduction due to exclusivity. This would be the case for specialist holidays or desirable products or services, which appeal to high-end customers such as the rich, celebrities or early adopters. Often prices will reduce as the product or service moves through the product life cycle.

PENETRATION Market penetration is used to push a product or service on to the market. Heavy discounting techniques are used to establish longevity, e.g. launch of a new transport route.

PRICE-BASED PROMOTIONS Discounts, special offers and freebies are all ways of making a product more appealing to consumers and therefore inducing buyer behaviour. Often promotions are put in place to get the product to market at the early stage of the product life cycle. At product development stage, customer testing will help to judge the price point. At introduction stage, promotions are expected by consumers as an inducement to switch brands (for loyal customers) or to try something new (for price-sensitive consumers). Discounting is often used at the later stages of the product life cycle in an attempt to keep the product in line with competitors.

SPECIAL OFFERS These are temporary promotions aimed at attracting purchase behaviour. The list price remains unchanged when the special offer period is completed, e.g. BOGOF.

DISCOUNTS Flexibility for discounting allows the product or service to be adjusted to a number of buyer groups consecutively. Loyalty discounts, supplier discounts and customer discounts are all examples. Yield management relies on the ability to discount the rack rate in order to fill hotels. The list price will remain unchanged.

Discounting is a good method of testing price sensitivity. It will involve market research to position the product by price.

FREEBIES Freebies are often subsidized by sponsorship. Brands sponsor events or distribute at trade fairs, which represent the target market they are aiming to win. Instead of providing money towards an event's cost, they provide samples, vouchers, discount codes or branded merchandise (gifts).

BUY ONE GET ONE FREE Although used extensively in the industry, care needs to be taken at the middle to high end of the market not to devalue the brand.

Organizations must be careful not to emphasize discounts and low prices to attract customers; do not buy customers, win them.

Place (distribution)

The *place* part of the marketing mix is getting the product or service to the target market, via the right distribution channels, in the right amount of time, at profit.

Distribution channels are the routes by which companies deliver their products or services to customers. Channels can be direct, straight to customer, or indirect, via a channel intermediary. Intermediaries link businesses to customers; the more intermediaries involved, the more the potential for complications to arise in the supply chain. Intermediaries may be: wholesalers, travel agents, retailers, distribution companies or the Internet.

The supply chain consists of all the intermediaries involved in the life cycle of a product or service, from conception to post-consumption. During the life cycle of a product or service, it may be exposed to production, operation and transportation by different intermediaries, through a variety of distribution methods (each of these with connections to products and services of other companies) with a potential global geographical distribution.

Supply chain management is the most difficult to control as it involves more than two intermediaries in the process: the manufacturer of the product or owner of the service, the distribution company or intermediary who moves the product to the place ready for the customer to purchase, e.g. warehouse and on to travel agents, Internet web site and the sales process travel agents, group sales and on to customer. The management of the supply chain is a threat to brand management and needs to be operated and monitored to brand specifications.

From a marketing perspective, control of place (distribution) involves management of relationships within the supply chain and many companies avoid this by owning all the processes within the distribution chain.

Distribution strategies are designed to place the product or service in the most appropriate place (distribution channel) to match the buying behaviour of the target market and achieve the desired buying behaviour. Marketing communications are the methods used to design distribution strategies.

Customer relationship management

Customer relationship management (CRM) involves working with other departments to form a value chain in order to serve customers.

THE INTERNET The Internet has had the biggest impact on the place in which the travel operations industry chooses to pass its products and services to consumers. Technology is being introduced by the hour and companies race to innovate in this area. Current fads will be yesterday's news. The last decade has seen the increase in web-based bookings, holiday brochures allowing virtual tours of planned locations, travel books, blogs and an increase in the ability to DIY holiday plan using the Internet.

PUSH OR PULL   Push and pull are terms used to describe the method by which companies place their products and services within distribution channels.

Companies push products to channel members from the distribution channel to encourage distribution, e.g. using a travel agent or a trade fair to sell specialist holidays.

Products and services are promoted to customers using a pull strategy to raise product awareness and encourage buyer and purchase behaviour either through direct or indirect marketing channels. Pull techniques include merchandising, advertising and customer loyalty schemes.

Physical evidence

Physical evidence encompasses the tangible face of service products including premises, vehicles, company web sites and appearance and behaviour of staff.

The growth in the use of e-communications and, in particular, the Internet has changed the face of customer service for this method of product distribution. Customer call centres have been contracted out to countries in continents where the services are cheaper to purchase (e.g. Asia). Call centres based overseas have gained bad press because they are so far removed from, and unable to provide information and advice on the features and benefits of, the product or service. Recent developments see companies returning call centres to the country and hub of the organization to remedy this criticism.

> **CASE STUDY: COMPLAINING THROUGH E-COMMUNICATIONS TECHNOLOGY**
>
> Technology allowing customers to complain is now at consumer's fingertips, enabling a problem to be solved as it arises.
>
> A customer using National Express Coaches was unhappy with the cabin temperature. Seeing a customer service number inside the vehicle (displayed by the company to actively seek customer feedback in order to meet customer needs), the customer telephoned this number using his/her mobile phone while en route. The call centre relayed the message to the driver who was able to adjust the heating and solve the problem.

Process

The process relates to the processes involved in the life cycle of a product or service from conception to after sales; it is the key to brand management. Brand management is standardization of a product, service or brand. The process part of this involves producing a product or service that reflects the mission, vision and values of a company, operationalizing the product or service through documented standard operational procedures

D. Wale

(which clearly describe the operational process of products and services). Standardized processes are audited through internal and external audits. Internal audits include operational checklists, external mystery-guest audits. These in turn are linked to bonus-related key performance indicators (KPIs) of a company (linking back to values), adding an incentivized reason for conforming. Is there a complaints procedure or an auditing system in place to alert you of customer problems before dissatisfaction sets in?

People

The people part of the marketing mix relates to all stakeholders involved in the product or service during its life cycle. They portray and benefit from the brand values.

In service, operation staff are the face of the brand whether in person or voice and need to be trained in customer service techniques relating to quality excellence.

Staff must be trained to deliver the brand in a standardized way. The holiday sold in a brochure in a travel agent must live up to all the elements in its marketing mix. Staff tend to represent the consumer from the market being targeted, i.e. companies selling high-end products and services will be able to attract the best staff. For specialized markets, staff will match the demographic and lifestyle characteristics of that market. This is important as they will need to be able to advise or lead the particular holiday segment, e.g. sport tourism.

Promotion

Promotion is the part of the marketing mix that uses marketing communication methods to sell products and services to targeted consumers. The choice of method depends on the message that needs communicating, the budget and time constraints. Communications are usually visual or verbal in nature. Promotion is a balancing act; methods that target mass audiences may be value for money, but the skill is creating sales from communications and getting return on investment. Integrated communications are coordinated promotional methods used to get maximum coverage and returns.

Marketing communications has a promotions mix, which consists of advertising, merchandising, sales, PR, direct mail and sponsorship. E-communication incorporates the promotions mix in a variety of electronic formats. Targeted marketing campaigns are designed by developing marketing tactics with elements of the marketing mix.

Integrated marketing communications is a holistic approach to promotion. Advertising cannot always work in isolation to other promotional mix elements. The benefit of integrated marketing is that, at planning stage, finances can be allocated to a number of marketing methods best suited to getting the product or service to the intended consumer over a specified time period.

Military tactics

Marketeers competing in an aggressive marketplace have adopted promotional campaigns employing marketing tactics using military metaphors. Two methods utilizing military tactics are stealth marketing and guerrilla marketing.

STEALTH MARKETING Stealth, undercover or buzz marketing is a method used to promote a product or service to a target group without them realizing they are being subjected to a marketing campaign. This method of marketing requires actors from the targeted market segment (who appear to be peers). Internet marketing uses stealth marketing within chat rooms, forums and blogs. They provide a fast, inexpensive method of reaching a segment over a large geographical reach.

GUERRILLA MARKETING Guerrilla marketing is an unconventional form of promotion, usually on a small budget. Guerrilla marketing involves a very publicly staged promotion using people (in costumes) or objects in a creative or controversial way, either at the site of the product or service to be marketed or at that of a competitor.

Advertising

Advertising is paid-for marketing communication aimed at getting the right message, at the right time, to the right audience, using the right imagery.

Advertising is communicating a message to a target market through the most suitable channel that motivates purchase behaviour. Advertising techniques include e-tools and print methods. Advertising channels include media such as cinema, television, Internet, radio, print, information kiosks (touch screen) and billboards.

Advertising campaigns are designed to fit with the target market the tourism operation is attempting to win or keep. Financially, targeting allows budget allocation to be used to push or pull a product or service to the intended purchaser. Failure to provide targeted advertising would result in inability to attract prospective consumers and waste of capital. Target marketing is about spending money effectively. There would be little benefit in a specialist walking company operating treks in the mountains of India sending out marketing materials to the whole population.

Advertising is linked to the product life cycle at the beginning of the product life-cycle development. Advertising is piloted in the product development stage. At introduction, marketing spend on promotion will be at its optimum. The product or service will be pushed to consumers.

Advertising must appeal to market segment, hit the target market and achieve the desired effects of positioning, e.g. make the customer feel and think the positioning, high-quality, high-cost such as first-class travel.

Advertising needs to be simple, put the product or service in the mind of the consumer and gain the ultimate aim, sales. It needs to be better than the advertising of competitors.

Advertising communicates the brand image and personality to the consumer. Memorable advertisements have used characters, mottos, colours, personalities and music; all of these reflect brand attributes.

There are many possibilities to get free advertising product placement. Travel companies may provide a 'free' holiday for television presenters on prime time television spots. Radio shows such as British Broadcasting Corporation (BBC) Radio Four's Excess Baggage provide a good medium for independent companies.

D. Wale

Public relations

Public relations (PR) is the practice of managing the flow of information between an organization and its public (Levy, 2007). The practice of PR is planned around the core business activities of an organization (in line with the mission, vision and values). Public relations is about reputation: the result of what you do, what you say and what others say about you. PR is about making sure that communications truly represent the organization and that this message is relayed to the public. In practice, the PR role is a balancing act of providing 'good image' information, e.g. positive working practices, adoption of practices aimed at reducing carbon footprint and managing 'bad news' stories such as disasters. It involves making sure that all activities carried out by the organization, its intermediaries and stakeholders maintain the reputation of the business. External PR interaction may consist of putting out the right message about the company through communication channels such as the media, television or conferences. Good image information includes: good news stories such as achievement of industry awards, sponsorship of, or product placement via, high-profile events or celebrities, or cause-related marketing (CRM) or socially responsible initiatives. Bad news stories management involves responding to, and either preventing print of or reducing, negative impact of press coverage (often before it breaks to the public) by a planned PR strategy for crisis or a disaster.

CAUSE-RELATED MARKETING   CRM is the partnership link and initiative between profit and not-for-profit (charities) organizations. The value of adoption of a charity by organizations includes enabling a good image to be communicated to the public. Charities are big business for organizations; they can complement good working practices by giving organizations a cuddly, feel-good image, which is particularly useful when companies are constantly investigated and targeted by the media in search of bad news stories from unethical or socially irresponsible business practices. Charities are keen to link with businesses that reflect their values, stakeholders and cause in order to raise their profile and capitalize from fund-raising. The financial benefits for charities from this relationship include profile raising which translates to the bottom line from company and public fund-raising and the potential to adopt lifetime and inheritance donors.

Sponsorship

Specialist areas tourism such as film tourism, music tourism, sport tourism and lesbian and gay tourism are all having their impact on the travel operations industry. These specialist areas are providing good income for sponsorship and partnership working. It is not uncommon to lay on special services to transport tourists to specialized events, e.g. National Express runs dedicated events services to Wembley (www.national express.com). Sponsorship of sports events and sports products provides opportunity for high-profile and media exposure. Alignment and quality match of brands is crucial in partnership, e.g. Emirates sponsors Arsenal Football Club. Sponsorship of specialist events by major tour operators and travel brands is a way of introducing fringe aspects of a brand personality; companies are realizing that minority groups will recognize these brands as user-friendly, and knock-on sales and loyalty will pursue. Recognizing the value of the pink pound and in order to align themselves with the target group, Air France sponsored the London Lesbian and Gay Film Festival.

BBC Radio One promotes music tourism opportunities through its coverage of Glastonbury and other music festivals. Gaining exclusive media rights to such festivals provides revenue for the broadcasting company (BBC), the destination (Glastonbury) and the Festival organizers (Michael Envis).

Merchandising

Merchandising is selling a brand through producing and selling (or distributing free of charge) related products, which appeal to a consumer's cognitive processes (put and keep the brand in their mind) and induce buying behaviour. Merchandising is often used by companies for relationship marketing purposes, providing branded 'freebies'. The travel company Exodus provides a flight bag for customers using their service on a regular basis. This acts as a convenience measure; it standardizes operations for the company, but en route to a destination. Exodus is promoted through holidaymakers' use of branded flight bags.

Merchandise includes t-shirts, children's toys, mugs, pens and bags. Companies will often have a number of merchandise products for each of their umbrella brands; choice of products will reflect market segment of target audience and elements of the marketing mix.

Merchandising crosses over with promotion when used at point of sale to advertise a brand.

In retail, merchandising is the display of related materials used to gain interest in, and sell, products, e.g. travel brochures. Companies strategically place this merchandise in order to generate sales.

TRAVEL BROCHURES   Travel brochures are tailored to the market segment the holiday the brand is selling is aimed at. Selling a holiday is selling a dream. A brochure displays these dreams. Images need to conjure up the desired state the consumer wants to experience. With holidays to poor countries, if people are included they need to draw the person in. A true reflection of a destination may be too shocking or unattractive to sell, e.g. child poverty, cruelty to animals. Companies should warn about shocks, but these do not sell holidays. Travel brochures are easily accessed online offering virtual tours of resorts or can be downloaded to a computer in portable document format (PDF).

TRAVEL AGENCIES   Major companies have the major share of the travel agency marketplace and more prominent positioning, e.g. high street for attracting the mass market. Smaller independent companies cannot compete. Travel agencies allow the customer to buy a holiday and all the extras from an expert in a safe environment for the exchange of a large amount of money; therefore, travel agencies appeal to people who are not confident of the safety of the Internet and prefer this exchange to be person to person. Travel agencies have had to adapt to the technological change in the marketing environment, which has led to the rise in Internet home usage. Travel agencies now incorporate additional features and services, e.g. computer screens (kiosks) and provide refreshments and comfortable and private seating, to make the process an easy and relaxing experience.

D. Wale

E-marketing communications

The noughties (the term used to describe the years 2000–2009) have seen an explosion of e-marketing spurred by a rapid revolution in the development of communications technology. Globalization has enabled consumers to travel to once inaccessible destinations actually and virtually. Portable technology enables real-time access to travel information and systems globally. The race to get the best online systems to provide product information and convert enquiries to bookings is helping the rapid Internet expansion. Internet provides customers with an online travel supermarket at their fingertips. User-friendly touch screens and portable devices enable ease of navigation to this cyberspace network of sites. Planning a trip is facilitated by online intermediaries, partner web sites, travel blogs and special interest (segmented) social networking sites.

Larger operators are swallowing up smaller specialist companies enabling the volumes of scale to capture niche and mass markets with their portfolio of brands. With lack of differentiation between the main tourism suppliers, customer loyalty has become a high priority, and social networking, blogs and loyalty cards are the vehicles for communicating with, and capturing, special interest groups.

THE WEB-BASED TRAVEL INDUSTRY, BLOGS AND SOCIAL NETWORKING The noughties have seen the growth in the use of the blog in the travel industry. In the consumer behaviour stage of information search, blogs can influence a consumer's choice and subsequent purchase behaviour.

A blog is a web-based diary. One of their original uses was as an online travel diary for travellers across the world. It enabled them to keep regular contact with friends and relatives and meet other travellers through the Internet (socially network). The Internet café facilitated this method of communication, which was cheaper than previous methods such as the telephone and helped to increase usage and popularity.

There are numerous travel web sites both related and unrelated to travel brands. Sites differ in content, but all are funded by revenue from advertising. www.travelbag.co.uk is a virtual travel agency which provides a worldwide tailor-made travel service; its USP is a 'travel expert' feature where advice is available on any travel-related enquiry. www.wikitravel.org aims to provide an up-to-date and reliable worldwide travel guide; content is provided from the public in the same method as Wikipedia (the main brand). Extra navigation includes Wikitravel Extra, which features blogs and forums. Forums are web-based discussions through question and answer. The Wikitravel Extra forum covers discussions on travel destinations all over the world. www.tripadvisor.com and www.TravelBlogs.org provide travel advice and information and forums for exchange of travel hints and tips, including companies not to buy from.

Social networking provides specialist sites for mass communication over a global geographical area. Specialist sites provide opportunities for people from the same market segmentation categories to network. Companies offering specialist products for these target groups can easily market (relatively cheaply) and sell their holiday products, e.g. food tourism, adventure holidays.

Forums and blogs are often accessed via search engines and provide a quick reference guide for a consumer on any product or service. This method of travel information search is popular due to its unbiased nature; however, stealth marketing techniques are

---

used to ambush these forums, whereby actors associated with travel companies and pertaining to be peers attempt to influence purchase behaviour through suggestion.

PORTABLE DEVICES AND WIFI With portable devices such as the iPhone and access to WiFi (it will pick it up automatically as soon as you hit a zone), the planning, organization, booking (through to seat selection) and route planning (door-to-door maps, local and global) can all be performed up to the minute and on the go.

WiFi is provided free of charge in a number of travel destinations either in zones, on monitors set up in areas for customer use, e.g. at airports, or on transport, e.g. free WiFi access on buses in Singapore.

DESIGN AND INTERNET MARKETING The Internet provides a global, fast and relatively inexpensive opportunity to reach a large number of people from a target market. The key to successful web sites is to design what the target market wants, make the navigation easy; many people access web sites through search engines and will not necessarily hit the home page first, so indexing needs to work throughout the site. A navigation bar at the top of each page will facilitate this.

Design rules stay the same as other forms of advertising, avoiding overuse of words and information and detracting from the intended message. Images, fonts, colour schemes and features including multimedia such as podcasts, virtual tours and PDFs all need to attract the target market and comply with branding. Material should always be up to date.

Tourism sites tend to use image maps due to the nature of the product being sold; these can take the form of maps, plans of seating on trains and planes. A successful web site will make sure that clickable areas (hot spots) lead to desired content and not to blind URLs.

In web site design, the company providing the most user-friendly sites, with the fewest technical errors, more facilities (i.e. links to other sites, features), promotions, support and after-care are likely to appeal to consumers preferring to find the convenience of the one-stop-shop approach that the one-site Internet travel supermarket provides. The speed at which the Internet provides information can be its demise for a company not able to keep up with the times. In designing web sites, information or promotional material at the analysis stage, check out competitors, trends and make sure you know what your target market wants and will be able to use. Think about where, when, who, what, why. Building loyal customers is facilitated through loyalty clubs and member login access, which provide companies with registered users who can only access member areas. Sites providing online sales require customers to register and this in turn provides segmentation data. Customers returning to the site to purchase extras, track the progress of their order and check-in online will need to engage with the customer relationship mechanisms that registration creates.

Customer after-sales tends to be a hit and miss on web sites, often requires contact via a different medium, e.g. telephone, and is not immediate as are all other functions within a web site.

Promotional tactics

Figure 7.15 outlines the process of designing and communicating a promotional message.

D. Wale

Communicating a promotional message
1. Determine target market
2. Select communication channels considered best fit (one or more) for target market depending on budget
3. Design a message that will provide the right information to arouse interest and purchase behaviour

AIDA is used as the framework for designing a promotional message:
A: Get attention
I: Hold interest
D: Arouse desire
A: Obtain action

4. Promote features and benefits to target market, e.g. low cost/economy/bargain, safe, faster
5. Consider appropriate format to attract attention: position, colour, copy (words), headline or strapline
6. Message structure: who, what, when, where, why

Fig. 7.15. Communicating a promotional message.

COLOUR IN PROMOTION Colours are used to sell products by appealing to consumers in a variety of ways. Colours may be culturally representative, e.g. colours in a nation's national emblem; colours may represent different meanings to different cultures, e.g. green is seen both as unlucky and, in the ecological green movement, as environment-friendly. Colours often get their connotations from previous uses, e.g. Coca-Cola red was used in an advertising campaign and inherited as the colour of Father Christmas's outfit, which was originally green.

In repositioning its image in order to appeal to a more culturally diverse population, British Airways has changed its traditional red, white and blue national colour choice.

Colours can be matched to demographic categories, e.g. sex and age group. Red and yellow are often used together to appeal to children. Colour can represent a brand, e.g. Cadbury's purple. Behaviourally, colour can affect mood. Red is used to stimulate appetite, yellow to calm and purple to represent luxury.

Colours may be matched to other segmentation categories such as lifestyle. Gay and lesbian travellers have adopted the rainbow flag. The flag acts as a sign and a unifying symbol for this segment. Each colour represents the different values of this community with the colour and order of the stripes varying from flag to flag. The Equality Act (Sexual Orientation) Regulations 2007 has made it illegal for accommodation providers such as hotels to discriminate against gay and lesbian travellers. Travel companies promoting gay and lesbian tourism will use the flag to signal that their product is provided for the user group. To maintain market share, companies seen as gay-friendly prior to this legislation use the rainbow flag to signal that they are part of the target group or particularly welcome this market segment.

POSITION IN PROMOTION Advertising rates for newspapers are set around the projected sales for advertising space. Pricing factors include position of advertisement: readers scan a page from right to left, so an advertisement on the right-hand side of a page will be expected to deliver better returns on investment of advertising spend. Page location, e.g. front page, will affect price and returns as will colour, size and frequency of the placement of the advertisement. All of these factors can be negotiated. Cheap rates will be offered when space has not been sold and so companies willing to gamble on availability may pick up a bargain.

ATMOSPHERICS Atmospherics refers to the term used to describe methods targeted at the senses of customers in order to sell products and services. Techniques include space, smell and materials. In travel superstores, the space by the door as a customer enters is referred to as a decongestion chamber. This space is deliberately empty to allow the customer to adapt to the environment and absorb the stimuli, which have been designed to induce buying behaviour by appealing to the senses of the consumer (selection will match product to target market).

Summary

The chapter has outlined principles, practices and the process of marketing in the context of the travel operations industry. Models and examples have been provided and will facilitate student's application to products and services relating to organizations accessed in their work and related studies.

Acknowledgement

Martina Venus, Starwood Hotels and Resorts.

References

Johnson, G. and Scholes, K. (1999) *Exploring Corporate Strategy*, 5th edn. Prentice-Hall, London.
Kotler, P. and Armstrong, G. (2008) *Principles of Marketing*, 12th edn. Prentice-Hall, London.
Kotler, P., Makens, J.C. and Bowen, J.T. (2006) *Marketing for Hospitality and Tourism*, 4th edn. Prentice-Hall, London.
Levy, S. (2007) *Public Relations and Integrated Communications*. Lotus Press.
Lumsdon, L. (1997) *Tourism Marketing*. International Thomson Business Press, UK.
Middleton, V. (2001) *Marketing in Travel and Tourism*, 3rd edn. Butterworth-Heinemann, Oxford.

D. Wale

8 Financial Awareness for Travel Operations Management

CAROLINE A. WISCOMBE

Objectives of the Chapter

This chapter considers the role of financial affairs within travel organizations. The approach taken ensures step-by-step building of financial awareness and provides an overview of financial issues in the sector. Financial management is often considered as financial reporting and performance measurement but it is much more than this. The chapter therefore divides the debate on finance and financial issues from performance measurement into two sections.

Part A of this chapter, which seeks to improve financial awareness, will:

- explain the role of financial affairs within travel organizations;
- analyse and collate the information and data needed for financial decision making; and
- consider the development of systems to assist the finance function.

Part B of this chapter, which seeks to develop financial performance measurement, will:

- evaluate business performance using recognized analysis techniques.

PART A: DEVELOPING FINANCIAL AWARENESS

Introduction

The introductory chapter to this text defines the travel industry as an amalgam of multinational market leader companies, such as Thomas Cook and TUI AG, national multiples, such as Leger and Midland Counties Cooperative, regional multiples and small independent niche operators. Operating companies may be involved in some or all of the following activities: accommodation services, airlines, attractions, coaches, cruises, ferry companies, taxis and trains. Thus there is a wide scope of organizations; however, they all have one thing in common. They exist in order to make a profit.

Profit is the term used to define the difference between income and all expenditure used to make that income occur. For an airline, this would mean number of ticket sales multiplied by price charged for each ticket (income) less cabin crew wages, airport taxes, head office bills, travel agent commission, aircraft lease, fuel and so on (costs and expenses). Our first introduction to an accounts 'equation' or calculation therefore is:

Income − (Cost + Expenditure) = Profit

Profit is used by organizations to grow and develop by investing in new plant, machinery, products and buying new companies or is used to pay dividends to shareholders who have invested in the organization. The balance of how to use profit is a tricky one and takes time to assess according to the strategic direction of the company. For large companies with many shareholders, the chief executive may have to defend those decisions at shareholders' meetings. Walt Disney Corporation's theme parks and resorts have to make incredibly difficult investment decisions. A new theme park can cost in the region of US$2.2 billion. They have to weigh up this investment against the costs of new cruise ships, which can cost in the region of US$800 million each. Disney's total investment in their growth strategy in the cruise market stands at about US$1.6 billion and needs to sign contracts for the ships up to 4 years in advance of delivery. Finance managers will help to assess those decisions using a number of techniques, but when making recommendations have also to assess against non-financial parameters, such as sustainability or impacts. For small independent organizations the decision process is just as difficult as the costs associated with investment are so high; a new black cab for instance costs around £28,000. The payments on such investment may affect personal income levels of the self-employed driver who currently earns around £23,000 after expenses. A taxi operation is not cheap to run and the taxi owner has to be sure that business will thrive before making the investment.

Consumer protection is paramount. In the late 1970s and early 1980s when air travel first began to develop as the industry it is today, there were number of high-profile cases that saw travellers stranded in foreign countries through the demise of their tour operator. Before granting Air Travel Organizers Licences, the Civil Aviation Authority (CAA) demands financial evidence of a solid base for business development, substantiated by appropriate investment.

To ensure companies make profit is not easy. Financial management helps large and small organizations keep on track, by the use of budgets and forecasting. This allows control of their decision making, thus ensuring profitability. Financial planning helps considerably when serious issues affect the travel industry; 9/11, severe acute respiratory syndrome (SARS), the tsunami in Asia and the outbreak of foot-and-mouth disease in the UK are all serious non-forecasted disasters which affected the travel sector. Businesses with sound financial management techniques were able to quickly implement strategies to offset the effects of these disasters by understanding their business costs, reducing these where possible and finding ways to help find marketing strategies to increase the much reduced sales. (This type of planning is discussed further in Chapter 6, this volume.) At the beginning of 2008 a worldwide fuel shortage drove up oil prices which impacted on travel costs. Different companies used differing financial management tools to help offset this cost.

CASE STUDY: THE CRUISE INDUSTRY – STRATEGIES TO OFFSET THE RISING COST OF FUEL

The cruise industry has restructured its pricing strategy to promote lower prices, and as a result has reduced commission payable to travel agents. Non-commissionable fares are added to the advertised ticket price and might include fees for port services such as shore power or piloting. Cruise lines are free to raise and lower them to reflect their costs. The fuel surcharge, however, while used by airlines for some time as an add-on fee, had not been seen in cruise ship charges. Carnival Corporation

Continued

began a trend among cruise line operators by imposing fuel surcharges upon passengers to cover rising fuel prices. In November 2007 Carnival added a fuel charge of US$5 per person per day. This was followed by Oceania Cruises announcing a levy of US$7 per day through to April 2009 and Silver Sea Cruises, who operate in the luxury category, charging US$10 per day. By July 2008, Fred Olsen Cruises had announced five rises in 8 months and while some companies had capped charges to a maximum per person, or limited fees to the first and second passengers in a state room only, most were charging customers who had already paid their cruise fare in full. As a result, for an average consumer on a 7-night cruise the add-on fees increased 22% from US$159 to US$194 per person.

(Sources: various)

Financial accounting will ensure the recording of financial data. The quantitative nature of the approach means that objectives can be set which are 'measurable' and thus the reporting of activity against the objectives becomes crucial; however, 'finance' and 'financial management' is much larger than just measurement of performance. Travel organizations are dependent on their finance divisions to help provide appropriate solutions to particular problems and to help develop strategic planning. Thus financial affairs contribute to planning, improvement, monitoring, control and evaluation of organizational development. They are not just the 'yardstick' by which the organization may be judged.

Accountants and Accounting Systems

An account is an explanation or a report of certain actions or events. In the travel sector accounts are given of the performance of a company for external and internal audiences in a number of ways. The account is supported by a number of systems. Depending on the size and scope of the organizations activities, the reports will contain a greater or lesser amount of detail, and be written with their audience in mind. Many of the accounting techniques that are used today were developed in the 19th century; however, these have developed over the intervening 100 years in order that accountants can provide the service that their clients need to plan, monitor and control their businesses.

Financial management: Financial management has grown rapidly in the last half century. Financial managers have a boardroom responsibility to contribute to the strategic direction of the company. This may mean setting clear SMART financial targets in order to safeguard assets, promoting standards that will enable capital finance to be obtained for strategic development or investigating alternative solutions for company growth. While they rely on financial data to underpin strategic planning, there is also a reliance on non-financial and more qualitative data. Thus if Walt Disney Corporation were to consider the building of a new theme park in say, South Africa, Russia or Dubai, financial managers would need to weigh up not just the financial costs but wider economic considerations such as organizations and markets, economic and environmental impacts, funding mechanisms, competitor activity, world economic situations and trends, as well as other capital investment plans. Decisions made by financial managers have legal implications. The training and qualification of financial managers should reflect this level of responsibility as consequences can be serious.

Financial accounting: Financial accounting classifies and records monetary transactions of an organization according to a set of principles, the Generally Accepted Accounting Principles (GAAP), and legal requirements and presents these using profit and loss accounts, balance sheets and cash flow statements. Financial reporting communicates this information to the external stakeholders in an appropriate format. External stakeholders are illustrated in Fig. 8.1.

In limited companies this may be in the form of the Annual Reports and Accounts where additional information is supplied providing both some quantitative and qualitative analysis of the data. In recent years, annual reporting has included the wider trends affecting the business including such aspects as corporate social responsibility, ethical trading, carbon footprint and other environmental analysis as the investor increasingly seeks assurances for company actions and expenditure.

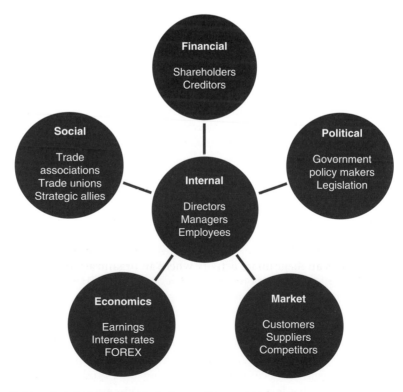

Fig. 8.1. External stakeholders in travel operations companies.

Management accounting: Management accounting was developed post Industrial Revolution when the importance of costs and stock valuation to businesses' worth was understood. Early forms of this branch of accounting were termed cost or cost accounting. Operations Managers use management accounting to help monitor cost data and information for managerial decision making and to ensure that stakeholders receive value from the organization. Management accounting has been developed for a largely internal audience.

Bookkeeping: Underpinning all financial records is bookkeeping. Originally a sub-branch of financial accounting, it can now be seen as a foundation stone upon which the discipline of accounting is built. It is a 'mechanical task', supported by the use of computer technology. It records the collection of financial data in 'books of accounts'. Bookkeepers traditionally followed the practice of 'double entry' bookkeeping, which records credits and debits in separate pages of ledgers. Bookkeepers also record the results of stocktaking activity. This may be accomplished by internal or external stock-takers depending on the industry sector. In restaurants and bars, it is common to use external stocktaking services to provide a check on the activity of management or employees. At the end of a period the ledger accounts and the stock results compile to form the 'trial balance' for an organization. Computerized systems follow the same principles but the layman no longer needs to spend long periods calculating the columns of figures that make up the ledger pages. Nevertheless, salutary lessons have been learned about the importance of keying in the correct data with the right code, in order to be as specific as possible when contributing to the financial records.

Auditing: Large limited liability (Ltd) companies are required by law to have their books audited. External auditors are appointed by the shareholders and ensure that the accountants of the organization have provided a 'true and fair' view of the business activities. Trained accountants will sample a selection of the activities of the organization in order to test the merits of the reports. While independent of the business, they occupy a difficult area as they are employed by the shareholders and can be dismissed. The directors can influence this decision. Sometimes the auditors can become too involved and this is where cases of fraud can go undetected. Some organizations, particularly in the not-for-profit sector, employ internal auditors to check the accounts process. They report to the management on routine tasks and in addition may look at the whole planning and control process ensuring 'value for money'.

Specialist services (SS): Other branches of accounting deal with specific accounting services such as taxation, bankruptcy or liquidity. Companies that make a profit have to pay the government taxes on that profit. It is perfectly legitimate to employ accountants who can seek as much reduction in that tax as possible. This is termed 'tax avoidance'. 'Tax evasion' is an illegitimate activity where an organization or individual does not declare all its income thus trying to avoid paying taxes. Bankruptcy is a formal legal procedure where an individual's financial situation is so serious that they need some legal protection against those to whom they owe money, their creditors. Where a company gets into trouble financially, the first step that would be taken is the appointment of an 'administrator'. They will assess the company and freeze creditors' rights while trying to save the business. If this cannot be achieved the company may have to go into 'liquidation' and its affairs have to be arranged to go out of business in an orderly fashion. Loan creditors to such companies may appoint a 'receiver' who acts to obtain the property on which the loans were secured and either secure an income from the property or try to sell it to raise some funds to repay the loans.

Those who operate the financial accounting and reporting systems internally and externally to organizations are termed 'accountants'. They operate in the 'accounting profession' where each branch informs the decision making and development of the other aspects, illustrated in Fig. 8.2. In the UK anyone can set themselves up in business as an accountant; however, they would be restricted as to the type of work that they could do. Thus they could act as an accountant for a sole trader or partnership but could not audit large limited company accounts. In the UK those accountants who do study and pass recognized awards term themselves 'qualified accountants', which allows them to join one of the six major accountancy bodies. All hold Royal Charter status but only those belonging to the Institute of Chartered Accountants in England and Wales (ICAEW), the Institute of Chartered Accountants in Ireland (ICAI) and the Institute of Chartered Accountants in Scotland (ICAS) are referred to as 'chartered accountants'. This terminology shows that the training had to be undertaken in a practising office where accounting services are given direct to the public, rather than in industry or in central or local government. Some accountants qualify in a practising office before entering commerce or industry in order to gain this additional status.

Those not training in practising offices can become members of the Association of Chartered Certified Accountants (ACCA) who may obtain their training in the office but include experiences from elsewhere. Members of the Chartered Institute of

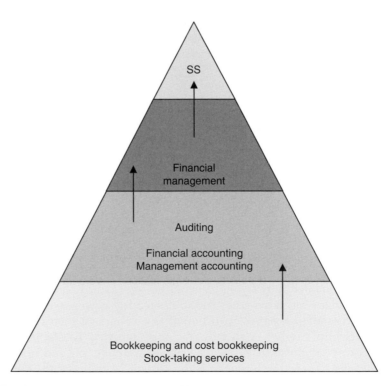

Fig. 8.2. The hierarchy and information trail in accountancy.

C.A. Wiscombe

Management Accountants (CIMA) usually train and work in industry and Chartered Institute of Public Finance and Accountancy (CIPFA) members train and work in central or local government.

Supporting the preparation of accounting information on behalf of chartered accountants is a group of technicians. Through the taking of a series of less technically demanding but practical qualifications they can gain membership to the Association of Accounting Technicians (AAT). However, these are not the only types of accountant that could be involved in the preparation of your companies financial records; there are a number of smaller, though no less important, accountancy associations and services but these have not yet achieved the status of membership of one of the six major bodies. Such accountants may belong to The Association of Authorized Public Accountants or the Institute of Company Accountants.

Organizational Structure

Before we move into discussing financial management and accountancy in any detail, it is imperative that we first consider the size and scope of the organizations within the travel industry. We have already commented in the introduction to the section about the profit-making nature of the organizations and that many are huge multi-national corporations while others are small owner-/operator-run. Each of these differences means that travel operators will work for organizations with very different financial and management accounting systems.

There are a number of different categories we can use to try to build a picture of organizational structures in the travel industry. Size and scope do not fully explain the industries structure but companies can all be classified into profit-making and non-profit-making organizations, illustrated in Table 8.1. For both categories financial management is important, but this can be for very different reasons.

Private sector of the economy

The private sector business aims are to make profits for the owners. To start up a business an investment is needed. This investment is termed 'capital'. The capital purchases all the things the business needs to operate and hopefully leave some cash in a dedicated bank account to help the organization run on a day-to-day basis. This cash is termed 'working capital'. For a restaurant business the capital invested might

Table 8.1. Public and private sector companies in the travel industry.

Private sector organizations	Public sector organizations	Voluntary organizations
Funded by private investment, organizations vary in structure they include: • sole trader • partnerships • limited companies • public limited companies	Largely funded by national or local government	Largely funded by voluntary subscription or donations

purchase the cooking equipment, tables and chairs, plates and cutlery, the lease or a freehold premises in which to operate, food to turn into meals and drink 'stock' to accompany the meals. These we term the assets of the business.

In business terms, the capital invested becomes the worth of the business. The business is made of all the tangible assets that the capital bought plus our 'cash left in the bank'. This is the same for large companies with multiple shareholders, as for sole traders or partnerships. Our second introduction to accounts 'equations' then looks like this:

Capital = Assets

Sole trader: One person owns the business although this does not preclude two people trading as a sole trader (married couples often trade in this way rather than forming a partnership agreement). Sole traders invest capital in to the start-up costs of the business. They may also take out long-term loans from banks and financial institutions. Any profits after the long-term interest has been paid can be used for the growth of the business, or withdrawn from the business and repaid to the owner. Money withdrawn from the business by the sole trader is termed 'drawings' rather than wages or salaries and reduces the capital that the business owes the owner. Recent research has shown that some sole traders operate on a 'lifestyle' rather than a 'profit' basis. This means that some expected financial objectives, such as maximizing sales revenue or investment for business growth, may not be considered vital by the operator. While the sole trader may be content to operate on this basis, they put themselves at greater risk of insolvency as external factors or rising costs affect their operation. **Risks:** There is no distinction between the business assets and private assets of the sole trader. If the business collapses the sole trader may have to sell part of his/her private assets so that the debt of the business can be paid.

Partnership: Two people, or more, working together and jointly raising capital to start up in business and to continue trading. Usually the partners will jointly manage the business and share the financial risks. Occasionally groups of partners will invest in a project with one taking a non-management role. This agreement may be formed in order that they invest capital and yet have no experience to offer but they see the business as being able to provide income. They are termed 'silent partners'. Partners draw down the profits from the business by agreement. There may be different agreements over the sharing of that profit according to workload or risk factor. Legal agreements are drawn up to agree partnership terms. **Risks:** As with sole traders there is no distinction between the partners' business assets and other private possessions. Collapse of the business may mean selling private assets; therefore, if one partner invests more capital than another, they may agree a higher share of any profit so that they are repaid for the additional risk they have taken.

Limited Companies (Ltd): Limited companies allow large groups of people to combine resources to form and invest in organizations. The 'share' of the company can be termed 'ordinary' or 'preference' and each gives different benefits to the investor. Operational control will be given to a board of elected directors who report performance at an annual general meeting (AGM). They are employed to provide 'stewardship' or management of the company and its funds invested in the interests of ordinary shareholders. At the AGM shareholders may be asked to vote on constitutional or strategic change. **Risks:** The ownership has a different legal identity from the owners, who will not be asked to pay business debts from their private wealth. If

C.A. Wiscombe

the business was to collapse the shareholders will be 'limited' in their liability, often to as little as a nominal £1; however, they may also lose their original capital investment, the share value and receive no return on assets.

Public Limited Companies (plc): In the UK a company with limited liability that has over £50,000 of share capital and a wide spread of shareholders can apply for those shares to be traded on the stock exchange. Although boards of directors run public companies, shareholders own them. However, this can lead to a conflict of loyalties as managers pursue objectives that help their own careers. This has led economists to talk about a 'divorce of ownership and control' within plc. **Risks:** A loss of control and the share price fluctuations which accompany quotations on the stock exchange. Both Richard Branson of Virgin and Alan Sugar of Amstrad decided that, having become plc, they wished to revert to private limited company status.

Each of these types of ownership will bring a range of challenges to the financial management of the business. Limited companies accounts have to be submitted to auditing by Companies House on an annual basis. The Companies Acts of 1948, 1967, 1985 and 2006 cover the basics of these requirements. The latest updates can be found on Companies House web site at www.companieshouse.gov.uk. A company secretary who can follow and ensure compliance with the requirements of legislation is usually employed. Company accounts will be distilled from the detailed lines of sales, income, costs and expenses that have been collected by the bookkeeping system of the organization into very broad categories such as 'administration' or 'employee costs'. The fact that 'administration' may include printing, stationery, computer expenses and so on does not concern Companies House but it does concern the management of the organization.

At sole trader and partnership levels, annual accounts must be submitted to HM Revenue and Customs on demand. These submissions support the declaration of tax earnings of the trader or partners. It is usual for all but the smallest sole trader to employ an accountant to make these tax returns so that, first, they ensure that they are complying with the law but also that they are reclaiming as much as possible against their tax liability. No one wants to pay more tax than they have to! Again the detail of the accounts produced for the tax office will reduce the lines of accounts into broad headings and the detail needed to operate the business may be lost.

Not-for-profit sector of the economy

The 'not-for-profit' sector of the economy includes public sector organizations and charitable or voluntary groups. Travel operations no longer have a large presence in the UK 'not-for-profit' sector since most travel organizations were denationalized in the early 1980s. However, other countries' travel operations are still part of government-developed services.

Not-for-profit sector organizations require different detail levels of both management and financial accounting according to their aims (see Table 8.2). Public sector organizations have often been termed bureaucratic in their approach to maintaining financial records. In order to purchase a box of paper clips, three forms may be needed to audit the chain of command that approved permission for the expenditure. It is difficult sometimes to accept these issues, but when dealing with public money the accounts must show that the purchase, no matter how small, is legitimately made. Voluntary organizations

Table 8.2. Non-profit-making organizations in the travel industry.

Non-profit-making economic sectors	Aims	Typical ownerships
Public sector organizations	Provide leisure and tourism facilities and travel infrastructure on a non-profit-making basis. Not for profit, they produce other non-financial benefits for the community. Thus, a leisure centre that is part of the tourist attraction of an area is supported for the health of the local community and may support the multiplier effect from travel businesses	Often owned by local authority or by a semi-independent organization set up by central government. Until the late 1980s the travel companies such as buses and trains were all operated by the government in what were termed 'nationalized industries'. The train service was instrumental in helping tourist resorts develop. Torquay in South Devon and Blackpool in the North West were both seaside resorts that greatly benefited from strategic decision making to take public-funded transport to the area
Charitable or voluntary organizations	A service provided by a voluntary group where they may manage a facility or facilities. Not for profit, they may also be given grants by public sector organizations so that they can break even	Based on a 'community' sharing overall management and control of finances and operational activity on a not-for-profit basis; examples include The National Trust, The Settle & Carlisle Railway Trust and Alnwick Tourism Association

may have different accounting needs according to size. Where organizations are part of a charity, however, accounting becomes very specialized. In requesting charitable status organizations have to undergo a rigorous applications process. They will need to satisfy the Charities Commission that they are bona fide and that all funds raised go to the charity they are supporting. Financial reporting of these activities is a specialist function and organizations will employ specialist auditors to monitor activity.

The structure and organization of the business will dictate the complexity of the financial information needed to manage it both for external stakeholders (financial accounting) and for internal audiences (management accounting). Financial accounts drive forward the measurement of company performance and their analysis provides finance managers with key performance measures in order to plan, improve, control and monitor business strategies.

Questions

Using the Companies House web site, investigate the steps a business would have to take to ensure compliance with the rules of limited companies.
1. Evaluate the differences between that and being a sole trader or partnership. If you were setting up a business as a self-catering apartment operator with a like-minded friend, buying a small complex with around five or six apartments, which structure would suit the project best?
2. How might your decision change in 5 or 6 years' time?

C.A. Wiscombe

Financial Management

Financial management is a decision-making process which draws, as a main but not a sole source, on accounting information to provide strategic financial direction. Financial managers have a number of responsibilities. At a more complex level in travel operations, financial managers will develop the business by controlling investment, developing growth strategies, sourcing income, ensuring profit on foreign exchange movements, considering foreign exchange hedging and reducing loan interest while ensuring systems and accounting support the organization. At a simple level, they must set targets, maintain cash flow, ensure solvency, monitor external factors that may affect performance and ensure internal factors are understood and monitored. Some financial managers will be responsible for setting prices and fixing any rates of discount. In some organizations this less strategic level of work is undertaken by the role of management accounting. The way financial managers undertake their responsibilities may make, or break, the company for whom they work.

CASE STUDY: A COMPARISON OF THE FINANCIAL MANAGEMENT OF FRONTIER AIRLINES AND ARRIVA

If travel operations companies do not employ sound financial management techniques they will encounter some branches of accountancy that they may have hoped to avoid. Frontier Airlines is one of the four US carriers to seek bankruptcy protection during April 2008. However, at first glance it is not the external factor, that of increased fuel costs, that has been to blame. Had the rise in global fuel prices been the legitimate factor, shareholders might take comfort that the business was well managed and blame world recession. The company, however, declared the reason for their difficulty was that the principal credit-card processor would be withholding a greater share of proceeds from ticket sales. The competitive nature of the industry means that this increase in direct costs adversely affects the ability of the company to remain in business. Better financial management should have provided some alternative strategies in advance of this crucial situation. This example of poor financial management is even more exemplified when comparing it to Arriva, bus and train operator. Arriva has ensured it is protected from the rising fuel prices experienced in the UK during 2008. By June 2008 it had fixed all its fuel requirements for 2008 at £0.28/l and has already fixed 75% of that needed in 2009 at £0.39/l. In an industry where fuel is vital, this procurement of such a resource at such good prices provides sound financial management. It is not the only strategy to be working well, however: revenues are up by more than 50% in the first half of 2008. This puts Arriva in a good situation to address the continuing rise in costs to the business and allow time to plan for the further expected rises in fuel prices.

(Sources: various)

Controlling investment: Companies need to invest in new plant, machinery and products and in buying other businesses. These investments need to be controlled. The investment of US$1.6 billion into a growth strategy for the cruise industry which Disney Corporation is making must be part of a well-developed plan of action and will have rested on answering a series of very detailed questions that include how much net profit the investment will make over its lifetime, whether the rate of return be acceptable to shareholders, how quickly the investment would pay for itself, whether the marketplace is sustainable, whether the investment will provide a cash surplus within its lifetime and whether other projects would provide a better rate of return. The evaluation of alternative ways of achieving the long-term aims of the business may result in larger scale of operations that will add to the cost of the project outside the initial decisions to develop particular markets. Thus the doubling of capacity of Disney Cruise ships entails additional investment in land-side terminals for the berthing of the ships and construction of a new parking garage, adding US$22 million in capital investment to the US$1.6 million for the ships themselves. The process of allocation of funds into a long-term project is often termed 'capital budgeting' where capital is part of long-term funds. Payback on the investment is a major part of the budgeting process and there are a number of ways of ensuring an appropriate rate of return. These are termed 'accounting rate of return', 'payback', 'net present value' and 'internal rate of return'.

$$\text{Accounting Rate of Return (ARR)} = \frac{\text{Average annual profit generated by investment}}{\text{Average investment}}$$

Payback = the time taken to recoup the cash invested in the asset

Net Present Value (NPV) = finding today's value of future cash flows associated with an investment proposal by multiplying the future cash flow by the appropriate factor. A project's NPV is calculated by deducting the initial investment from the present value of the cash inflows that the project will generate.

Internal Rate of Return = the discount rate that causes the present value of the project's inflows to equal the present value of the project's outflows, i.e. the discount rate that causes the project's NPV to equal zero.

Most large companies use more than one technique and will ensure that the concept of 'time value of money' which is used in the NPV is considered. This concept realizes that money today is not worth the same as it is in a year's time. The concept uses discounting tables to assess the likely worth of currency in future time periods. The development of the project will be analysed and reported on by the financial controller and budgets will undoubtedly change through the period of development.

Developing growth strategies: This will be part of the remit of financial managers within the board of directors. Often the financial managers will take away ideas from other directors and develop realistic implications of undertaking these and alternative strategies for delivering the same outcome. In April 2008 Star Cruises sold two of their ships to Louis plc for a total amount of US$380 million while retaining the option of chartering them back until November 2008 and December 2009, respectively. This is a strategic growth strategy for Louis plc, which, unlike Disney Corporation, wants to increase its growth in the Mediterranean quickly and not wait for ships to be built. For Star Cruises it gives the opportunity to raise capital to invest in other areas of their business. Developing growth strategies depends on many aspects of the internal and external environments of the organization and is discussed further in Chapter 6 (this volume).

Sourcing of income: The quantity, type and cost of finance invested in businesses is essential knowledge to assess where new avenues of funding can be raised. How much of the business is supported by borrowed money and at what rate of return can make a huge difference to the profitability of the business. Whether financial markets are stable or volatile, the financial manager will ensure that the costs associated with borrowing are the best that can be obtained and that they are providing a rate of return to shareholders that they will accept. To invest in capital projects funding may need to be sought from banks or, in the case of large organizations, from investment houses.

FOREX: Foreign Exchange (FOREX) is a fundamental part of the travel sector. Many businesses will offer services to exchange cash into different currencies and suppliers of currency make a profit by buying or selling currency at below or above a central rate at which they can change currency themselves. Often the transaction also draws a commission-based fee. However, in the travel operations sector FOREX becomes a major profit (or possible loss) centre as, for companies like TUI Travel, they are paid for holidays in US dollars, German euros and UK sterling according to where their offices are located. They create cash flow within the countries they operate in, for instance travel representatives selling trips on the river in Goa, India, will be paid in rupees. The currency exchange, particularly in volatile markets, can cause big differences in the exchange rates between currencies. The FOREX market is worth US$2.4 trillion globally per day and in London, where the main centre for trading occurs, US$75.3 billion. Working in these markets, financial managers for travel companies must learn to buy and sell foreign exchange at appropriate times as differences could be very expensive.

Activity

In August 2004, £1 could buy AUS$2.56, US$1.82 or €1.49, whereas in June 2008, £1 bought AUS$2.05 US$1.988 or €1.25.
1. Work out the difference in purchasing power for £1000 in August 2004 and June 2008.
2. Which currency has performed better/worse in the 4-year period?

Hedging: This is defined as the process of undertaking a transaction to reduce or eliminate risk and financial managers of large corporations will ensure that they take best advantage. Hedging depends on trying to 'best guess' the marketplace in a number of areas that can include short-term interest rates, share prices, government bonds, currency or foreign exchange rates. The idea is that the financial manager looks to 'futures' performance of share price or foreign exchange rates and enters into a transaction to try to offset a potential decline by making profit out of a different transaction. For example, a company holding £1 million in cash would want to get the best interest rate possible. Currently that interest rate might be 4%. The financial manager could commit to an 'interest rate future' by lending that money at a predetermined rate of interest, say 5.15%, for 3 months. This is called a 'futures contract'. The risk is that the interest rate might have risen from 4% to 6% and thus the financial manager would lose (6% − 5.15%) interest. Alternatively, the rate could have fallen and the hedging capacity grown. Calculating the earnings from such a futures deal depends on the rise in the 'futures market' and is calculated in 'ticks', each tick being worth 0.01%. This may not seem a lot, but £1 million over 3 months could earn £12,800 if the difference in interest rates is 1.15%.

Loan interest: This can rise and fall. The differences in loan interest payments can be substantial and the financial manager's acumen in ensuring the best rates of interest are paid

---

on any loan is imperative to success. Often long-term loans can be negotiated on 'fixed-rate' terms. The financial manager must calculate if the financial markets are expected to rise or fall to ensure that a fixed-term rate is the most viable. Interest rates, whether short or long term, are linked to macro economic policy and, as the global economy has grown, so too has the impact of world phenomena. This has meant that where economies, such as the USA, undergo difficulties and see rises in interest rates, equivalent market forces impact on the EU. Most travel organizations operate in an 'open market economy' and policy announcements on short-term interest rate rises will be significantly impacted by governments. However, the overall determination of interest rate rise and fall is extremely complicated, with factors including availability of funds, the rate of economic growth, inflationary expectations and the risk associated with the borrower all having an impact.

Target setting: While organizations will always set implicit targets, they are usually ensconced in a vision and mission (see Chapter 6, this volume). They follow a series of SMART (specific, measurable, achievable, realistic and time-bound) objectives. Carefully thought out targets will ensure that planning objectives can be met. Tools to assist the attainment of targets are set in budget and forecasting statements.

Budgets will drive down into an organization and affect managers, supervisors and employees. They will be based on sales targets (e.g. number of holidays to be sold or number of fares attained), price achieved for those sales (maximizing the sales opportunity and getting the best price possible for the sale), cost control (keeping costs and expenditure to a minimum, ensuring maximum efficiency from the resources used including assets, materials and labour) and fixed asset maximization, thus achieving strategic and operational plans. If budgets are going to be a useful financial tool, then they must be rigorously designed. The essence of the budget is a forecasting tool that allows the financial performance of the organization to be monitored and controlled. It will identify how much money a cost centre should spend within a stated period of time.

A cost centre is any part of an organization to which specific costs are allocated. There may be a large number of budgets within one large organization and they need to be coordinated and combined into one overall budget. Managers and other employees will have considerable control over expenditure so long as they remain within the budget limits.

Keeping within the budget is an important target. Budget structures form the basis of management accounting and will be monitored on a regular basis, usually monthly. They will be amended on a regular basis in line with a range of internal and external factors. In particularly difficult trading periods where sales may not have reached capacity it is not unusual to find changes to planned capital expenditure to ensure budget targets and expenditure are controlled. It is also not unusual for travel organizations to change their pricing structure to encourage the sale of their holidays when demand falls.

Cash flow: Financial managers must monitor the flows of money that result from the financial activities of the organization. This will ultimately result in accounts that show the profit, or loss, engendered by those activities. In the meantime, however, monies will flow in and out of the business at different rates. In the short term, income can be less than expenditure, despite the company being in overall profit (see Table 8.3). Financial managers will monitor the 'cash flow' of the business and take steps to ensure that expenditure can be paid for. They will arrange short-term loans or 'credit', such as an overdraft.

If a serious cash flow problem exists for a period of time then the company could become 'insolvent' and unable to meet the demands of its creditors. It is therefore the responsibility of the financial manager to prepare and monitor cash flow forecasts.

C.A. Wiscombe

Table 8.3. A simple cash flow forecast.

		January	February	March	April	Etc.
		£	£	£	£	£
Receipts						
Sales						
Loans						
Total receipts						
Less payments						
Cash purchases						
Business rates						
Wages/national insurance						
Electricity						
Gas						
Telephone						
Water rates						
Loan repayments						
Bank charges						
Professional fees						
Insurance						
VAT						
Drawings						
Total payments						
Net cash flow	Receipts – payments					
Opening balance	From December closing balance					
Closing balance	Opening balance + net cash flow					

A cash flow balance, either positive or negative, does *not* indicate whether the company is making a profit or loss.

Solvency: The most basic reason why any organization monitors financial performance is to ensure that it remains solvent, i.e. has the ability to pay its creditors. If a company cannot meet the demands of its creditors then it would be wound up and the assets sold in the hope of meeting, at least partially, the demands. Sometimes creditors will take the assets themselves as part payment for the debt.

CASE STUDY: LIQUIDATING ASSETS

In 2002, a subsidiary company of American Classic Voyages, who had been loaned capital from The Maritime Association, filed for bankruptcy. In order to get some of its capital back the association took possession of two cruise ships, which they subsequently sold for US$9 million each.

(Sources: various)

A sole trader could be declared bankrupt if the liabilities of the business exceed the assets so that all outstanding debts cannot be paid.

External factors: Travel organizations will flourish when the rate of the growth of the economy allows people to have money to spend on non-essential items, 'discretionary expenditure' or 'the leisure pound'. The growth of the economy is measured using a number of methods but is basically the total of all incomes received in the country. Rapid expansion, such as seen in China and India in the first part of the 21st century, can indicate a new market or opportunity for travel organizations to expand. The economy will not always expand at a steady rate and during a serious recession the total wealth will 'contract' and economies in leisure spending can occur. Local economies can have a serious impact on some travel organizations; coach and taxi companies operating in regional locations would be in danger when large factories operating locally close down. If local economies are attracting new businesses then there may be considerable competition for labour, which results in higher wages. While this may create more demand for travel organizations, it can also increase the operational costs of the business. Seasonal demands for different types of travel organization can also affect the operational activity within companies. In the UK, more people take holidays in the summer than the winter; those operating businesses dependent on this type of travel must make all their income in a relatively short season. Operators will use a number of strategies to counteract the seasonal problem from offering cheap weekend break holidays to summer season resorts during the winter months or coach operators may work as 'school buses' during term time. The impacts of external factors will affect the number of customers and how much they spend. The financial manager will monitor and act on this information.

Internal factors: The internal factors that financial managers need to exercise control over are limitless. While fixed costs cannot usually be altered, variable and semi-variable costs including stocks need not only monitoring but also active reduction. Within the remit of financial control are aspects of purchasing and personnel, which in large organizations become target-driven units within, or external to, the finance function. Other internal factors that occupy the financial manager's attention will be the level of credit and, debit the organization has. Most goods are bought on credit from suppliers and, while convenient, could also cost money in interest payments. Credit is also offered to many consumers, but there is a serious risk of delay if payment is not made. Travel organizations such as holiday companies insist on payment in advance in order to alleviate this problem. Flexible labour contracts are often used for travel organizations; a coach tour guide, for instance, will work what may feel like 24/7 while the tour is on the road but will then get time off when back at base. Where companies can they will try to employ part-time or temporary employees who can be called in on demand in order to keep payroll costs to a minimum. The strategies around labour costs have begun to be challenged within the corporate social responsibility (CSR) agenda; this has cause to affect how companies have traditionally operated their employee policies. Internal factors affect 'cost control', which, if it rises, affects profit.

Pricing structures and discounts: Revenue generation is as important as cost control in determining profit and is a direct function of price multiplied by quantity sold. There are a number of pricing policies that can be adopted that include pricing based on cost data (sometimes called cost plus pricing), if indeed it is possible to determine the full cost of the product. Others include pricing based on market conditions, pricing to optimize profit based on cost and market information, pricing in special situations and finally pricing based on contribution. Usually the strategy of the business will begin with determining the full cost of the product and seeking to see if the cost structure will support a price that the customer is willing to pay. This works by absorbing all the costs and adding on an acceptable profit margin. However, a business with little or no competition, a 'price maker', could charge much more for the product or service than one operating in a crowded market, a 'price taker'. The demand for a product, say overseas travel during school holidays, sees a higher price being charged than during 'off season' but there will be a limit to what people may pay. This is called the 'price elasticity of demand'. The financial manager would work alongside marketing to ensure that the price charged was the optimum that the market would stand. Pricing based on contribution is a strategy that understands the costs of the business but also the concept that some sale is better than no sale. For instance, if an aircraft is to fly with three empty seats the operator may say, at the last minute, that the fare could be reduced in price in order to get something rather than nothing for the seat. In hotels the reception team may have been given a 'walk-in rate' that operates after 6.30 pm when no more full-paying guests are likely to check in. Consumers could take the risk and wait until then to try to get a reduced room *but* they would also risk not being able to be accommodated at all. Given adequate cost and revenue information, a sales price and quantity can be deduced that would ultimately maximize profits. This is the financial manager's goal. Very occasionally they may sell at below cost in order to take advantage of a business opportunity or to meet short-term competitive threats, thus no single strategy on pricing can be used all the time.

Summary

While financial managers draw on a wide range of information to inform their decision the financial accounts provide the main source of data. Understanding financial accounts, though, is not just the role of the financial manager. It is imperative that all stakeholders fully understand their message.

Financial Accounting

All organizations are 'accountable' to their investors, to the taxing authorities and, in the case of public or voluntary organizations, to the public. The branch of accounting that accommodates the 'accountability' of organizations is 'financial accounting'. In the case of limited companies and public limited companies, the financial documents produced will be published and are able to be reviewed by a wide number of stakeholders. Each stakeholder in the business, the owners or investors, long-term financiers (the banks), the employees, the suppliers and the government, will have their own agenda and read into the accounts the story that they feel should be told. However, in order to make financial accounting as transparent as possible the documents produced, the 'trading account', 'profit and loss account' and 'balance sheet', will be written using GAAP. GAAP are accepted in today's global marketplace and enable consistency in the reading of accounts across nations and nationalities.

Trading, profit and loss accounts

Trading, profit and loss accounts are written for a 'period of time'. They measure the profits of the company within that period, which is usually annually but could be prepared more often if required. Therefore, the financial document will be prepared and clearly labelled 'for the year ending'.

The trading account is used to measure 'gross profit'. Gross profit is the difference between the cost of goods sold and the income from the sale of those goods. The costs of goods are those which are incurred only when making that one sale; for a restaurant that will include the ingredients of the food and the beverages consumed, but not the wages of staff as the staff would be there whether the customer came into the restaurant or not. See Table 8.4 for an example of a trading account layout.

The separation of costs is not easy. In some businesses such as airlines the costs would include the direct staffing of the aircraft, the fuel to run the aircraft and the airport fees incurred by each flight, on the premise that if the flight did not take off those costs would not be incurred. However, for many operations managers, this analysis of gross profit is too simplistic. Some companies therefore change the trading account to measure operational profit. Walt Disney Corporation reports on the operational performance of each segment of their business. Thus, the annual accounts look at the operating profit of Media Networks, Theme Parks and Resorts (subdivided into domestic and international results), Studio Entertainment, Consumer Products and Corporate (Walt Disney Corporation, 2007). See Table 8.5 for an example of an operating account layout.

The figure of 'gross profit' or 'operating profit' only tells part of the expense of providing a product for consumers. Other costs and expenses will result from the need to lease or buy premises, consume energy, employ staff and, in the case of large companies, pay head office overheads. Once all expenses of the organization have been met, what is left is 'net profit'. This amount will form the basis on which a sole trader or partnership will pay income tax, and on which a company will pay corporation tax. It is usual in sole trader or partnership accounts for all expenses to be listed, which can be very detailed. See Table 8.6 for an example of a full trading profit and loss account.

Sole traders or partnerships will not usually wait until they know the final net profit before 'drawing' some money from the business in order to pay their own personal bills. This money is not part of the profit and loss account of the business but is accounted for in the balance sheet. In effect, the sole trader or partner is 'borrowing'

Table 8.4. Trading account.

	£	£	(Previous year) £
Sales			
Cost of sales			
Gross profit			

Table 8.5. Operating profit account.

	£	£	(Previous year) £
Sales			
Direct cost of sales			
Direct labour costs			
Other direct expenses or costs			
Operating profit			

C.A. Wiscombe

Table 8.6. A full trading, profit and loss account structure for a sole trader or partnership.

	£	£	(Previous year) £
Sales			
Cost of sales			
Gross profit			
Less expenses			
Business rates			
Wages/national insurance			
Utilities			
Administration			
Loan repayments			
Bank/accountancy charges			
Insurance			
Depreciation			
Total expenses			
Net profit			

money throughout the year from the business, against what they invested, and care is needed to ensure they do not take too much cash.

In limited company accounts the annual report will be far less detailed in operational activity (see Table 8.7). The report is to the shareholders and they will be less interested in the amounts spent on individual expenses, for instance on utilities or business rates, than in overall profitability. The business may also have other investments which could generate income for the organization and other costs that relate to strategic planning. The shareholders cannot be paid any share of the profits, called a 'dividend', until the company has paid its taxes. Therefore, while the principles of 'trading profit and loss accounts' exist, the overall look of limited company accounts may differ from company to company.

Table 8.7. Structure of company profit and loss accounts.

	£	£	(Previous year) £
Sales			
Cost of sales			
Gross profit			
Operating expenses			
Operating profit			
Net interest income[a]			
Reorganization costs[b]			
Profit before tax			
Tax on profit			
Profit for the financial year			

[a]Interest income is income made from the financial investments made by the business.
[b]This company reorganized during the financial year and has included these costs as a separate item to show shareholders where monies outside the operational activity of the business have occurred.

Once profits are declared limited companies then decide, bearing in mind their strategic plans, how much of the profits to pay shareholders as dividends. Taking too much cash from the business in order to pay out dividends could leave the company without enough capital to engage with their growth plans. Currently Walt Disney Corporation is growing their theme parks and resorts operations through the purchase of cruise ships. These are expensive purchases and to finance the development they have not paid out as much dividend as their profit might have indicated. Shareholders will need an explanation for these strategies and an assurance that it is in the long-term best interests of their investment to leave the profits with the company to support further growth.

Balance sheet

The balance sheet measures the 'worth' of the organization at a specific point in time on the basis that the capital invested in the company bought the assets. Profits retained by the business may have purchased more assets, be sitting idly in a bank account owned by the business or have bought stock that is waiting to be sold. Alternatively, the business may not have been producing profits, the organization may be borrowing money to stay in business or the worth of the company has fallen. The balance sheet reflects the equation introduced earlier:

Capital = Assets

Some accountants use a horizontal format to reflect this equation with the assets listed down the left-hand side of the page and the capital to the right. However, most use a vertical format. Whichever format is used the balance sheet must always balance. To determine the 'assets' of the business, i.e. what it owns, the organization must also consider the 'liabilities', i.e. what it owes. Assets will be either 'fixed assets' (those which remain in the business for longer than a year), or 'current' (those which only exist in the business for a short time, such as stock, debtors or cash). Liabilities will be 'current' (those which are short term such as debts owed to suppliers called 'creditors' or a bank overdraft which is a short-term loan repayable in less than 1 year). Total assets will be fixed assets plus current assets. The total value of the current liabilities is deducted from the assets to give a net assets figure. Assets will always be equal to capital and thus, on the balance sheet, the net assets figure must equal the capital invested. For sole trader and partnership accounts, the capital account is made up of cash invested by the sole trader or partners plus possibly long-term loans from finance institutions.

In the example of a sole trader balance sheet in Table 8.8, the long-term liabilities of the company are such that they contribute to the assets purchased by the business in the form of premises. While the business owns the premises, they become security for the long-term loan and if sold contribute to the worth of the business. It seems logical therefore to consider those long-term liabilities as part of the worth of the business.

The differences between sole trader and partnership balance sheets and those of limited companies lie in the definition of 'capital investment'. In the sole trader or partnership balance sheets, the capital invested by banks and building societies, perhaps mortgages or long-term loans, is deemed as part of the capital invested in the business. In limited companies, the capital invested is the shares issues or debentures. Any long-term loans are part of the long-term liabilities which reduce the total assets

C.A. Wiscombe

Table 8.8. Balance sheet format for sole trader or partnership.

	£	£	£
Assets			
Fixed assets			
Premises			
Equipment			
Current assets			
Cash in hand			
Cash at bank			
Stock			
Debtors			
Less current liabilities			
Creditors			
Net assets			Balance
Financed by			
Long-term liabilities			
Capital invested by owner			
Profit account			
Total capital employed			Balance

of the company. Depending on the structure of the shares, the balance sheet may look like that illustrated in Table 8.9.

Dividends are entered into the accounts as part of the capital contributing to the worth of the company but are actually owed to the investor. A figure for dividends will usually be negative; in accountancy negative figures are often put in brackets (thus).

It is interesting to note that different countries may use slightly different terminology to describe the same thing. Thus 'stock' may be listed as 'inventory'; 'ordinary shares' become 'common stock'; 'preference shares' become 'preferred stock'; these are the vagaries of a common system. The terminology is a little different but the meaning is the same.

Despite the differences in layout in the balance sheet from one organization to another the principles on which they are based do not change. In all cases, they reflect the equation Capital = Assets and assets are defined as total assets of the business which must include the liabilities.

There are some other key terminologies that the balance sheet highlights, but this is not intended to be a finite listing and further research will be necessary as new terminology is encountered.

Depreciation: When a fixed asset is used, for example the car used by the taxi driver or the cooking range used by the chef, it reduces in value. This reduction in value is termed 'depreciation'. Depreciation appears as a figure in the balance sheet to reduce the value of the fixed asset. It also is accounted for in the profit and loss account as an expense incurred during the course of the year. Accepted accounting principles are used to determine the amount of the expense which is gauged on the life cycle of the asset. For instance a cooking range may be expected to last for 10 years. At the end of the 10-year period the asset would probably be worth nothing if the business tried to

Table 8.9. Balance sheet for limited company.

	£	£	£
Assets			
Fixed assets			
Premises			
Equipment			
Current assets			
Cash in hand			
Cash at bank			
Stock			
Debtors			
Less current liabilities			
Creditors			
Net assets employed			
Less long-term liabilities			
Lease payments			
Bank loans			
Other			
Provision for liabilities[a]			
Deferred tax			
Total assets – Total liabilities			Balance
Shareholders' funds			
Ordinary share capital			
Preference share capital			
Dividends			
Profit and loss account			
Total shareholders' funds			Balance

[a]In limited companies where known expenditure will be made in the very near future, such as an expense that will have to be paid, a 'provision' may be made in the accounts to show a much clearer, real picture of the worth of the company. This may be used to allay shareholders' interests, particularly if the dividend being offered that year is not as high as might be expected.

sell it 'second hand'. If purchased for £15,000 then the asset would be written off over 10 years and the depreciation would be £15,000 divided by 10 or £1500 per annum. Accountants will ensure that the concept of depreciation is explained in the 'notes to the accounts'. Whichever concept is used, this will remain the same year on year.

Amortization: Sometimes organizations buy business interests for more money than the worth of their assets. The price paid reflects the intangible assets which cause the business to run profitably. (This could be location, reputation, skills of employees and so on.) The intangible assets are referred to as 'goodwill'. Goodwill has been bought and paid for but must be accounted for. The solution in accounting terms is to write off the goodwill (i.e. to reduce its value to zero) over a number of years. This process is called 'amortization'.

Derivatives: Derivatives are a contract, the price of which is dependent on the value of the underlying asset. Examples of derivatives are futures (these are a standardized agreement to buy or sell a security at predetermined prices at a given date in the future), forwards (an agreement to lend or borrow money at a predetermined interest rate in the future for a given amount of time, for example an agreement to lend/borrow £1 million for 3 months in 6 months' time at 4%), options (the right but not the obligation to sell or buy shares, foreign exchange or commodities at a given price at or before a predetermined date in the future) or swaps (an exchange of cash flow obligations between two parties). Money made from derivatives could be termed 'derivative financial instruments' in the balance sheet. Success or failure in the derivative markets could cause problems for organizations; however, the ability to create income using cash, shares or commodities that are not needed in the short term can be a lucrative source of income. Travel companies that sell foreign exchange to another company to create profit are an example of a derivative transaction. The purchasing of fuel ahead of need, or the disposing of same at an increased price if not needed is another.

CASE STUDY: 'HEDGING' IN THE TRAVEL SECTOR

By June 2008 Thomas Cook Group plc had hedged all its crude oil and 93% of its jet fuel needs for the remainder of 2008/09. In addition the group had hedged 100% of its foreign currency requirements. This financial management of resource needs was complimented by a 6-month performance announcement reporting average selling prices 14% ahead of the previous year with overall selling prices up 5% after creating demand by reducing the number of holidays sold by 19%.

(Sources: various)

Summary

While the balance sheet for a public limited company may appear more complicated than that of a sole trader the structure is still relatively straightforward. Once mastered, the structure gives us access to analysis and evaluation that through interpretation tells us the story of the company.

Management Accounting

Management accounting refers to the collection, recording, storage and summary of financial and other data, usually for internal parties of an organization that include managers, supervisors and employees. It may be of interest to external organizations, such as the government, but it has a very different role from the accounts produced for external audiences, which are produced in the annual format.

Management accounting has no mandatory format, can be produced when and how it best suits the organization or department, contains both quantitative (financial, numbers) and qualitative information, uses forecasted and planned data sets for comparative purposes and should be as easy to compile as possible. In large organizations, companies will employ a management accountant to provide information on a timely basis. In small independent organizations the owner/operator may take on this role. In some very small businesses the role may be ignored and this becomes a threat to their existence.

Management accounting is concerned with long- and short-term planning, control of the business, recording and monitoring the costs to the organization, providing information for decision making, providing the information necessary for financial management and providing audit trails. It developed as a branch of financial management when the necessity of more detailed and timely information was needed. In the food and beverage sector of the travel industry stocktaking is one such aspect of management accounting and is monitored closely to ensure profitability is maintained. In the airline sector the price of fuel is monitored on an almost hourly basis and fuel surcharges applied to customers' ticket prices so that the airline maintains its profitability. In large organizations management accountants will set budgets for departments or units based on the strategic or long-term plans for the business. Department or unit managers will then be responsible for understanding and implementing that budget. It is important that the department and unit managers fully understand the terminology and role of the management accounts, but in doing so will learn aspects of financial accounting. As we have already seen, financial accounting refers to the classification and recording of monetary transactions of an entity in accordance with established concepts, principles, accounting standards and legal requirements, and their presentation during and at the end of an accounting period. This by necessity follows GAAP in both the UK and in many overseas countries. Often the information used by management accountants feeds directly into the information used to create the annual accounts and must therefore be accurate. It is also indicative that many of the systems and procedures used to create the financial accounts define and assist the development of management accounts.

In order to assist the development of management accounting processes a number of bespoke and 'off-the-shelf' computer software companies have produced appropriate software solutions. More often than not the computer software is dedicated to the particular sector of the industry and will have a number of add-on packages to build into a complete business overview. In the accommodation sector organizations can purchase integrated reservations systems that can link with sophisticated checkout systems linking housekeeping, human resources, restaurants and leisure services together. In restaurants and bars stocktaking packages link with sales information and purchasing to give comparisons to expected and achieved results. The US lodging industry created a 'uniform system for accounts in hotels' published in 1926 with revisions since. It provides a consistent presentation of management accounts with 30 supporting schedules and has enabled management accounts to develop across an industry sector with consistency in concepts and terminology. It will always need to be recognized that software alone will not provide solutions to management accounting functions. The information they produce will always need interpretation.

Management accounts are necessary to ensure the business is following a planned course of action that enables it to remain solvent, profitable and operational. Employees will expect their salaries and wages to be paid on time; suppliers will expect to be paid for their goods and services; and those to whom we have sold goods and services that the organization supplies should pay their debts.

Sometimes we work in businesses where the performance against those management accounts will dictate some or part of our salary and it is important that we understand their meaning and where this can help to develop our income further. For instance, a chef in the restaurant kitchen may have a bonus linked to the number of customers served, the sales made and the 'gross profit' achieved. A travel agent may earn higher commission on holidays that generate better 'operating profit'. For sole traders or partnership organizations their sole income may be dependent on the performance of the business.

It is important that the management accounts show clearly where and how the operations happen, the cash flow linked with those operations, and that we understand the financial terminology that will help us to interpret those accounts. But it is not as difficult as it might first appear. There is a series of essential elements that must be included to provide: the ability to plan and budget (this includes aspects of yield management); the ability to cost a product or service; and the ability to price a product or service, accounting for contribution (particularly in seasonal businesses). The evaluation of plans and any variance analysis must be done on a regular basis; for established businesses this would usually be on a monthly basis. One other aspect remains and that is the ability to account for capital investment decisions. This is a function of both management accounting and financial management, as capital investment is the largest expenditure of organizations. Both internal and external audiences may feel the implications of capital expenditure.

Plans, budget and variance analysis: The majority of management accounting begins the year as the budget based on targets. It 'operationalizes' the overriding strategy. The monitoring of variances revises the original budget and becomes a working document upon which changes may be made. A real example is too large to invert into the context of this page but an idealized one-page example is given in Table 8.10. This shows some of the costs for some of the centralized resources of a travel operations organization. In the last year they have bought and altered an office premises that they previously rented (capital expenditure), rented additional accommodation that became available next door and stabilized their staff recruitment – the previous year they headhunted a new management accountant.

The lines of account, see column 1, ran to 1205 lines in the year illustrated. Thus numbering these helps discussion in management meetings. Column 2 allows management to look at notes to explain some of the differences, perhaps for the original budget, the year to date, the variance or the revised estimate prepared at the last management meeting. Some clear directions have been taken in defining last year's rent and rates costs and this has expanded the explanation to specific overheads. This has allowed management to see clearly the costs of storage facilities (used for brochures) and the impact of a decision to buy Saxon House instead of renting it: reduced rent but increased depreciation that has resulted in a reduction of costs of around £70,000. However, the decision to purchase brings with it overheads of repairs and renewals: roof repairs, alterations to accommodation and building repairs are (hopefully) one-off costs which make the property fit for use. Finally, in looking to reduce costs the level of detail allows the highlighting of postage and stationery as areas for investigation. While not over budget, there may be more cost-effective ways of distributing information other than by post.

Costing a product or service: It can be seen from the example that management accounting needs to classify expenses to the business in a very sophisticated manner. This provides a basis for decision making. Managers need to know what expense occurs, in which department it occurs, where it occurs, when it occurs, how it occurs and why it occurs. The financial accountant will group very generically all expenditure

Table 8.10. Example of a management accounting system year to December (date).

Line No.	Note	Total budget for the year £	Year to date (December) actual £	Variance £	Year end previous year £	Revised estimate (September) £
95	1 **HR costs**					
96	Staff recruitment	25,000	17,468	7,532	101,800	15,000
97	Staff training and development	45,000	39,852	5,148	72,098	45,000
98	Professional subscriptions	6,000	6,816	(816)	8,066	7,500
99	Health and safety	7,500	7,819	(319)	4,856	6,000
100	Car parking	40,000	44,057	(4,057)	35,257	46,000
101	Staff conference	15,000	14,296	704	19,306	17,000
102		138,500	130,308	8,192	241,383	**136,500**
103	2 **Overheads**					
104	Rent and rates				191,361	
105	Rent – Saxon House	150,000	35,848	114,152		35,848
106	Depreciation – Saxon House	–	35,354	(35,354)		45,500
107	Rent – Overwater House	–	10,797	(10,797)		10,614
108	Rates	11,200	11,875	(675)		15,000
109	Storage	22,800	15,805	6,995		19,000
110	Cleaning	12,000	16,865	(4,865)		18,000
111	**Rent and rates subtotal**	196,000	126,544	69,456	191,361	143,962
112	**Repairs, renewals, security and air conditioning**					
113	Roof repairs	–	24,522	(24,522)		24,522
114	Alterations to Saxon House	–	23,949	(23,949)		25,000
115	Air conditioning	–	16,875	(16,875)		5,000
116	Equipment repairs	–	6,085	(6,085)		6,000
117	Building repairs and alterations	–	34,651	(34,651)		25,000

Continued

Table 8.10. Continued.

Line No.	Note	Total budget for the year £	Year to date (December) actual £	Variance £	Year end previous year £	Revised estimate (September) £
118	Car park alterations	–	3,000	(3,000)		
119	Other	–	2,089	(2,089)		1,000
110	**Repairs and renewals subtotal**	**25,000**	**111,171**	**(86,171)**	**71,407**	**86,522**
111	Insurance	13,000	15,301	(2,031)	12,658	15,031
112	Light, heat and water	11,000	15,787	(4,787)	10,808	12,500
113	Office equipment maintenance	16,000	15,108	892	10,046	16,000
114	Office equipment lease	12,400	10,501	1,899	16,462	12,400
115	Depreciation of office equipment	5,612	23,355	(17,743)	21,571	17,279
116	Office expenses	27,000	27,182	(182)	26,151	27,000
117	Computer consumables/ supplies	17,000	3,289	13,711	15,114	4,200
118	Stationery	70,000	73,611	(3,611)	65,747	75,069
119	Postage	145,000	120,345	24,655	128,093	124,932
110	Telephone – landlines	24,000	16,950	7,050	34,357	16,381
111	Telephone – mobiles	18,500	18,526	(26)	16,110	18,677
112	Internet broadband usage	8,000	10,392	(2,392)	–	6,000
113	**Subtotal**	**588,512**	**587,792**	**720**	**619,885**	**6,000**

in certain areas, for instance wages and salaries, to one sub-heading. Management accounting will be much more specific and identify specific costs and specific purposes and classify them according to sector. By being so definitive, they can ensure that the costs incurred are necessary, are at an appropriate level and provide the consumer with the product or service they require. The more remote expenditure is from the consumers' consumption the harder it is to provide that level of definition; thus, wherever possible, management accounting classifies generic expenses into 'cost centres'. For the travel organization illustrated in Table 8.10, the centralized management accounts subdivide expenses into central services, marketing, communications, IT, finance and travel operations and each department will have lines for staff costs, motor expenses, telephone, stationery and so on.

Hotel group accountants have organized this structure expertly for a number of years. The cost centres are sometimes dependent on the 'revenue centre' (such as bars or restaurant, sales, banqueting and conferences) or within the 'locus of control' (for instance 'marketing' department or 'finance function'). Even though this seems very detailed, some expenses will be charged to departments from control centres where particular activity happens. If the marketing department works with the restaurant manager to develop materials for the restaurant, new menu designs for instance, which are then put in guest bedrooms to encourage use of the facilities, marketing may well charge the restaurant manager for these services. This may sound a little odd if they are all working for the same company but it is the responsibility of the marketing manager to meet their performance targets and be as cost-effective as possible. In this type of accounting costs become termed 'direct costs', 'indirect costs' and 'remote costs'.

Direct costs are those easily associated with the revenue-generating activity and will include direct materials, direct labour and direct expenses. Indirect costs are those which are necessary to produce the revenue but are difficult to allocate on anything but an agreed 'overhead recovery rate' (ORR). The ORR is divided into revenue- and non-revenue-earning departments on an agreed rate. For a restaurant only serving meals and drinks the ORR would be overheads divided by the number of customers, and this amount is used to provide the price of the product. In a hotel the ORR may be divided by floor area, by sales or by other determinants to revenue-earning departments only. There may be some terminology to describe costs which are direct, indirect and remote, such as wages, which confuse the bookkeeper and may get apportioned wrongly. Managers in different areas will monitor this closely to ensure they are being 'billed' for the appropriate costs. A system of cost codes is easily developed using computer programs.

C.A. Wiscombe

> **Activity**
>
> The following list describes the menu offerings for two different types of breakfast served in first-class carriages on a regular commuter service. Using prices from your local supermarket, or information from the Internet, calculate the cost per person of each dish.
>
> *Cooked breakfast:*
> Two pork sausages
> One scrambled egg
> Two rounds of toast
> Spinach (approx. 50 g)
> One cooked tomato
>
> *Continental breakfast*
> Three slices watermelon
> One slice cantaloupe melon
> Six mandarin orange segments
> One-third of an apple, sliced
> Eight grapes

Pricing up this recipe provides an illustration of just how complicated costing processes can be. The cost of a one grape or the cost of 50 g spinach can be complex. Calculating direct labour costs is no less complicated. The reality on board the train is that there may be as many as six breakfast choices. The direct costs in the preparation of meals are easy to assess historically, by collating all the hours of work and salaries paid to kitchen and waiting staff. To get an average cost per meal this total can be divided by the number of meals served. It is much harder in a fledgling business to assess accuracy of costs in advance. Thus monitoring becomes absolutely essential.

Of the indirect costs, 'allocation' takes place when the overhead is indirectly associated with a particular department. This would include specific insurance cover associated with an activity, such as for the leisure centre in a resort complex. Where the cost is remote, there is a measure of subjectivity in 'apportioning' the cost.

Pricing: Management accountants will follow the strategy adopted by their companies to ascertain pricing policy. In large organizations with multiple regional units there may be local needs which dictate alternative strategies or the consideration of promotions to achieve individual sales targets. For instance, a local branch of Let's Go Travel may host a seminar on a particular cruise line in order to promote sales. They may offer discounts or prize draws to attract consumers to attend. For a cost of £350 in wine and buffet achieving sales of £3500 would make such an event worthwhile and create a profit from the travel agent's commission.

Contribution and break even: To adopt pricing policies that offer discounts the individual unit must also consider its break-even position. The understanding of how many sales are needed to cover their fixed costs is essential (this is the point at which the unit does not make a loss but neither does it make a profit). The theory behind contribution is that if the fixed costs are already covered then there can be different evaluations of the pricing policy to be adopted in order to maximize profits. This has allowed companies such as Travelodge to offer a set number of rooms in their portfolio for as little as £19 if they are booked, and paid for, in advance. This non-refundable payment ensures cash flow for them, booking indications well ahead of competitors and allows consumers to be attracted by the deal to be had. As the company gets nearer to the available dates, the price rises according to availability. The original price has already covered fixed costs.

CASE STUDY: THE IMPORTANCE OF CONTRIBUTION

Explore and Exodus are specialist travel companies competing to provide holidays to exotic locations for niche groups. Those groups could be looking for adventure, walking or hiking, culture, arts or a mixture of all of these. Usually they travel between small holiday destinations using very basic accommodation in order to see the real country culture, rather than the distilled version available in major tourist centres.

Holidays are taken in groups of six to 15 and bookings can be made on an individual basis. Clients will be met by a leader at the main destination, usually the airport, and accompanied to the start of the trip. Maximum groups relate to the sizes of coach (or other transport) used to travel between locations; thus the company books airline seats up to a year or longer in advance, based on the size of mini bus available *in situ*. Accommodation is booked by the companies on a tentative proviso, as are local services.

The companies retain the right to cancel the holiday up to 6 weeks in advance of the trip. Clients who book take this risk. Holidays will be cancelled then as this is the last date of confirmation that the airline will accept without the company losing the fare. Decisions on whether to run a trip will depend on the contribution a trip that has not filled up would make. If it did not break even it would not run. Once confirmed to the client the trip has to go ahead, otherwise the companies will face penalties.

(Sources: various)

Yield management and overbooking: Maximization of sales is a key driver in travel operations. To maximize sales, the assumption is that someone will cancel before final payment, or simply not turn up. Air travel, particularly among low-cost airlines, has followed hotels' maximization technique in overbooking flights in order to increase sales (of both fares and the extra in-flight services). Many consumers seem to accept that until they actually check in they are not guaranteed to fly on the booked flight. Some will be transferred to other flights (often with a seat upgrade to placate them). With occupancy ratios, a key efficiency driver for both industries, the practice of maximizing yield will be a double-edged sword. (Yield management is also discussed in Chapter 4, this volume.) Measurements of yield are in occupancy rates (e.g. rooms occupied/rooms available × 100%), labour costs as a percentage of sales, overheads as a percentage of revenue and extra spend per guest or passenger.

Summary

Finance is a crucial underpinning role of travel operations management. The planning, budgeting, organization and systems that a business uses depend upon the collection and analyses of financial data in a logical and ordered manner. While computerized systems support the work of the finance function, understanding and knowledge of how these operate is essential. Where companies operate a proactive and searching approach to solution management through financial awareness, they are successful and can contribute greatly to profitability.

C.A. Wiscombe

PART B: PERFORMANCE MEASUREMENT

Introduction

Performance measuring systems should be able to improve the way people work and support strategy. They must be dynamic, balanced, integrated and improvement-orientated. Operations managers may receive targets from process-based measurement techniques which look at reliability, speed and quality. Thus airlines are measured by how often their flights take off on time and whether luggage arrives at destinations and trains are measured by punctuality. Some of these process-driven targets contribute to overall performance measures. Performance measures will look at reliability, speed, price, flexibility and quality. The importance of these performance measures to customer perceptions cannot be underestimated. Trailfinders, a travel service company, is finding that the trend for individuals to book their own holidays via the Internet has impacted on business but advertises strongly their distinct unique selling point (USP), 'the highest standards in terms of speed, convenience, sound advice and pleasant booking process', as adding value to the consumer experience. In terms of operations management, they look 'to deliver, by every means' the best possible value and so remain viable in the changing travel marketplace (Gooley, 2008).

Historically, performance measurement of organizations has concentrated on financial analysis of sets of accounts. While these accounts measure sales, cost of sales, profits, assets and liabilities as performance standards, they do not consider the holistic performance of organizations. Twenty-first century operations seek to go much further than these financial measures. Brown *et al.* (2001) argue that companies should measure 'economicalness' with standards that are set about the use of resources to create and deliver products, 'efficiency' where standards measure the level of outputs (room sales, flight tickets) against the input (labour, resources) necessary, and 'effectiveness'. This last concept is concerned with whether the right product or service is being produced (thus providing market share), competitor benchmarking, customer service, human resources, brand image and many other factors. New approaches to performance measurement are being adapted by the travel industry. External awards, such as Investors in People (IiP), provide indicators of reaching standards that companies use to indicate good performance. The adoption of quality systems, such as ISO 9000, also provides a measurement tool which can help service organizations deliver to their customers. Quality systems and measures are discussed further in Chapter 5 (this volume).

Unfortunately, these performance measurement tools do not negate the use of financial data to plan, monitor and control modern service organizations. Rather, the additional tools enhance the complete reporting process which has become the driver in financial decision making and in management accounting. This complete approach has led to differing management reporting mechanisms that allow a holistic approach to performance measurement. Two of these mechanisms are introduced here:

- 'Activity-based costing' (ABC): This underpins service standard development by trying to apportion common costs to department or product activity thus attempting to reflect resource consumption. It is not an easy mechanism to put in place. Imagine a large corporate organization head office, such as that of Enterprise Inns plc, based in Solihull. They own some 7000 public houses in the UK. The concept of ABC would be to work out the exact costs that head office use according to each public house and charge those costs to the outlet concerned. At a more local level, a hotel might try to allocate the human resources used in housekeeping to the public areas of restaurant, front office, conference and banqueting, so that the cleaning and maintenance costs of those areas are accurately costed against any sales they may make. Each scenario provides a detailed analysis of costs to take place before true allocation against unit or department budgets can be made. This is such a complicated process that some businesses have had to abandon ABC as a systems approach; nevertheless the skills and knowledge gained from attempting its implementation have added to the financial knowledge of the company (Liu *et al.*, 2002).

- **The balanced scorecard:** It is interesting to see the growth of Kaplan and Norton's (1992) idea of the 'balanced scorecard' approach to performance measurement. Many companies are looking at the use of reporting mechanisms to different stakeholder groups very seriously and the balanced scorecard is a tool which can be used to help. The balanced scorecard looks at four key areas of the company: financial performance, customer perception, internal business processes, learning and development. Goals and measures are set for each area. The advantage of the balanced scorecard is that it combines the external awards of quality standards with the financial measures and consumer indices to create a holistic picture on which senior managers from different departments will report. For operations managers this can mean they are responsible for driving forward activities which feature in the balanced scorecard, possibly without being introduced to the whole picture.

Despite other alternatives all companies have to produce financial accounts. These enable the performance measurement of a company against historical figures, against the competition or market place (benchmarking) and against industry 'norms'. In this case performance measurement is clearly in financial terms and uses key data. The financial performance measures focus on five key areas: profitability, liquidity, debt position or 'degree of leverage', activity rates and return to shareholders. Limited companies will provide, alongside their annual financial statements, reports on each of these areas as they feel best serves their stakeholders. In order to achieve this measurement, financial managers use 'ratio analysis'.

Ratio analysis

Ratio analysis is the term we use to describe the translation of the lists of figures in the 'trading, profit and loss accounts' and 'balance sheets' into understandable data sets. Many of these data sets depend on comparing percentages or the ratio of figures on an historical basis (i.e. has the organization performed better or worse than last year) with the competition (whose figures, if a limited company, will be published) or with industry norms. HM Customs and Excise often use industry norms to determine the accuracy of sole trader accounts. In business the understanding of financial ratios is very important and the higher the level or responsibility within a company or

C.A. Wiscombe

organization, the more useful it is to practise this understanding. If starting your own business, the more you know the more you can earn!

One way of achieving familiarity is to compare sets of accounts. If you can use your organization's accounts then so much the better. This text has provided two sets of accounts from travel operation organizations of very different sizes in which to apply the concepts introduced. These accounts are real industry examples *but* have been adapted to provide students with the ability to compare and contrast similar ratios. It must also be acknowledged that the internal and external forces causing some of the results are due to the strategic changes within the organizations. These fall outside of our immediate discussions but prove the point that to truly understand accounts they cannot be read in isolation, but form only part of a holistic picture.

Company A Ltd was founded in 1970 and operated with a staff of four. It now operates 29 travel centres: six in London, branches in all major towns in England, Scotland and Northern Ireland, five in major centres in Australia and one each in Dublin and Cork in Ireland. In 2008 Company A will make travel arrangements for over 650,000 people. Turnover for the year ended February 2008 was £510 million, up by £35 million on the year to February 2007. The company remains privately listed and reports to Companies House on an annual basis. Interested parties can access annual accounts of the company by paying a small fee to Companies House.

Company B Group plc is a global corporation; it operates in the cruise sector, sailing in Alaska, the Bahamas, through the Baltic, in the Mediterranean, as well as other worldwide destinations. It owns tour companies, which, combined with its other travel operations, provides for 7 million guests annually. At any given time there are more than 225,000 people sailing aboard the company's fleet of 88 ships, 160,000 guests and 65,000 shipboard employees. In 2007, the company totalled US$13.1 billion in revenues, with a net income of US$2.4 billion, and employed a total of 80,000 people. Strategically, it is developing its business to attract a wide customer base that is very varied in terms of cultures, languages and leisure time preferences; thus it operates a number of brands within the portfolio selling its products not just across countries but across continents.

At first glance it may seem impossible to compare like for like performance in these two very differently sized organizations. Indeed, they even use different currencies. Any comparison must acknowledge companies using different groups of income, costs and expenses to develop the final accounts. That aside, using accepted concepts, the ability to apply ratio analysis enables us to compare and measure one performance against the other and an ability, despite the different currencies, to compare like for like. In comparing performance, however, we reiterate that this is for the benefit of students developing accounting skills rather than investors looking for key analysis. It is also worth knowing that databases exist that can provide comparisons of key data without the effort of doing the calculations – they still, however, need to be understood.

A set of full accounts from a small or large company can seem daunting to the untrained eye. Accordingly, this section breaks down the trading, profit and loss account into small sections to assist the student's development and then introduces a balance sheet. For each financial statement the key ratio analysis is given.

Trading, profit and loss account analysis

The first sets of ratios that measure performance are profitability ratios. There are four key profitability ratios measured from the trading, profit and loss account.

1. Gross profit margin: This measures how well the costs of the sales have been controlled. This examines the trading account of the company. It acknowledges the sales generated by the operational activity (i.e. not from other business interests that the company might be involved in) and measures costs as a percentage of the sales generated from them. Gross profit is therefore a cash amount showing Sales – Cost of Sales. To measure this as a ratio, we look at gross profit as a percentage of sales, and then costs as a percentage of sales. The ratio allows us to see if the company made £1, US$1 or €1 of sales what proportion would be used up in costs. Thus:

$$\frac{\text{Total Sales} - \text{Costs}}{\text{Total Sales}} \times 100 = \text{Gross Profit \% or Gross Margin}$$

The trading accounts of both companies indicate that sales have risen (Table 8.11). So too have costs and that would be expected. The test is whether the sales have risen at the same rate as costs, or at a lesser rate. If at a lesser rate, then the company has performed better at increasing sales while reducing costs, which is a great achievement.

Company A Ltd has performed better in the year to February 2008 than in the previous year. This has improved their gross profit by 0.56%. This may not seem a lot but on each £1 million this makes a difference of £5600 and as we are discussing a turnover of £510 million this will equate to £2.8 million.

Alternatively, Company B Group plc has a weakened gross profit by 1.17%, and thus shown that they have not managed their cost of sales as well in the year to 2007 as in the previous year. Fuel costs have risen globally and thus any comment on the rise in gross profit may, in a very full analysis, need to compare the challenge and management of rising fuel prices. Nevertheless, a drop in gross profit as a percentage of sales needs operational action to reduce costs.

Table 8.11. Trading account comparison.

Company A	To February 2008 £ '000	%	To February 2007 £ '000	%	Company B	To November 2007 US$ million	%	To November 2006 US$ million	%
Turnover	510,206	100	475,473	100	Revenue cost of sales[a]	13,033	100	11,839	100
Cost of sales	(448,027)	87.81	(420,167)	88.37		(7,628)	58.53	(6,791)	57.36
Gross profit	62,179	12.19	55,306	11.63	Gross profit	5,405	41.47	5,048	42.64

[a]The first adapation is to create a 'cost of sales' in Company B accounts. This has been done using accepted direct costs but is an illustration only. Company B may in fact use different costs to create their own management accounts gross profit figures.

C.A. Wiscombe

Costs of sales are very important drivers of performance. The lower the costs and expenses of a business, the more profit the company will achieve.

2. **Operating profit margin**: Operating profit is the area on which operations managers become really focused. Drivers for operations performance improvement will be directly related to improving this figure in the financial accounts. Financial managers will set performance targets which will directly impact on the results shown because operating profit margins measure how well the direct cost and those operating expenses that can be allocated to operational activity have been controlled.

Efficiency and economy can be illustrated through these figures. Detail within financial accounting can be limited. Sometimes 'notes to the accounts' will provide some detail of activity, which can be measured, but strategic targets to improve performance will need to be reflected through management budgets. In comparing like for like, differently structured organizations will have different detail in their accounts. However, the company can look at historical comparisons with their own performance as well as comparing final operating profit margins with competitors.

$$\text{Operating Profit} = \text{Gross Profit} - \text{Operating Expenses}$$

$$\text{Operating Profit Margin} = \frac{\text{Operating Profit}}{\text{Total Sales}} \times 100$$

Company A Ltd has a lower operating profit margin in 2008 than they had in 2007 (Table 8.12). Administration expenses have been reduced in both cash terms and as a margin. This is a very positive result and to be commended. Other operating income has, however, fallen by 0.8%. This means that the gain in gross profit, or improved performance in costs and administrative expenses, has been offset by a fall in operating income.

Company B Group plc profit from operations has risen year-on-year (Table 8.13). They create more operating profit for each dollar of sales than does Company A, but they have not done this as well in 2007 as they did in 2006. This is indicated by the operating profit percentage, down from 22.07% to 20.91%. Individual lines of costs and expenses provide operations managers with detailed information on how well performance against sales has increased or decreased. Selling and administration costs have fallen by 0.1%, saving the company US$13.63 million. However, other costs and expenses have not performed well and have contributed to the fall in operating

Table 8.12. Operating profit margin: Company A Ltd.

Company A Ltd	To February 2008		To February 2007	
	£ '000	%	£ '000	%
Turnover	510,206		475,473	
Cost of sales	(448,027)	87.81	(420,167)	88.37
Gross profit	62,179	12.19	55,306	11.63
Administrative expenses	(59,806)	11.72	(56,456)	11.87
Other operating income	1,557	0.30	5,294	1.11
Operating profit	3,930	0.77	4,144	0.87

Table 8.13. Operating profit margin: Company B Group plc.

Company B Group plc	To November 2007		To November 2006	
	US$ million	%	US$ million	%
Revenue	13,033		11,839	
Cost of sales	(7,628)	58.53	(6,791)	57.36
Gross profit	5,405	41.47	5,048	42.64
Selling and administration	(1,579)	12.12	(1,447)	12.22
Depreciate and amortization	(1,101)	8.45	(988)	8.35
Operating income	2,725	20.91	2,613	22.07

Table 8.14. Company B: analysis of costs and expenses by sales.

Company B Group plc	To November 2007		To November 2006	
	US$ million	Percentage of sales	US$ million	Percentage of sales
Commission, transportation and other	1941	14.89	1749	14.77
On board and other	495	3.80	453	3.83
Payroll and related	1336	10.25	1158	9.78
Fuel	1096	8.41	935	7.90
Food	747	5.73	644	5.44
Other ship operating	1717	13.17	1538	12.99
Other	296	2.27	314	2.65
Total costs and expenses	7628	58.53	6791	57.36

income. Company B provides additional detail that can be analysed to see where operational practices need to improve (Table 8.14).

Commission, payroll, fuel, food and other ship expenses have all risen as a percentage of sales while 'other' costs have been reduced by 0.4%. Overall the company has used more of the sales dollars on costs and expenses than the year before. Not all rises in costs are negative – a rise in commission paid is in line with a rise in sales, nevertheless operations managers would look to increase those areas of direct trade

C.A. Wiscombe

where commission does not have to be paid. Strategies to develop these areas are crucial for all tour operations.

On-board costs will inevitably rise as sales increase; volumes of food, all-inclusive beverages and on-board activities and tangible goods sold, such as gifts from on-board shopping, are some examples of these. However, they should rise in line with sales so a rise in such costs would reduce profits. An example of good performance is noted in 'other costs' which have reduced by 0.38%, equating to US$18 million, quite a saving.

With over 80,000 employees it is inevitable that payroll costs will account for a large proportion of expenses. Analysing personnel expenses by sales shows that it costs 0.47% more to create US$1 of sales in 2007 than it did in 2006, so while we would expect payroll expenses to rise as the company expands and grows the productive nature of that cost is not performing as well as it has in the past. Operations managers would seek to ensure payroll is productive and may set targets to lower these figures. Thus operations management will be charged to increase production from their staff or to question whether they really need all the staff that is employed. This type of evaluation can, in very serious cases, lead to redundancies or lay-offs; however, Company B Group plc is not in that position yet.

The second way of looking at personnel expenses is to measure them in relation to each member of staff. Staff numbers have risen. In 2007 the company employed 81,000 employees, and in 2006 only 75,000 employees. A simple division of payroll costs per employee shows that costs have risen per employee, rather than just because of a rise in numbers.

Finally, in evaluating performance of operations it is important to note that the operating account for Company B Group plc illustrates the terms amortization and depreciation. There is an increase in depreciation. This is largely due to the increased number of ships the company owns. As their largest fixed asset, each ship will depreciate; the more ships the company owns, the larger the figure for depreciation. This figure is not within the control of operations managers and is subject to the accounting principles already discussed but understanding this concept assists the setting and acceptance of operational targets.

3. (After tax) net profit margin: This ratio measures the final profits of the company in the accounting period. The relationship between this ratio and operational management may be tenuous as income is counted from other investments, outside core operational activity, and is affected by interest received from these. However, it is the company's main profit ratio for shareholders and therefore is of great significance to the performance of the company as a whole. The ratio is again a measurement of performance against sales thus:

$$\text{Net Profit Margin} = \frac{\text{Profit after Deductions}}{\text{Sales}} \times 100$$

Company A net profit margin has gone up by 0.02% (Table 8.15). In cash terms, this equates to £744,000. As we have already identified, operating performance has been reduced but the 'interest receivable and similar income' category has risen substantially. The notes to the accounts show this is from 'bank interest'. The reason for this is interest on deposits held for customers' payments, but it is enough to realize at this stage that it is very unusual to have a business hold cash reserves and get substantial interest from it. Usually cash generated would be invested into other businesses or fixed assets, equipment or product development, in order to grow the business.

Table 8.15. Company A net profit margin.

Company A Ltd	To February 2008		To February 2007	
	£ '000	%	£ '000	%
Turnover	510,206		475,473	
Cost of sales	(448,027)	87.81	(420,167)	88.37
Gross profit	**62,179**	**12.19**	**55,306**	**11.63**
Administrative expenses	(59,806)	11.72	(56,456)	11.87
Other operating income	1,557	0.30	5,294	1.11
Operating profit	**3,930**	**0.77**	**4,144**	**0.87**
Investment income	170		1,670	
Other interest receivable and similar income	9,952		7,502	
Profit on ordinary activities before taxation	**14,052**	**2.75**	**13,316**	**2.80**
Tax on profit on ordinary activities	(4,254)		(4,262)	
Profit for the year	**9,798**	**1.92**	**9,054**	**1.90**

Table 8.16. Company B Group plc net profit margin.

Company B Group plc	To November 2007		To November 2006	
	US$ million	%	US$ million	%
Revenue	13,033		11,839	
Cost of sales	(7,628)	58.53	(6,791)	57.36
Gross profit	**5,405**	**41.47**	**5,048**	**42.64**
Selling and administration	(1,579)	12.12	(1,447)	12.22
Depreciation and amortization	(1,101)	8.45	(988)	8.35
Operating income	**2,725**	**20.91**	**2,613**	**22.07**
Non-operating (expense) income				
Interest income	67		25	
Interest expense, net of capitalized interest	(367)		(312)	
Other expense, net	(1)		(8)	
Income before income taxes	**2,424**		**2,318**	
Income tax expense, net	(16)		(39)	
Net income	**2,408**	**18.48**	**2,279**	**19.25**

Overall the operational activity of Company A's core product, travel organization, has not performed as well in the year to February 2008 as it did in its previous year, but the overall profit has risen.

Company B Group plc post tax profits have risen in cash terms from US$2279 million in 2006 to US$2408 million (Table 8.16). To shareholders of the company this would be a very good indication that the organization has performed well and has provided a better return on investment (ROI) *but* in operational terms the changing of the net profit into net profit margin, as a percentage of sales, shows us the company has not performed as well in 2007 as it did in 2006. Had it performed at the same rate

C.A. Wiscombe

of 19.25%, the organization would actually have created US$2508 million net income; the analysis thus points to a poorer performance by some US$100 million.

4. Growth of profits: This measures the rate of growth of profits year-on-year. This ratio can be done for each level of profit being measured. Those who work with numbers a great deal acknowledge that pages of figures and calculations do not always illustrate the points well. Sometimes this type of comparison is illustrated by graphs or charts to better show results.

Growth of profits is defined as 'profit from this year divided by profit from last year'; however, there are clearer ways of showing the difference year-on-year of sets of figures. Analysts use terms like, 'profits have grown year on year by 10%' or 'sales have fallen year on year by 3%'. It is useful to work out how this is calculated.

Profit for the year earned by Company B Group plc was US$2408 million and the year before was US$2279 million. To work out the percentage growths take (2408 – 2279)/2279 × 100. The result measures the difference between the two figures, US$129 million, as a *percentage of the original figures*, 5.66%. This is a very good growth result and will be a figure which shareholders revel in.

Activity

Develop a chart or graph that illustrates the pattern of profit behaviour in Company A Ltd and Company B Group plc. Using a spreadsheet will help accuracy in presentation. Include gross profit, operating profit and net profit.

Charts or graphs that could be used include bar charts, pie charts, line graphs, doughnuts, scatter graphs and so on.

Try at least three different graph or chart types before deciding which one illustrates the information best. State why this is the case.

Balance sheet

The balance sheet, which measures the worth of the company at a given point in time, can be used to analyse performance in a number of areas. Profitability of the company in the trading, profit and loss accounts is looked at as performance against sales. Profitability in the balance sheet looks at how well the company has performed against the investment made. The balance sheet also illustrates 'liquidity', 'debt levels', 'activity rates', and 'shareholder return rates'. Activity rates are measures of operational performance and, while monitored by financial managers, are usually devolved to operational management for improvement. Table 8.17 gives the balance sheet for Company B Group plc.

The Balance of Capital (termed equity in these accounts) clearly equals Assets. In 2007 the balance was US$19,963 million and in 2006 US$18,210 million. Remember the equation Capital = Assets. Capital invested in the organization through shares, retained earnings, other accumulated income and treasury stock purchased the assets of the business. The net worth of those assets has taken into account the debts (or liabilities) that the company has acquired.

Table 8.17. Balance sheet for Company B Group plc. (Format adapted to GAAP.)

As at 30 November 2007	2007 US$ million	2006 US$ million
Non-current assets		
Property and equipment, net	26,639	23,458
Goodwill	3,610	3,313
Trademarks	1,393	1,321
Other assets	563	465
Total non-current assets	**32,205**	**28,557**
Current assets		
Cash and cash equivalents	943	1,163
Trade and other receivables, net	436	280
Inventories *(stock)*	331	263
Prepaid expenses and other	266	289
Total current assets	**1,976**	**1,995**
Total assets *(current assets + non-current or fixed assets)*	**34,181**	**30,552**
Current liabilities		
Short-term borrowings	115	438
Current portion of long-term debt	1,028	1,054
Convertible debt subject to current put options	1,396	0
Accounts payable	561	438
Accrued liabilities and other	1,353	1,149
Customer deposits	2,807	2,336
Total current liabilities	**7,260**	**5,415**
Non-current liabilities		
Long-term debt	6,313	6,355
Other long-term liabilities and deferred income	645	572
Total non-current liabilities	**6,958**	**6,927**
Total liabilities *(current liabilities + non-current liabilities)*	14,218	12,342
Net assets *(total assets – total liabilities)*	19,963	18,210
Equity		
Common stock	6	6
Ordinary shares	354	354
Additional paid in capital	7,599	7,479
Retained earnings	12,921	11,600
Accumulated other comprehensive income	1,296	661
Treasury stock	(2,213)	(1,890)
Total equity	19,963	18,210

Note: Labels in italics have been added for explanation.

Profitability measures

Return on total investment or assets (ROI): This indicates the return on total investment or assets and is measured by (profit after deductions/total assets) × 100. The importance of ratio analysis is very evident in this calculation. The assets of the

C.A. Wiscombe

Table 8.18. Return on total assets – Company B Group plc.

	2007 US$ million	2006 US$ million
Profit after deductions	2,408	2,279
Total assets	19,963	18,210
Return on total assets	12.06%	12.52%

company have grown from US$30.5 million to US$34.1 million. We might expect them to have a bigger growth in profits if those assets are working effectively for the company. Table 8.18 illustrates ROI.

The ratio analysis shows a good ROI. Twelve per cent is a much higher return than an investor might expect from leaving their money in the bank (in 2007 bank interest rates stood at around 6%). There has been a fall in ROI from 2006 to 2007, however, by 0.45%.

Liquidity ratios

Liquidity is the measure of an organizations ability to meet immediate demands on its cash which may fluctuate at different times. Emergency holdings of cash may be needed where travel is affected by unexpected trauma (war, natural disaster, terrorism and so on). There may also be fluctuations in income due to seasonality. Banks and lending institutions that provide short-term funds (less than 1 year) can sometimes request repayment at very short notice where industries face short-term problems. It is possible that a company may be fundamentally profitable but unable to meet their short-term obligations.

CASE STUDY

A travel organizer will have to accommodate a number of risks that both its clients and the business may face. Since the late 1950s there have been some very difficult situations for the growing tourist industry where airlines have gone out of business, leaving travellers stranded on foreign soil. In travelling to the Caribbean, Africa, Asia, the Middle East and even, after the Bali bombings, in the Indian Ocean, tourists may face the difficulty of pirates or terrorists impacting on their travel plans. War is also a problem facing many travel organizers as the world reacts to perceived threats against their national pride. Currency rate changes which react to global activity mean that the foreign exchange rates agreed when holidays are booked are not those in place when travel is undertaken by clients. Additional risks exist from natural phenomena such as that experienced in China, in earthquakes, and Burma, through flooding. Each of these risks will affect overall tourism business by putting potential clients off travel. Thus business per se may experience a downturn. However, travel as a leisure and business phenomenon is growing. The current debates on climate change do not seem to be slowing the number of tourists seeking more interesting and diverse destinations and many governments continue to expand the infrastructure of their countries to enable them to capitalize on this trend.

Trailfinders Ltd have found two particularly unique financial management solutions to these problems on behalf of their clients. The first is the creation of a

Continued

---

trust account in June 1993. This 'separate legal entity holds all clients' money received for travel arrangements until such time as payment is due to suppliers'. This account has held amounts exceeding £164 million but the company receives its commission only after the settlement of supplier accounts. Thus the monies of clients are safeguarded until after the funds are used. Then in 1996 Trailfinders signed a voluntary, but binding, agreement with the Civil Aviation Authority to protect any of their clients who might be affected by the financial collapse of an airline. The security of mind this service gives to potential customers, who might otherwise book holidays through the plethora of Internet sites, gives Trailfinders an USP. Thus they hold large cash reserves in order to be able to react to this situation, if it arises. Finally, they minimize currency losses by internal rates adjustment.

(Sources: various)

Current ratio: This indicates the extent to which the claims of short-term creditors, such as suppliers, can be met by liquidating short-term assets, such as selling inventory or chasing debtors for their payments. The ratio is calculated by dividing current assets by current liabilities. Accepted practice, and most financial writers, expects a company to show a current ratio of 1:1, i.e. for each £1 of current liability there is £1 in current assets to cover it. Some texts have suggested that the figure should be 2:1 but care needs to be taken in assuming this to be correct. The figure will be dependent on the industry. If a large amount of business is done in cash transactions, such as pub or supermarket, and not on credit then cash (or equivalent) will flow through the company, allowing easy access to funds with which to pay creditors as they fall due.

Company B Group plc has a worsening current ratio figure (see Table 8.19). For every US$1 of current assets it has US$3.67 of immediate debt (current liabilities). If all the creditors asked for their payment immediately Company B would be unable to pay them. One of the ways this problem can develop is to hold too much stock for the company's immediate needs as it takes some time to convert stock into sales. In addition, it costs money to store stock and thus this can also decrease profits. To see if this is the problem, we can analyse the figures further by using the 'acid test'.

Acid test (or quick) ratio: This ratio shows the organizations capability to pay-off short-term obligations without running down its stock (or inventory). The importance of this test is highlighted in Company B Group plc balance sheet. Look at liabilities first. 'Accounts payable', those that need payment within 30 or 60 days, amount to US$561 million. Cash and cash equivalents (look in current assets) amount to US$943 million. On the surface then the company has enough short-term cash or cash equivalents to pay its short-term debts. But to find the exact situation:

$$\frac{(\text{Current assets} - \text{Stocks})}{\text{Current liabilities}}$$

Table 8.19. Current ratio – Company B Group plc.

	2007 US$ million	2006 US$ million
Current assets	1976	1995
Current liabilities	7260	5415
Current ratio	1: 0.27	1:0.37

C.A. Wiscombe

Table 8.20. Acid test – Company B Group plc.

	2007 US$ million	2006 US$ million
Total current assets	1976	1995
Inventory	331	263
Assets less inventory	1645	1732
Current liabilities	7260	5415
Current ratio	1: 0.22	1:0.31

While Company B Group plc may at first appear to be vulnerable, with a ratio of less than 1:1, it must be acknowledged that they are a huge company with many assets (see Table 8.20). It is unlikely, unless the economic situation seriously worsened for the industry, that short-term creditors would demand payment all at once. This is far more likely for very small independent or sole traders where banks or creditors become worried that they will not get paid. Therefore, liquidity analysis, while a good indicator, must be read in context of the industry and sector.

Inventory ratio: Some ratio analysts of liquidity measure the level of inventory, or stock, to the net working capital. This would be a very valuable analysis in a high-inventory business. If you would like to work this out the ratio is measured by:

$$\frac{Inventory}{(Current\ Assets - Current\ Liabilities)}$$

Activity

At the end of this chapter you will find the balance sheet from Company A Ltd.
Apply the ratio analysis for profitability and liquidity to the balance sheet and comment on the differences with Company B Group plc.

Debt level

The third area of consideration when judging company performance is the debt position of the organization. In accounting terminology this is called 'degree of leverage'. It is important to understand the concept of debt level for two reasons. The first is to understand that debt costs money to service and this was illustrated in the profit and loss account for Company B Group plc in the line of account labelled 'Interest expense'. Interest payments are due on long-term liabilities such as mortgages; interest is also due, along with service charges, for short-term overdraft facilities. In both cases they are expenses which the company needs to pay. If a business has a large short-term overdraft but has stock unnecessarily sitting in storage facilities, it is paying to borrow money that it should not need if stock was managed more effectively. The second reason for understanding debt level is to know when an organization is able to borrow more long- or short-term finance. If a business has already borrowed to its limit, then the finance manager knows that to invest in new products or fixed assets, funding would need to be raised from profits rather than by borrowing. For shareholders there is a third reason. If the company cannot find enough cash to repay its loans then the ordinary shareholder may not get any money back if the company went into liquidation!

Companies can be funded out of a mixture of share capital, retained profits and loans. Loans can be short or long term and would include, for the purposes of true analysis, the credit given by suppliers such as trade creditors. The fact that creditors might not be paid for their goods or services for 30 or 60 days is in fact a 'loan'. Some companies, such as Marks and Spencer plc (M&S), have utilized this aspect of cash flow to support their business in difficult times, pushing the payments of trade creditors to 90 or even 120 days. For some very small trade suppliers this can be very difficult indeed as their cash flow depends on being paid on time. Hopefully you can begin to see that this could become a very vicious circle of liquidity, with M&S retaining their ability to remain liquid while small suppliers to whom they owe money become less liquid. The corporate social responsibility (CSR) debate is often applied to this aspect of financial management. Analysis of debt level needs an understanding of the difference between funds and loans, see Table 8.21.

The first difficulty can already be clearly seen. Preference share capital is seen by some accountants as a type of loan, rather than as a funding stream. The second issue is that in a complex organizational structure other items, classed as loans, might exist. Ratio analysis allows us to study the complexity of company debt in four ways, although some other analysts may include more aspects of this challenging area of financial management.

1. Debt to assets ratio: This indicates the extent of borrowed monies to finance the operation. Different industries will expect different levels of borrowing. In the 1970s and 1980s licensed retail sole traders were assumed to be investing up to 30% of their own capital in any venture before banks would consider funding. During the late 1980s and early 1990s this rose to up to 50% for a period. This protected the bank from some of the more wayward ideas of entrepreneurs; they worked on the assumption that if the sole trader was going to lose a substantial sum if the business did not work out, they would work harder and smarter to ensure its success! Some industries would suggest that a debt to asset ratio of more than 50% indicates a possible problem, others that the emphasis should be on the direction and rate of any change. If the ratio is rising rapidly then this may indicate a deteriorating position. The ratio is

Table 8.21. Difference between funds and loans.

Shareholders' funds	Loans
Ordinary share capital	Debentures
Share premium account	Loans
Capital reserves	Overdrafts
Revenue reserves	Provisions
Other reserves	Accruals
Profit and loss account	Current liabilities
	Other amounts due for payment
Preference share capital	

C.A. Wiscombe

more commonly used for sole trade or partnership accounts where shareholder funds are not defined. To calculate:

$$\frac{\text{Total Debt}}{\text{Total Assets}}$$

2. Debt to equity ratio: This indicates the division of shares of funds provided by creditors to those of equity or shareholders. It is calculated by:

$$\frac{\text{Total Debt}}{\text{Total Equity}}$$

3. Long-term debt to equity ratio: The indication of long-term ratio of debt to equity in the business. Calculated by:

$$\frac{\text{Long-term Debt}}{\text{Total Equity}}$$

4. Times interest earned or 'covered' ratio: This ratio examines how well the business can service the cost of the debt and is calculated by:

$$\frac{\text{Profits before Deductions}}{\text{Total Interest Charged}}$$

The debt ratios show that in 2007 Company B Group plc had 0.42:1 debt to assets, or for every US$1 of assets they had only US$0.42 of debt (see Table 8.22). If the company had liquidated all its assets it would have been able to cover all its debts and have capital left over. This is a very strong position to be in although the ratio is slightly down on the previous year's figure. The debt to equity ratio shows a 70/30 split of debt to equity and that figure falls to 30/70 in the consideration of long-term liabilities. Finally, the covered ratio shows the company can afford to fund the cost of the borrowings with a ratio of 6.60, although again this has fallen from 7.43 in the previous year.

Activity

Using Company A Ltd balance sheet compare the debt position of the company with the results of Company B Group plc.

Table 8.22. Company B Group plc debt ratios.

As at 30 November 2007	2007 US$ million	2006 US$ million
Total debt	14,218	12,342
Total assets	34,181	30,552
Total equity	19,963	18,210
Long-term debt	6,958	6,927
Profits before deductions	2,424	2,318
Total interest charged	367	312
Debt to assets ratio	0.42	0.40
Debt to equity ratio	0.71	0.68
Long-term debt to equity ratio	0.35	0.38
Covered ratio	6.60	7.43

Activity rates

The way a company uses its stock or inventory, manages its debtors and uses its assets are operational performance measures that can indicate detail of improvements to be made in future periods. The results are likely to provide performance targets for managers and supervisors within budgets and forecasts.

Stock performance: Unused stock deteriorates, creates a storage expense and ties up cash that can be used elsewhere in the business. The ideal scenario is to achieve a 'just-in-time' (JIT) purchase of materials that arrives, is converted into the sales product and sold as quickly as possible. While most businesses can get 24/7 delivery service on materials, there are cases where longer lead times for purchasing is an advantage, such as fuel at the right price. In most cases, however, the lower the storage figures the better. There are three potential performance measures that contribute to the analysis:

Average Stock = ½ (Opening Stock + Closing Stock)

$$\text{Stock Turnover} = \frac{\text{Cost of Goods Sold}}{\text{Average Stock}} = x \text{ times}$$

Days of Stock Holding = 365/Stock Turnover = No. of days stock held

In this case we cannot compare year on year as we do not have the opening stock figure for the year 2006, only the end stock (Table 8.23). However, we can complement Company B Group plc for holding very little inventory. The calculation shows that they perform excellent JIT purchasing with less than 14 days' stock held and a healthy stock turnover. In food and beverage operations, such as hotels, it would be expected that for some commodities very quick turnover is necessary, whereas others, such as fine wine, may remain *in situ* for some time.

Debtor management: Debtors can cost the company dearly. Debtors not paying their bills on time can create cash flow problems, cause the company to have to borrow to meet their short-term liabilities and, if not monitored, could become a bad debt (one that is not paid at all). Most companies operate on standard payment terms, 14, 30 or 60 days are the maximum periods. If a debt runs into 90 days and is still not paid then further action might be needed. Monitoring debtors for large and small organizations is a full-time job. Invoices sent are followed up by statements, and then telephone reminders, perhaps another statement then

Table 8.23. Stock performance for Company B Group plc.

As at 30 November 2007	2007 US$ million	2006 US$ million
Stock	331	263
Turnover (sales)	13,033	11,839
Cost of goods sold	7,628	6,791
Average stock	297	
Stock turnover	25.68	
Days of stock holding	14.21	

C.A. Wiscombe

debt recovery processes may need to be used. The usual ratio for trade debtor collection measurement is:

$$\frac{\text{Average Trade Debtors}}{\text{Credit Sales}} \times 365 \text{ days} = x \text{ days}$$

In most travel operations consumers pay deposits for goods and services they have yet to use; payment will be expected in advance of consumption. In the case of holidays this can be 6 weeks before the holiday is taken. This practice has prevented the creation of short-term debt for travel companies. For companies who offer events, such as weddings, they have adopted similar approaches. While most holiday clients accept that they have to pay 'in advance' for goods and services this is not without risks.

Asset utilization: The higher the level of fixed assets in a business the more sales that should be generated! Plant and machinery should enable the organization to operate more efficiently. Measuring this ratio can ensure that operations managers are making the most of the equipment and machinery that they have to maintain. The high cost of fixed assets in the travel sector, such as aircraft, hotels and land mean that it is essential that full utilization of these is made. Thus some companies are disposing of assets and leasing them back. The companies purchasing the asset will ensure maximum occupancy by selling the service to more than one client.

CASE STUDY: TUI TRAVEL

Sales of assets are used by financial managers in different ways. TUI Travel announced in June 2008 that it was to sell and lease back 19 of the 28 aircraft it owned in a deal to raise US$526 million. The deal included aircraft currently flown in the UK by Thomsonfly. The cash from the sale to a leasing company, AerCap Holdings, is used to reduce the group's £900 million debt, a write down in the group's assets, a paper loss on this of US$155 million due to the fall in value of the aircraft but greater flexibility in the use of aircraft amid the increasing economic uncertainty of the period. TUI plans a 12% reduction in aircraft capacity for the summer of 2009, the equivalent to taking out ten aircraft.

(Sources: various)

The asset utilization ratio is:

$$\frac{\text{Total Sales Revenue}}{\text{Fixed Assets at Net Book Value}} = x$$

However, this figure is not the only comparator that can be made. All assets should work to generate sales and thus we also measure total assets turnover. This is calculated as:

$$\frac{\text{Total Sales Revenue}}{\text{Total Assets}} = x$$

It is essential to compare performance year on year or benchmarked, as in isolation one figure does not mean very much (see Table 8.24).

Table 8.24. Asset utilization in Company B Group plc.

As at 30 November 2007	2007 US$ million	2006 US$ million
Total sales revenue	13,033	11,839
Fixed asset value	32,205	28,557
Total asset value	34,181	30,552
Fixed assets turnover	0.40	0.41
Total assets turnover	0.38	0.39

In Company B Group plc fixed asset use is at a ratio of 1:0.40. Year on year the analysis shows consistent use of assets but the huge value of its assets makes true judgement of performance difficult. Operations managers will spend time looking at occupancy levels, or standard measures of passenger capacity, in order to assess performance. For the cruise sector of this business this is computed by multiplying passenger capacity by revenue-producing ship operating days. Overall the sector needs to take a long-term view of asset utilization given the huge values and long-term usage of its assets.

Shareholders' return

Shareholders are interested in the dividend paid out at any time, and the capital gain made by selling the shares. Increases in the share price, due to good performance of the company, will increase the capital gain. If the company performs well, share prices will rise and enable organizations to raise capital more easily. If either dividends or share price fails to perform then management of the company could be at risk. Shareholders who are not happy with the performance of an organization may sell their shares. The more shares there are for sale in a company, linked with the overall performance of the company, the less the share price will fetch.

There are a number of shareholder return ratios. Some analysts are tempted to reduce these, but the more information gained the clearer the picture on performance. In comparing or benchmarking performance, shareholders will compare the performance of the company using stock market indices and seek to ensure their share portfolio is providing the best rate of return. There are very few shareholders in large plc who will simply leave their money in poorly performing companies. As you read through the indices it is clear that without a current market price per share all ratios cannot be calculated. The final dividend for year ended 2007 for Company B Group plc shareholders is US$1.375 per share and for 2006 was US$1.025 but this is only around 45% of the actual earnings per share.

1. Return on equity: This measures the net rate of return on the share investment. It can be classed as a profitability ratio but is vital to shareholders interests so is included again in this section of analysis. It is measured by:

$$\frac{\text{Profits after Deductions}}{\text{Total Equity}} \times 100$$

Shareholders in Company B Group plc receive a return of 12.06%, a slight fall on 2006 returns (see Table 8.25).

C.A. Wiscombe

Table 8.25. Return on equity results – Company B Group plc.

As at 30 November 2007	2007 US$ million	2006 US$ million
Profits after deductions	2,408	2,318
Total equity	19,963	18,210
Return on equity	12.06%	12.72%

2. Return on common equity: This ratio removes the debate on whether preferred stock, discussed earlier, is true capital or loan. Thus:

$$\frac{\text{Profits after Deductions}}{(\text{Total Equity} - \text{Preferred Stock})} \times 100$$

3. Earnings per share: This is usually declared in plc annual reports and indicates the earnings made per share. This is available as either distributed income (dividend) or may be retained by the company for reinvestment. If being retained by the company a full explanation will be required to shareholders at the AGM. Calculation:

$$\frac{\text{Total Profits after Deductions and Dividends on Preferred Stock}}{\text{Number of Common Shares}}$$

For Company B Group plc earnings per share in 2007 were US$3.04, and in 2006 were US$2.85. As the dividend to be paid is US$1.375 the balance of those payments becomes 'retained earnings', ploughed back into the business to help develop its growth. Shareholders of this business are well aware of the enormous costs of developing the fixed assets of the business and in total the company has US$12,921 million in this account.

4. Dividend on yield equity: This indicates the actual rate of return to shareholders based on the dividend that they will receive. Thus:

$$\frac{\text{Annual Dividend per Share}}{\text{Current Market Price per Share}}$$

5. Price/earnings ratio: This considers a shareholder's long-term view on the potential future income streams to grow and the risk this entails and is calculated by:

$$\frac{\text{Current Market Price per Share}}{\text{Earnings after Deductions per Share}}$$

6. Dividend/payout ratio: This puts a ratio on the willingness of the organization to distribute profit. This is, however, a complicated scenario and will always be addressed in annual reports to shareholders. For instance, Walt Disney Corporation theme parks and resorts have bought two new cruise ships in 2007. In order to ensure the capital investment needed, they did not pay out all the profits after deductions in dividends but retained capital in the company for this reinvestment. Company B Group plc has declared a rate of US$1.375 payout for 2007 or 45%. The calculation is made by:

$$\frac{\text{Annual Dividends per Share}}{\text{Earnings after Deductions per Share}}$$

Table 8.26. Balance sheet for Company A Ltd.

As at 29 February 2008	2008 £ '000		2007 £ '000	
Fixed assets				
Tangible assets		21,991		19,970
Investments		21,842		21,727
Total fixed assets		43,833	41,697	
Current assets				
Stocks	43		40	
Debtors	3,165		3,646	
Monies held on trust	132,842		108,205	
Cash at bank and in hand	66,037		61,763	
Total current assets	202,087		173,654	
Current liabilities (creditors' amounts falling due within 1 year)				
Net obligations under finance leases	310		–	
Trade creditors	95,922		81,948	
Amounts owed to parent and fellow subsidiary undertakings	26,758		17,984	
Corporation tax	1,560		1,777	
Other taxes and social security costs	877		812	
Other creditors	2,441		1,852	
Accruals and deferred income	2,948		6,344	
Proposed dividend	2,500		0,000	
Total current liabilities	133,316		110,747	
Net current assets (*current assets – current liabilities*)		68,771		62,907
Total assets (fixed assets + current assets)		112,604		104,604
Long-term liabilities				
Creditors' amounts falling due after more than 1 year		(621)		(–)
Provision for liabilities		(361)		(280)
Total assets less long-term liabilities		111,622		104,324
(Financed by) Capital and reserves				
Called-up share capital		94		94
Share premium account		27		27
Revaluation reserve		1,104		1,125
Other reserves		16		16
Profit and loss account		110,381		103,062
Total shareholders' funds		111,622		104,324

C.A. Wiscombe

Activity

Table 8.26 gives a balance sheet for Company A Ltd. To consolidate your learning of ratio analysis techniques it is important to practise. Apply all the ratio analysis techniques to Company A Ltd balance sheet and comment on the results. Reflect on the findings and put yourself in the position of a financial manager.
1. Based on your findings what (SMART) financial targets would you set the company for the year 2008–2009?
2. Think about the trends in the industry. How might external and internal factors affect the attainment of your targets?

Summary

This chapter has provided an overview of some of the financial affairs facing travel operations managers today. The production of profit is not easy as different sub-sectors of the leisure sector vie for business. The growth of holidays booked independently has impacted on travel operators and forced them to invest in quality services to attract consumers. The focus is changing from a purely financial performance measurement of success to a much more holistic one. The CSR agenda is questioning previously used financial management techniques as being unethical and there is a move away from a purely corporate agenda. Companies are being encouraged to invest in tackling climate change, environmental protection and sustainability. The research and development needed for this will reduce profitability. The challenge for companies will be to satisfy shareholders that their investment is used soundly for long-term profitability; shareholders may need to take a more long-term view.

The finance function underpins all levels of management and supplies data for improvement, monitoring and evaluation. The data needed for management information are immense. They include financial and performance targets, the collation of which is time-consuming and onerous. The provision of those data is not enough. Targets will be set that are essential to the success of the company. But the finance function alone cannot succeed in these targets because maximizing capacity draws on marketing techniques and maximizing productivity on human resource management. The improvement of activity measures is driven by operations managers and overall strategy and planning must be agreed by directors. Therefore, while financial performance targets are a driver for organizations, the financial managers can often be seen as authoritarian; however, they are the servants. It is up to other management functions to put those targets into practice.

Acknowledgements

Harvey World Travel; Marian van der Heidje FCCA, Anglo Dutch Accounting, Tring, Herts.

Further Research

ATA (2000) *Alnwick Tourism Association Constitution*. Alnwick Tourism Association, Alnwick, UK. Available at: www.visitalnwick.org.uk/pop/constitution.htm

Dyson, J. (2004) *Accounting for Non-accounting Students*. Prentice-Hall, Harlow, UK.

Guilding, C. (2002) *Financial Management for Hospitality Decision Makers*. Butterworth Heinemann, Oxford.

White, C. (2004) *Strategic Management*. Palgrave Macmillan, Basingstoke, UK.

White, M.P. (1990) *White Heat*. Reed International Books Ltd, London.

Further information on accounting for non-accounting students:

Dyson, J. (2004) *Accounting for Non-accounting Students*. Prentice-Hall, Harlow, UK.

Millichamp, A.H. (2002) *Finance for Non-financial Managers*, 3rd edn. Continuum, London.

Owen, G. (1998) *Accounting for Hospitality, Tourism and Leisure*, 2nd edn. Pearson Education, Harlow, UK.

Further discussion on financial and management accounting techniques:

Adams, D. (2006) *Management Accounting for the Hospitality, Tourism and Leisure Industries: A Strategic Approach*. Thomson Learning, London.

Pilbeam, K. (2005) *Finance and Financial Markets*, 2nd edn. Palgrave Macmillan, Basingstoke, UK.

Yeoman, I. and McMahon-Beattie, U. (2004) *Revenue Management and Pricing. Case Studies and Applications*. Thomson Learning, London.

Web Sites

Alnwick Tourist Association: www.visitalnwick.org.uk
Companies House: www.companieshouse.gov.uk
The National Trust: www. Nationaltrust.org.uk
Travel Weekly: www.travelweekly.co.uk

Review Questions

1. Visit a trade fair or use the Internet to investigate appropriate computerized management information systems (MIS) for the travel industry. Compare products. Include a pricing comparison. Write an analysis of your findings.

2. For the products investigated consider the capital investment needed to adopt the MIS of your choice. How could you persuade your organization's financial manager to invest in the asset?

References

Brown, S., Blackman, K., Cousins, P. and Maylor, H. (2001) *Operations Management – Policy, Practice and Performance Measurement*. Butterworth Heinemann, Oxford.

Gooley, M. (2008) *Realising Value; Chairman's Message*. Company A Ltd, London. Available at: www.Company A.com/aboutus/chairman.htm

Kaplan, R. and Norton, D. (1992) The balance scorecard – measures that drive performance. *Harvard Business Review* January–February, 71–79.

Liu, L., Martin, J. and Robinson, J. (2002) Double measure. *Financial Management*. October 2002, 22–24.

Walt Disney Corporation (2007) *Annual Review and Report*. Walt Disney Corporation, Burbank, California.

C.A. Wiscombe

9 Sustainability for Travel Management

Sine Heitmann and Peter Robinson

Objectives of the Chapter

This chapter addresses the range of impacts the travel industry can have on economies, natural and built environments and different societies and cultures. In order to minimize any negative impacts, the concept of sustainability, and its application to the travel industry, is analysed. An integrated consideration of the environmental, economic, political and sociocultural aspects of sustainable travel development includes principles of good practice in sustainable business management, travel and tourism planning and development of travel management strategies. The chapter will:

- explain the impacts travel and tourism can have on destinations;
- explain the concept of sustainable tourism and the importance of sustainable travel and tourism planning; and
- identify good practices of sustainability.

Introduction

Tourism is a booming industry with 898 million arrivals in 2007 and the travel and tourism industry contributes an estimated 10% to the worldwide gross domestic product (GDP), providing almost 240 million jobs worldwide. Within the UK, the data show a similar picture in terms of the importance of the travel and tourism industry, with a 9.2% contribution to the country's GDP and 2.7 million jobs (8.6% of total employment; WTTC, 2008). Many countries, not only the UK, are building on tourism as a source of income as it provides an attractive alternative to declining industries such as agriculture and manufacturing. From a consumer's perspective, travelling has become an essential part of life. Tourism is a broad system characterized by the movement of people, goods, capital and knowledge, among other things, between tourist sending and receiving regions which are linked by means of routes and transit regions and associated with many other societal processes. Tourism is steadily becoming a part of the global economic system and culture.

In 2008, Heathrow Airport, the busiest in Europe, extended the capacity of the airport through the construction of Terminal 5, and plans for further expansion exist to cater for the constantly rising demand (such as a sixth terminal and a third runway). Similar plans have also been drawn up by other UK airports including Stansted and Birmingham. These expansion plans attract large movements of protest. While an expansion of airports would obviously increase capacity to deal with growing passenger numbers and create new jobs, new tourism income to the region and the country as well as new business opportunities, the protesters raise concern about the negative consequences of these developments, such as increased noise pollution, increased levels of emissions, congestion and overall loss of quality of life to those living near the airport. These discussions present a very good example for the impacts that travel and tourism-related activities can have on a region or an entire country – these impacts are both positive and negative and can be of different magnitude, depending on the volume of travel activity within the region concerned. The first part of this chapter will give an overview of the general impacts a destination can experience as a result of travel and tourism activities.

Sustainable tourism is the concept that is discussed throughout the chapter and although, for the most part, the book focuses on travel, in this instance it is impossible to get away from the underpinning ideas that are embedded in tourism theory, and consequently adapted for travel. Sustainability as a key aspect of tourism has become a top point on every agenda concerned with tourism development. The key idea of sustainability applied to tourism is the minimization of any negative impacts tourism can have on a destination while enhancing and maximizing the positive impacts in order to guarantee that not only today's generation of tourists and locals can enjoy the natural and cultural resources a destination has to offer, but that these resources are also made available to future generations of hosts and guests.

Historically, countries, regions and cities have focused on the positive economic impacts that tourism can bring to developed destinations. Considering the development of tourism within the Mediterranean countries, particularly Spain, the focus was on rapid and uncontrolled development of mass tourism in order to reap as many economic benefits as possible. However, as the protest against the Heathrow expansion well exemplifies, there is a range of negative impacts that has to be taken into account when developing a region into a tourist destination. Over the past two decades countries like Spain have come to realize that the lack of planning for tourism development during the 1950s and 1960s resulted in the destination having massive urban tourism zones along the coasts, which caused pressure on natural resources (coastline, water resources, natural habitats), changed demographic structures and loss of traditional communities. The importance of tourism planning as part of sustainable tourism is discussed in more detail in this chapter.

The final part of the chapter will introduce the reader to a range of good practices of sustainable tourism. Drawing on a history of roughly 30 years, different practices and initiatives such as community involvement, zoning, pricing, interpretation, education and alternative forms of tourism have been introduced to comply with the underlying principles of sustainability, safeguard the destination and its community from negative impacts and enhance its potential to survive within the travel and tourism industry for as long as possible. While there is no intention to go into much detail (as this would go beyond the scope of this chapter) the introduction of different concepts is included to enhance the reader's awareness of concepts that contribute to the idea of sustainability.

Impacts

The chapter starts with an explanation of why sustainability has become important. This is generally understood within the knowledge that every action by a tourist has an impact on the environment they are in. This may be a positive or negative impact. For

S. Heitmann and P. Robinson

example, spending money in a local shop will help the local economy, but taking coral from a coral reef will damage the very sites people have come to see. These impacts can be classified under a range of headings, and are discussed here in greater detail.

Tourism impacts

Tourism's core activity is to 'sell' physical and human environments – a destination depends on natural and cultural resources for its success. Much research has been carried out into tourism impacts, as tourism is an activity that leaves many prints on a destination, both visible and invisible. Impacts in tourism studies are generally categorized into physical/environmental, economic and sociocultural impacts.

Economic impacts

A range of positive economic impacts can be identified from any travel or tourism activity within a country or a destination. The influx of tourists and their spending power has positive impacts on the economy of a destination in terms of an inflow of revenue which contributes to the turnover of travel (and other local) businesses, and increases opportunities for employment and household incomes. To governments, tourism is beneficial as they will earn extra tax and revenues directly through business rates and community taxes. Furthermore, with a focus on travel, the industry has become a major contributor to national GDP.

When discussing economic impacts, the multiplier effect has to be taken into account, which describes the knock-on effect that money generated from tourism activity has within a destination (see Fig. 9.1). Direct impacts are those outlined where tourists' expenditure has an immediate impact. For example, more overnight visitors result in more sales for the accommodation sector and restaurants, nightclubs and event venues. Indirect impacts are secondary effects that result from the spending

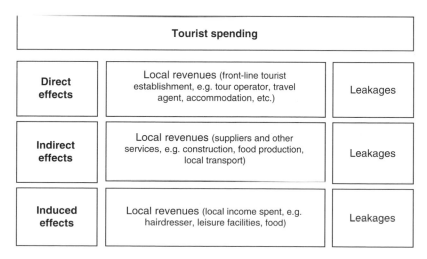

Fig. 9.1. Multiplier effect and leakage.

of tourism receipts, for example more sales in the accommodation sector results in more demand for the suppliers in the accommodation sector. Finally, induced impacts are changes that result from the increased household incomes (e.g. household earns income from tourists' expenditure which is then spent within the economy, for example in supermarkets, housing, etc.).

At a destination level, wider positive economic impacts stem from the improvement and diversification of economic structures; while a country might have previously relied on primary (agricultural) or secondary (manufacturing) industries, it can develop its economy with tertiary (service-oriented) industries. Tourism is also often seen as an important driver for economic regeneration through the establishment of alternative income sources. In addition, tourism is credited with encouraging entrepreneurial activity by providing new income-generation opportunities to local business owners.

Finally, after discussing tourism in general, it is worth pointing out the economic contribution specific events and particular tourist industry activities can have. For example, the Olympic Games or World Cups have received much attention and many countries and cities compete to host these events because of the benefits in terms of economic gain and image enhancement. Other events that have similar impacts include festivals such as Edinburgh Fringe Festival, Glastonbury Music Festival or Munich Beer Festival. Niche tourism activities can also have considerable economic considerations to destinations, such as skiing in Switzerland, golf in Ireland or cruises in the Caribbean. While many impacts are similar to those described above, there are impacts specific to these activities, particularly considering the encouragement of entrepreneurial activity and the development of small businesses that cater for these niche markets.

However, despite all the obvious benefits of tourism, there can be heavy financial burdens brought to the destination's community. The cost for infrastructural development (e.g. road construction, accommodation construction, police services, public transportation, water supply, waste disposal) has to be borne by the local government, which has to be financed through increased taxes. Rising costs that come with tourism development can lead to inflation, if not controlled properly, and increased land value, leading to many locals not being able to afford the prices asked for products, houses and land. Many developing countries (but also destinations within developed countries) experience the problem of leakage (see Fig. 9.1). While multinational travel companies might bring the tourists to a destination, they will also keep the profit, particularly if they also import the products offered in their business (e.g. foreign food being imported for a restaurant). Tourism is an activity characterized by seasonality, so while much money and many employment opportunities are provided to the community, it only happens during the tourist season, and throughout the low season, income has to be secured from alternative sources. In addition, while many employment opportunities might be generated through tourism development, this can lead to migration (people leaving their homes and families to find work in resorts), or labour has to be imported (migrants working in tourism resorts and thus competing for jobs with the locals). Low productivity, low wages and semi-skilled and unskilled jobs are further negative features of tourism employment. Furthermore, the attractiveness of working within the tourism sector may lead to other industries (such as agriculture or manufacturing) not being able to attract enough workers. On a macro economic level, if a destination receives its main income from tourism, there is

S. Heitmann and P. Robinson

a significant danger of over-dependence. This dependency will only pay off if nothing happens that could affect the profitability of tourism activity, such as witnessed in recent years by the impacts of global events such as 9/11, SARS and foot-and-mouth disease.

Environmental impacts

Environmental impacts have received the most attention, as these are the most visible form of impact that tourism can have. When talking about the environment, reference is made to the natural environment (mountains, sea, lakes, rivers, beaches, forests, etc.), natural resources (air, water, land or the climate in general) and the built environment (buildings, villages and towns, transport infrastructure). Tourism and the environment have a very close relationship, as many destinations are famous for their environmental qualities, making the environment the main attractor of tourists to the destination.

Increased tourist numbers and tourism activities can have a direct impact on the environment through pollution, be that air or water pollution, but also noise pollution and visual pollution (e.g. theme parks). Further damage can be caused to the ecosystem through the loss of flora and fauna and disturbance of wildlife. Erosion of beaches and soils is another problem many destinations are faced with. More tourists also cause more waste through litter or solid waste and incidents like increased risk of fire from discarded cigarettes. Human behaviour also leads to vandalism and over-utilization of resources. Finally, it should not be forgotten that urbanization, crowding and congestion can result in a loss of aesthetic value. This is a vicious circle because the very features which draw tourists to certain destinations can lose their attractiveness through increased visitation, making them less attractive to visitors.

Tourism can, however, have positive impacts on the environment. The increased attention paid to a destination fosters awareness of conservation as both tourists and locals are educated about the value of conservation and preservation of natural areas and historic sites. This in turn can lead to environmental improvements, e.g. through community improvement programmes, improvement of infrastructure, redevelopment of old/redundant buildings and other measures.

Sociocultural impacts

Sociocultural impacts are less visible but can have more severe consequences as they affect the society and culture of a community (e.g. values, lifestyle, morals, religion, family structure, language, traditions, customs). Among the sociocultural impacts, again we can find positive and negative impacts. Tourism activity within a destination contributes to the maintenance and support of local services (e.g. public transport, health care) as well as the provision of new facilities and attractions, such as cultural or entertainment facilities and sports centres which are not only accessible to tourists but to locals as well.

Furthermore, tourism can provide opportunities for cultural exchange, thus facilitating increased social contact in more isolated communities. The establishment of partnerships for tourism-related activity could contribute to better communication within the destination. The interest that tourists show for local culture can trigger greater awareness and the preservation/revitalization of local customs, crafts and cultural identities among locals. If a destination offers new opportunities (such as the economic effects outlined above), rural areas can benefit through repopulation and a reversal of the trend towards decline and migration. In more traditional or isolated rural communities, the role of women can change and provide opportunities for women to participate in tourism activity through employment that was previously denied to them. Many rural areas, picturesque though they seem, often hide significant and serious pockets of social and financial deprivation.

On the other hand, tourism has been criticized by many for the negative sociocultural impacts that it can bring to a local community. Disturbances occur, particularly in high season, through congestion, crowding, noise, litter and pollution. Invasion of privacy (see Fig. 9.2) and reduction in local services as well as increases in crime and antisocial behaviour (by tourists, but also by locals as a result of increased tourism activity) have significant impacts on community life and can add to social stress. Due to demand, tourist shops might drive out local businesses. Besides the positive impacts of more employment, tourism can have an impact on population structure through the migration of workers. Jobs tend to be seasonal and working conditions might not be very good. In developing countries it is common to employ expatriates for the higher paid management jobs while locals take up the front-line menial jobs.

The increased influx of tourists has a significant influence on the traditional way of life and can lead to transformation of values among the community as they are witnessing tourists' behaviour (see 'Demonstration effect' in Chapter 10 (this volume) for further explanation).

Fig. 9.2. Sign in Binibeca, Menorca, asking tourists to respect the environment and the need for residents' privacy.

S. Heitmann and P. Robinson

CASE STUDY 1: SANI PASS, LESOTHO

Lesotho is one of the poorest countries, with difficult access due to its mountainous location. Sani Pass is located at the border to South Africa and only accessible by 4 × 4s. In 1955, the first tour operator was established and many companies have followed to take tourists, mainly daytrippers, from Underberg in KwaZulu-Natal (South Africa) up the Sani Pass across the border to Sani Top Chalet, the highest pub in Africa, which offers meals and basic accommodation for travellers. There is a small community living in traditional huts who earn most of their money from herding animals and some agriculture, but have now become part of the tourism system by offering insights into their communal life (such as bread making, see picture). They receive small change from the tour operators and tips from the tourists. One of these visits can provide them with enough money for a week's living expenses.

Questions

What impacts can you identify from these pictures, both visible and invisible?

If there was a proposition to tarmac the road up to Sani Pass, would you argue in favour or against it? Consider the points of view of the tourists, the locals, the pub owner and the tour companies.

(Photographs courtesy of Sine Heitmann)

Having outlined the various impacts that tourism can have, it is important to bear in mind that the discussion above is a rather generalized picture and there are several determinants of tourism impacts that have to be taken into account. Tourism can have short- or long-term impacts (think of events like Glastonbury or the Olympics, which have massive impacts for a short space of time, while tourism activity taking place throughout the year might have a lesser but steadier impact). Impacts can be on a global scale (aviation is often seen as a main culprit for global climate change through CO_2 emissions) or just pertinent to the local level (overcrowding in historic city centres). Some tourism activities have direct impacts (the building of hotels on the immediate environment), while other activities have indirect impacts (the changing employment structure within a destination). Furthermore, we should take the different sectors into account. The transport sector for example causes different impacts on a destination than the accommodation sector, not just the direct environmental impacts of pollution from emissions, but also in the development of transport infrastructures, such as roads, airports and parking facilities. Further determinants of tourism impacts are the volume of tourists (200 people have less of an impact than 20,000 considering they are all participating in the same type of activity at the same rate), the types of tourism activity (e.g. golf tourism requires more and different resources than visiting a museum), the structure of the host economy, the difference in sociocultural characteristics between the host and the guest (see Chapter 10, this volume, for a more detailed discussion) and the fragility of the local environment (e.g. the Galapagos Islands have a unique, fragile environment which has to be safeguarded from any influence from the mainland).

Sustainable Tourism

The underlying philosophy of sustainability and sustainable development is very much based on the saying 'We do not inherit the Earth from our forefathers, but borrow it from our children' (Indian proverb). The positive economic impacts outlined above led many regions to embrace tourism as an agent for change and to trigger economic development. Historically, much emphasis was placed on the economic prospects and quite often there was no proper tourism planning in place; this led to uncontrolled tourism development with many negative environmental impacts. Since the 1980s there has been a break from this economic growth-based focus. In 1987, the World Commission on Environment and Development (The Brundtland Commission) defined sustainability as 'meeting the needs of the present generation without compromising the ability of future generations to meet their own needs'. This definition is rather wide and subject to many different interpretations; nevertheless, it provided a suitable basis for further development of ideas.

With regard to tourism, many academics have taken this definition as a basis for discussion and several further definitions have been developed and proposed. Sustainable tourism development has not only received much attention from scholars, but governments are becoming more and more concerned about the concept of sustainability applied to tourism. The definition proposed by the WTO (1999) reflects the ideas put forward by the Brundtland Commission by suggesting 'sustainable tourism development meets the needs of present tourists and host regions while protecting and enhancing opportunities for the future'. Similarly, sustainable tourism is defined as 'tourism which is economically viable but does not destroy the resources on which the future of tourism will depend, notably the physical environment and the social fabric of the host community' (Swarbrooke, 1999, p. 13) This means that tourist resources (natural, historical, cultural and others) are managed in a way that allows them to be used in the future, while benefiting today's society; planning and management of tourist development is conducted in a way that minimizes ecological or sociocultural problems in a host region. The overall quality of the environment is preserved and, if necessary, improved; levels of tourist satisfaction maintained that destinations continue to be attractive and retain commercial potential. In short,

S. Heitmann and P. Robinson

tourism should benefit all members of society, be they locals, businesses, government or tourists.

Leading on from the impacts discussed above, sustainable travel should aim to minimize any negative impacts while at the same time enhancing the positive impacts. The principles of sustainable tourism include the sustainable use of resources, which means that any natural or cultural resource within a destination should be used to the extent that it will be preserved for future host and tourist generations to use it in the same manner. Hence, tourism should contribute to ecological sustainability through:

- preservation and protection of ecosystems;
- conservation of resources;
- reduction of emissions;
- social and cultural sustainability;
- intercultural exchange;
- mutual understanding among people of different nationalities, languages, religions;
- conservation of social and cultural values;
- economic sustainability through qualitative economic growth;
- protection of local sources of income; and
- improvement of living conditions.

As sustainable tourism adapts many of the key ideas of sustainable development, the contribution of tourism towards sustainability is seen as essential. Figure 9.3 outlines how tourism and sustainable tourism fit into the overall picture within the wider sustainable development environment, which considers town planning and wider involvement through manufacturing and agricultural industries also striving to develop environmental best practice.

Over the past decades many initiatives have been established in order to contribute to sustainable activities. These initiatives range from international collaboration, legislative changes, public–private sector collaboration, pressure group movements, etc. Particularly non-governmental organizations (NGOs) have been very active in pushing for sustainability to be added on any development agenda within destinations. One of the key organizations to be involved is Tourism Concern.

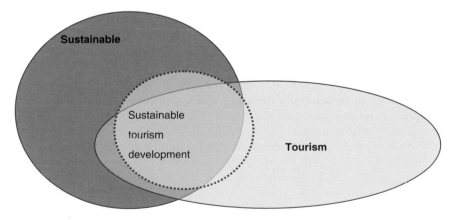

Fig. 9.3. Sustainable tourism. (Adapted from Hall, 2008.)

CASE STUDY 2: RESPONSIBLETRAVEL.COM

Responsible travel is about bringing you closer to local cultures and environments by involving local people in tourism. It is about doing this in a fair way that helps ensure that they will give you an even warmer welcome. For example, a local guide from the destination will open your eyes to their culture and way of life far better than an expatriate guide could ever do – they will also earn a much-needed income from you. Responsibletravel.com brings together over 270 operators and hundreds of villas, lodges, bed and breakfasts (B&Bs) and small hotels. Some of their environmentally sensitive travel suggestions include the following:

- Plan routes to minimize carbon emissions – travel by train and public transport where possible, and minimize internal flights.
- Minimize flying time and stopovers – the worst carbon emissions take place during take-off and landing.
- Ask to see the tour operator's policy for responsible tourism. All responsible travel.com members have to have one. Make sure it explains how they minimize environmental impacts *and* support the local economy.
- Read up on local cultures and learn a few words of the local language – travelling with respect earns you respect.
- Remove excess packaging – waste disposal is difficult in remote places and developing countries.
- Ask your tour operator for specific tips for responsible travel in your destination.
- Ask your tour operator/hotel if there are useful gifts that you could pack for your hosts, local people or schools.
- Ask the tour operator whether there are local conservation or social projects that could be visited on the trip, and if/how they could be supported.
- Buy local produce in preference to imported goods.
- Hire a local guide – you will discover more about local culture and lives, and they will earn an income.
- Do not buy products made from endangered species, hard woods or ancient artefacts.
- Respect local cultures, traditions and holy places – if in doubt ask advice or do not visit.
- Use public transport, hire a bike or walk when convenient – it is a great way to meet local people on their terms and reduce pollution and carbon emissions.
- Use water sparingly – it is very precious in many countries and tourists tend to use far more than local people.
- Remember that local people have different ways of thinking and concepts of time, this just makes them different, not wrong – cultivate the habit of asking questions (rather than the Western habit of knowing the answers).

In addition, responsibletravel.com founded The Responsible Tourism Awards in 2004 and run the awards in partnership with Telegraph Travel, World Travel Market and *Geographical Magazine* – the magazine of The Royal Geographical Society. Virgin Holidays has been headline sponsors of the awards since 2007.

The central tenet of the awards is that all types of tourism – from niche to mainstream – can and should be operated in a way that respects and benefits

Continued

230   S. Heitmann and P. Robinson

destinations and local people. These awards recognize individuals, companies and organizations in the travel industry that are making a significant commitment to the cultures and economies of local communities and are providing a positive contribution to biodiversity conservation.

The Responsible Tourism Awards are different from other awards schemes in that winners are nominated by tourists. One of the founding principles of these awards is always to seek out new responsible tourism ventures that deserve to be celebrated and public nominations are fundamental to this process.

(Source: Case study provided by Katie Fewings, www.responsibletravel.com)

Tourism Planning

Tourism planning is closely related to tourism policy. Very simply put, tourism policy is whatever a government chooses to do or not to do in relation to tourism – it includes the actions, inactions, decisions and non-decisions, thus implying the deliberate choice of a government between alternatives. A policy is heavily influenced by the political environment, values, ideologies, institutional frameworks and decision-making processes that are pertinent to a country. Studying tourism policy is very useful in order to understand the consequences of decisions and to seek solutions for any potential problems (such as tourism impacts). Tourism planning on the other hand is the more practical approach of putting a policy into action as its purpose is to create plans of action and to assure their implementation.

With the recognition of the negative impacts of narrowly planned or unplanned tourism development, many ideas have been generated for the reorientation of tourism planning and development towards sustainable, 'alternative', forward-looking approaches as opposed to typical corrective planning. Four traditional approaches towards tourism planning were identified (see Hall, 2008).

Boosterism was characterized by the extensive promotion of a destination to encourage demand and the facilitation of rapid and mainly uncontrolled growth of tourism. This type of approach could be witnessed in many Western countries that developed mass tourism in their destinations during the 1960s and 1970s (e.g. France, Spain and Italy). Attractions were established, transportation infrastructure provided and services created in order to provide the basis for massive tourism generation. Residents of these tourist destinations are usually not involved in the process of tourism development. This rather unbalanced form of planning still remains a dominant approach towards tourism planning in many regions whereby tourism resources (be it natural or cultural) are exploited, resulting in many of the negative impacts identified above. The underlying belief of this approach is quantity over quality.

The *economic approach* towards tourism planning evolved as an alternative approach to boosterism. Tourism is not only seen as a creator of jobs and revenue but also as a stimulator of other, associated economic activities (see multiplier effect) and as a tool for modernization; thus, this approach was favoured among developing countries. However, given its similarity to the boosterism approach, the economic approach was also heavily criticized for ignoring potential negative sociocultural and environmental impacts. Many of the Mediterranean countries were characterized by this approach towards tourism planning, but it can be argued that most countries and regions take this approach.

A *physical/spatial approach* towards tourism planning includes a higher focus on land-use planning as planning of facilities from a more geographical perspective. It is concerned with the development of specific tourist resorts and complexes with the primary purpose of developing new destinations. External planners and international agencies providing the financial back-up and technical know-how mainly influenced this approach. This last point gave rise for the main criticism of this approach – the non-involvement of locals and local governments, which in turn led to major economic leakages. Further negative impacts were the restricted access to public areas and overcrowding in coastal resorts. While it is uncommon to find a country that adopted the approach for tourism on a national level, this approach is quite common at a regional level.

A more bottom-up approach is the *community approach*, which implies the direct involvement of community in the tourism planning process in order to prevent any potential conflicts between hosts and guests, thus increasing the benefits of tourism to the community. As this requires a very democratic approach it has often been seen as an idealistic approach which may work in smaller communities but is less feasible in larger regions which are characterized by varied communities with unique requirements and different perspectives on tourism development.

Hall (2008) added a fifth dimension, *sustainable tourism planning*, which is 'a concern for the long-term future of resources' and thus in line with the underlying philosophy of sustainable development as outlined above. This approach is more holistic in its nature as it takes all impacts into account, sees tourism as one element within the overall economy of the destination and as an element of the overall destination development plan. The focus here is on long-term planning, public–private partnerships, continuous monitoring and cooperation among all stakeholders affected by tourism within the destination. This notion of partnership has developed since Hall's model and is now the preferred delivery method of most destination management organizations, working closely with a wide range of stakeholders, rather than just being a tool for sustainability. This means that all planning and operational management in the sector is governed by the needs of host and visitor communities within the destination.

Table 9.1 summarizes the planning traditions with the core ideas and the questions that are formulated in order to direct the process for finding solutions and making decisions.

Mass tourism, encouraged by the early approaches towards tourism planning, has generally been seen as the culprit for all the impacts and negative consequences of tourism, and thus many have been quick to argue that mass tourism is unsustainable. This has led to the search of many alternative forms of tourism. However, these arguments can be seen as quick responses to the question 'who is to blame?'.

These planning approaches should be regarded as general strands that can be overlapping with each other (you hardly find one particular planning approach within a destination), rather than in a chronological order. However, although traditional approaches still exist (many destinations view tourism as an economic development option), more recent concepts concerning sustainable planning prevail. A further note of caution has to be mentioned here, that tourism planning is considered to be more complicated than other planning, as there are many stakeholders involved and tourism

S. Heitmann and P. Robinson

Table 9.1. Planning traditions. (Adapted from Hall, 2008.)

Planning tradition	Underlying assumptions	Questions to be asked and answered
Boosterism	– Tourism is good and should be developed – Cultural and natural resources are to be exploited to maximum use – Development defined in business terms – industry as expert	– How many tourists can be attracted and accommodated? – How can obstacles be overcome? – How can locals be convinced to be good hosts to tourists?
Economic	– Tourism equal to other industries – Use tourism to create employment, earn foreign revenue, encourage regional development – Development defined in economic terms – planner as expert	– How can tourism be used as a growth trigger? – How can income be maximized and employment multiplied? – How can consumer choice be influenced?
Physical/spatial	– Tourism as a resource user – Ecological basis to development – environmental conservation – Development defined in environmental terms	– What is the physical carrying capacity? – How can travel patterns and visitor flows be manipulated? – How can visitors be concentrated or dispersed? – How can wilderness and national parks be managed, how should environmental areas be designated?
Community	– Need for local control – Search for alternatives to 'mass' tourism development – Development defined in sociocultural terms – planner as facilitator rather than expert	– What are community attitudes towards tourism? – What are the impacts of tourism on the community? – How can community control be fostered?
Sustainable	– Integration of economic, environmental and sociocultural values – Tourism planning integrated with other planning processes – Preservation of ecological processes and protection of human heritage and biodiversity – Inter- and intra-generational equity	– How can all elements of the tourism system be integrated? – How can public and private sectors work together? – How can local needs be met and local trades be successful in the marketplace?

is therefore not under the control of one owner. Tourism has no solitary aim but many different objectives (although for governments and businesses involved the economic ones usually prevail). Given that tourism is based on voluntary travel, it seems that tourism planning is almost an oxymoron, attempting to tackle such an unplanned phenomenon. In addition, tourism planning requires creativity that is difficult to achieve in consideration of the unpredictable nature of tourist demand.

Structures for Sustainability

Tourism planning happens at the international, national and regional levels and a range of different bodies are involved in the tourism planning process. At the international level, there are international agencies working together in order to harmonize tourism activities across national boundaries. While there may not be many examples for tourism-specific organizations, there are generic trade organizations such as the International Monetary Fund (IMF), the Organization for Economic Cooperation and Development (OECD) and the World Trade Organization (WTO) which indirectly influence tourism planning through economic policies. Further international organizations with a more travel-related focus are the World Tourism Organizations (WTO), the World Heritage Committee (UNESCO), the World Travel and Tourism Council (WTTC), the International Civil Aviation Organization (ICAO), the International Air Transport Association (IATA) and international organizations with a focus on human rights and environmental issues such as Greenpeace, Tourism Concern, World Wildlife Fund and ECPAT.

International example: European Union

The European Union (EU) does not have specific, direct competence in tourism, but its involvement in tourism activity has evolved over the past three decades. In 1986, the Tourism Advisory Committee was established to facilitate exchange of information, consultation and cooperation on tourism. The year 1990 was the 'European Year of Tourism', which emphasized the role of tourism and the importance of developing a coherent policy approach across the member states. The Maastricht Treaty in 1992 was the first treaty to mention tourism and authorized the EU to provide guidelines for tourism-related activities. Today, the importance of EU to tourism is twofold: directly through the EU Tourism Policy and indirectly through other common policies.

In 2006, 'A Renewed European Tourism Policy: Towards a Stronger Partnership for European Tourism' was published and the main aims were to improve the competitiveness of the European tourism industry and to create more and better jobs through the sustainable growth of tourism. The main areas within the document included the review of legislation and improvement of regulation, a coordination of tourism policies across the member states, the promotion of sustainable tourism, the enhancement of the understanding and visibility of European tourism through common promotion (www.visiteurope.com) and the improvement in use of available European financial instruments.

The indirect influence of the EU on tourism in Europe is further manifested through EU legislation, policy and programmes which affect the tourist, the economic and social environment and the field of culture and environment – some examples are presented in Table 9.2.

S. Heitmann and P. Robinson

Table 9.2. EU legislation, policy and programmes.

Policy	Purpose	Examples for influence on travel and tourism
The Single European Act (1987, completed by 31 December 1992)	The free movement of people, goods, services and capital Harmonization of VAT	Facilitates travelling across national boundaries Facilitates operation of business across national boundaries
EU Consumer Protection Policy	The 1990 Directives on Package Travel	Affects tour operators and their duties to comply with these regulations
Economic and Monetary Union	The euro	Removal of currency exchange when travelling to most countries
EU Environmental Legislation	The European Blue Flag Scheme (1987) The Sixth Environmental Action Programme (2002)	Designation of beaches that comply with environmental guidelines Review of environmental policies affecting transport and tourism
EU Employment and Social Policy	Community Charter of Fundamental Social Right of Workers	Harmonization of employees' rights (including tourism-related organizations)
EU Transport Policy	Liberalization of the transport of goods and passenger Trans-European networks	Open Air Policy for the aviation industry Channel Tunnel
Structural Funds	European Regional Development Fund (ERDF) European Social Funds (ESF) European Agricultural Fund for Rural Development European Fisheries Fund	Support of socio-economic development Funds sustainable tourism-related projects Co-finances projects targeting educational programmes and training Improving the quality of agricultural production and products Improving the environment and the countryside Encouraging tourist activities as part of the diversification of the rural economy objective Studies and investments associated with the maintenance, restoration and upgrading of the cultural heritage Sustainable development of fisheries areas through restructuring and diversification (e.g. ecotourism)
The European Investment Bank		Loans to small- and medium-sized hotels Loans for other tourism and tourism-related businesses Large-scale projects contribution to the EU's tourism appeal

On a national and international level, it is mainly the public sector that is involved in tourism planning with some additional input from multinational corporations in the sector. Generally, the public sector works at a national level through central government, then through regional government to local government. Often, tourism is similarly managed nationally through a government department or through a destination management organization working with national government, supporting and supported by regional and local destination management.

The reasons for public sector involvement on a national level are to earn foreign currency, gain increased tax revenue, attract foreign capital for investment, revitalize areas, stimulate interest in the arts, project a good image and increase friendship with other countries. The roles are equally varied. The national tourism policy is framed and drawn up to provide the basis for tourism planning. The national government controls tourist activity through legislation and regulation in order to stimulate or restrict tourism development and to assure the smooth running of tourism activities. The public sector plays an important role in terms of coordination of tourism activities and the cooperation between different agencies, and furthermore in the provision of necessary education and training within the tourism sector. Another role is the stimulation of entrepreneurial activity and investment or direct ownership through financial or fiscal incentives, research funding and funding for national tourism organizations. Finally, the public sector is responsible for the marketing and promotion of the overall destination.

The role of the local authorities is established in the Local Government Act of 1948 and 1972 which identifies the local authorities' main responsibility as ensuring:

- provision of information and publicity services for tourism;
- provision of tourism and leisure facilities;
- upkeep of historic buildings;
- environmental protection;
- engagement in tourism planning;

S. Heitmann and P. Robinson

- production of statistics;
- assistance in funding;
- staffing of local tourist information centres;
- public health and safety and licensing; and
- provision of other public services.

Effective tourism planning requires the harmonization of the local development plans, often referred to as the Local Plan, which identify the objectives of national and regional plans (see Fig. 9.4), guidelines for successful tourism development, applying sound principles and methodological processes, public–private sector coordination, conducting pilot projects, securing incentives leading to successful implementation, establishing high quality standards, effective training/education initiatives, appropriate tourist information and education, continuous monitoring, political commitment and strong leadership, satisfying stakeholder demands and community involvement.

Liaising with stakeholders is more difficult than it seems, as the stakeholders of a destination are wide and varied and include local residents' groups, business groups, special interest groups, external consultants/advisers as well as regional and national tourism groups. On the local level, it is achievable; however, on the regional and national levels, it is much more difficult to achieve. Furthermore, taking the example in Fig. 9.4, for a populous destination like London, it is an immense challenge to include all stakeholders. This requires careful consideration as to who is to be represented in the liaison over tourism planning issues.

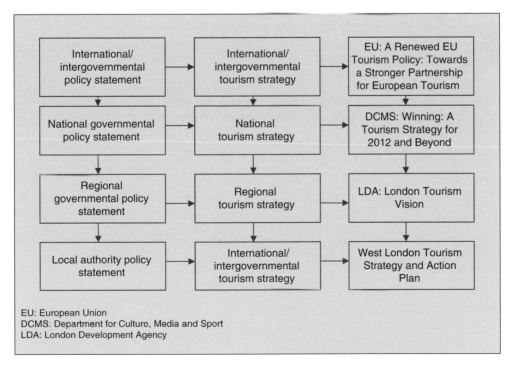

Fig. 9.4. Planning at international, national, regional and local levels: example UK.

Baobab Travel Ltd is a UK-based specialist ecotour operator, born out of a combination of a love of Africa and travel and a desire to actively work with and support local communities in the developing world. It is the company's belief that travel and tourism have an enormous capacity to provide much needed economic growth within developing countries. However, we also recognize the fact that it has the potential to inflict irreversible damage on fragile environments and communities. It is our aim to reconcile these two conflicting aspects and provide a form of sustainable tourism that is sensitive to the destination and yet still provides clients with a holiday experience of a lifetime.

In order to assess both the quality and sustainability of the lodges and activities offered, representatives from the company visit each location before offering it within itineraries. Time is taken to talk with, and assess, staff in terms of commitment to responsible tourism principles. In some countries, there are existing accreditation standards which allow an easy assessment of a lodge's commitment to responsible tourism – e.g. Fair Trade in Tourism South Africa (FTTSA). Where such accreditation is not in place, it is often left to the company to assess claims towards sustainability/ fair trade made by suppliers. In order to better quantify this, the company has worked with the University of Wolverhampton and Tourism Concern to produce a questionnaire-based assessment system which has proved vital in assessing new suppliers.

The company relies on customer feedback to ensure that lodges maintain their responsible tourism standards. As well as asking for customers to provide feedback on their holiday experience, questions are asked regarding their impressions of sustainability/fair trade practices at each destination. A detailed pre-departure pack containing responsible travel guidelines is posted to each customer prior to departure to ensure that they are informed of these issues before departing. A reasonable return rate of around 40–50% of feedback forms has been achieved and, where negative feedback is given, this is always passed on to the supplier concerned.

As business develops Baobab Travel expects to widen its portfolio of destinations offered and also to include more locally managed cultural tourism programmes in customer programmes. New programmes in Namibia and Malawi have been offered in the last 12 months as the company strives to offer both mainstream and more off-the-beaten-path destinations. As each new location is developed the emphasis will always be on promoting itineraries focused around locally owned and/or managed lodges to ensure that as much of the guests' money as possible will remain in the host country.

(Source: Case study provided by Paul Geiss, Baobab Travel)

Having outlined the characteristics of tourism planning and its importance in achieving sustainable tourism development, we are now taking a more focused approach and providing an outline of sustainable tourism initiatives that have been implemented at various levels and in various destinations and which are generally considered to be good practice in assuring the sustainability for tourism resources.

Sustainable Tourism Initiatives

Over the years there has been a range of initiatives designed to meet the requirements for more sustainable development of tourism. As indicated above, mass tourism has always been considered to be inherently unsustainable, which automatically implies that all forms of tourism that are an alternative to mass tourism have to be sustainable. Under the general heading of alternative tourism, an outline is given for some of these alternatives, although research in tourism academia and practice will give further examples which may include niche tourism, special interest tourism and green tourism.

Further, initiatives are those implemented and encouraged by the government. These include regulatory control and legislation for the designation of protected areas. Practices originating from the field of geography are outlined, explaining how they fit into the idea of sustainable tourism. Finally, good practices from the industry are exemplified.

Alternative tourism

Generally, effective ways of encouraging sustainable tourism practices involve looking at the bigger picture. Alternative forms of tourism to be offered to the consumer have emerged over the past decades and include, among others, ecotourism, propoor tourism (PPT) and fair trade tourism (FTT).

Ecotourism

Ecotourism is commonly defined as 'tourism that consists in travelling to relatively undisturbed uncontaminated natural areas with the specific objective of studying, admiring and enjoying the scenery and its wild plants and animals, as well as any existing cultural manifestations (both past and present) found in these areas' (Ceballos-Láscurain, cited in Weaver, 1998). The focus with ecotourism is on the environment and minimizing any negative environmental impacts, while later redefinitions have added fostering awareness among tourists and locals about the importance of preservation and conservation to the key principles. Ecotourism has been subject to much discussion, and the problems with a precise definition have led to different classifications of ecotourism (hard and soft forms) and ecotourists ('do-it-yourself' to scientific, hard core to casual, rough to smooth) that reflect the attitudes of the planners, developers and consumers. Consequently, the range of products includes eco, responsible, green, cultural, soft and ethnic tourism. However, given the contentions surrounding the definition, the key aspect of sustainability within ecotourism lies with the motivations of tourists. Ecotourism is targeted on the conservation and preservation of natural resources, social awareness and a non-consumptive character. The concept receives much support from international organizations, such as the WTO, which provide recommendations for adequate ecotourism planning reflecting the ideas of sustainable tourism:

- Integrate ecotourism policies across national boundaries and across national, regional and local levels.
- Create a planning framework for protected areas, including more funding.
- Develop tools for sustainability, such as visitor management and land use.
- Integrate planning: involve all stakeholders.
- Build local capacity (WTO, 2002).

Ecotourism has been rejected by some as a viable practice for sustainable tourism as it focuses primarily on environmental issues and less so on sociocultural and economic aspects. Furthermore, this focus on the environment as the primary attraction results in more tourists being pulled towards the environment and thus putting more pressure on natural resources. Therefore, it is argued that ecotourism is a contradiction in terms and seems to contribute to the negative cycle of tourism development. Finally, many companies or tour operators adopting ecotourism as a product have been accused of using ecotourism as a marketing tool and jumping on the bandwagon in order to satisfy the changing demand of their consumers, without necessarily implementing any ecotourism practices. Nevertheless, many destinations have adopted ecotourism as guidelines, primarily on a local or regional level, but also on a national level (e.g. Costa Rica). Furthermore, although the focus is on nature and the natural environment, there have been recent examples of urban ecotourism (e.g. Toronto, London, Dubai).

Question

Is urban ecotourism a reality or a contradiction in terms?

Propoor tourism

PPT is based on the idea that tourism has the potential to improve the quality of life for many of the world's poor and is broadly defined as tourism that generates net benefits (meaning benefits outweighing the costs) for the poor. The principles underlying PPT are participation of all stakeholders involved, a holistic livelihoods approach, distribution, flexibility, commercial realism and learning. The strategies for PPT are outlined in Table 9.3.

Useful in its ideology, PPT is not without its problems. Like other alternative forms of tourism, PPT focuses mainly on one aspect – poverty. Environmental concerns are part of it, but play a minor role. As with any other form of sustainable tourism it requires the involvement of all stakeholders, which always proves to be difficult given the different ideas of each stakeholder as to what constitutes good practice. Furthermore, PPT focuses directly on tourism destinations in the poorer developing countries (ProPoor Tourism, 2005).

Table 9.3. Propoor tourism. (Adapted from ProPoor Tourism, 2005.)

Increase economic benefits	Enhance non-financial livelihood impacts	Enhance participation and partnership
1. Boost local employment, wages 2. Boost local enterprise opportunities 3. Create collective community income sources – fees, revenue shares, donations	1. Capacity building, training 2. Mitigate environmental impacts 3. Address competing use of natural resources 4. Improve social, cultural impacts 5. Increase local access to infrastructure and services	1. Create more supportive policy/planning framework 2. Increase participation of the poor in decision making 3. Build propoor partnerships with private sector 4. Increase flows of information, communication

S. Heitmann and P. Robinson

Fair trade tourism

Similarly to PPT, FTT is an approach to tourism development that is characterized by underlying principles that reflect the ideas of sustainable tourism. FTT is built on the ideas of the fair trade movement that was originally applied to products such as coffee and bananas, as it demands a fair share of benefits for local stakeholders through reducing leakages and increasing linkages. Tourists are asked to pay a fair price instead of asking for a bargain holiday. Revenues should be distributed fairly among the stakeholders instead of exploiting the local labour. Further principles include fair competition among businesses without any dominance by larger companies. The use of local products and materials should be encouraged by using local suppliers instead of relying on the import of foreign goods, and employees should be able to enjoy fair pay and working conditions. Furthermore, open and transparent information and education for the consumer is encouraged. FTT is not a widespread idea yet but growing in importance, particularly in South Africa.

Again, there are potential negatives to consider. While fair trade might be tapping into the market of the conscious consumer, FTT has less potential to become a mainstream market as the mass consumer is less likely to be prepared to pay the premium price that comes with fair trade products. This last point leads us to a more general criticism of these alternative approaches to tourism and ways of travelling. Tourism is inherently a market-driven industry which is determined by demand and supply and subject to the principles of consumerism and consumption. While these alternative approaches towards tourism might give us alternative products and reflect the trend of alternative consumption, mass tourism and the mass consumer will not just disappear, but are instead more likely to be the dominant market sector. Thus, as long as consumer patterns do not change, the travel industries will cater for the demand of the masses. Even if alternative tourism can become the more dominant market, it will then create the paradox that the alternative tourism has become the new mass tourism.

Community participation

Community involvement or community participation in tourism planning and development is one of the key ideas behind sustainable tourism development. Unlike the alternative approaches to tourism outlined above, community participation can be incorporated in any type of tourism development. Involving the local community in the decision-making process is facilitated by:

- establishing permanent advisory and consultative tourism committees or forums;
- ensuring the widest possible community representation;
- providing consultation and financial support by government bodies at all levels;
- informing communities of the implications of proposals through outside speakers and experts;
- holding public hearings and meetings on planning issues;
- providing materials and documentaries, design workshops and visual presentations to inform and educate;
- balloting the community on key issues with opportunities to vote for alternatives;
- using small group processes and focus groups;

- initiating education and training programmes to raise the career profile and quality of tourism employment; and
- ensuring the widest possible local community participation through events, festivals and other activities.

Again, as the list makes clear, these are all good ideas with a sound ideology but community participation is none the less difficult to achieve.

As Bahaire and Elliot-White (1999) list, among the obstacles to effective community involvement are the following:

- As there is lack of proprietorship over land and natural resources, participation in tourism is limited to cooption in ventures controlled by outsiders.
- There is a lack of appropriate skills, knowledge and resources to develop tourism ventures.
- There are difficulties in accumulation/attraction of capital necessary to develop tourism facilities/attractions.
- Range of different interest groups within a community might compete for potential tourism ventures – through local elite who might control the decision making.
- Local community versus global players in industry could be compared to a David versus Goliath situation.
- Community participation is only viable on the local level; on a mass scale, it is too 'idealistic' (think of a large city like London, for example – how could consultation be planned so that *all* voices are heard?).
- The need for governmental support is crucial to match local initiatives with national policies.

Regulatory control and legislative methods

Government legislation can be a very effective measure to minimize negative impacts on the environment. As outlined above, the government is heavily involved in the planning for tourism development – just as they can plan for tourism use they can also encourage the restriction of land use for tourism purposes. Land can be designated for certain purposes to spread specific types of development activities across a designated area and thus prevent overuse. The National Parks and Access to the Countryside Act (1949) is a good example of conservation through government-protected sites such as national parks, areas of outstanding natural beauty and heritage coasts. The Wildlife and Countryside Act (1981) focuses on marine nature reserves and sites of special scientific interest.

On an international level, EU Directives can lead to conservation of the national environment, such as the EU Bathing Water Directive 1976. UNESCO in turn is responsible for the designation of World Heritage Sites, which requires the following of certain guidelines to conserve the site.

Other initiatives introduced by the government are through taxation, for example a pollution tax which encourages visitors *not* to pollute, or visitor payback schemes where visitors to national parks have to pay for entry.

Debate: visitor payback

National parks in the UK traditionally appeal to a daytrip market, whether through individuals travelling in cars or through organized tours. Whichever mode of transport is chosen, neither group makes much in the way of economic contribution to the local area. Most daytrippers buy petrol before they leave home and bring a pre-packed picnic or buy lunch in a local supermarket, so this money never enters the economy, and once at the destination they possibly pay for admission to an attraction or purchase an ice cream.

One commonly proposed solution is visitor payback, where an entry fee is levied for visitors to the national park. Taking the estimated Peak District visitor figures, as this is the second most visited national park in the world, of 24 million visitors and assuming this translates into approximately 4 million vehicles, then a charge of £2 per car and £10 per coach would quickly bring in several million pounds in revenue, but at what cost?

If visitor payback was implemented, would visits to attractions drop in response? Certainly, the scheme does little to encourage people to spend money with local businesses, so while the local authority benefits and has additional income to spend on the maintenance and development of infrastructure, there is still no more money coming into the local economy, where it would be of greater benefit through the multiplier effect.

But what are the alternatives? EU funding has supported numerous projects in the Peak District, providing business support, setting up local food producers' groups and increasing skill levels for the service industry in traditional farming communities. These projects make some difference to local businesses, indeed research suggested an average 33% increase in turnover over a 2-year period, but some of this could be apportioned to a strong economy.

Another strategy is to consider the 'shoulder months', the off-peak periods where there is additional capacity. There is no point encouraging more visitors when overcrowding and congestion are already an issue in the high season. A visitor payback scheme could address the issue of overcrowding, but this might mean fewer people around to spend money or the same number spending less in the destination. The challenge with increasing business out of season is the fact that the same barriers to access still exist. The weather is unpredictable and most attractions are, at least in part, outdoors. Heritage attractions have to limit opening hours anyway for conservation, another consideration for sustainability, and, as it goes darker earlier in the day, travelling becomes more difficult.

It may be that there is no real solution, but the raised awareness of the issues through contemporary concerns about the environment and the wider debate about sustainability, not just from an environmental perspective but from a business perspective as well, has done some good in bringing together stakeholders to share ideas, create new initiatives and work together to manage the natural resources of national parks upon which destination success is built.

As a footnote, it is crucial to remember that sustainability is not necessarily just environmental, but must also consider the sustainability of businesses. If businesses cannot survive in a rural environment in order to bring in money to the local economy, then this has a knock-on impact on the management of the natural resource, which could be as detrimental as if the business was taking advantage of the natural landscape through quarrying and erosion of access.

(Source: Peak District Sustainable Tourism Forum, ERDF funded project 2004–2006)

Local Agenda 21

The United Nations Conference on Environment and Development in 1992 saw the inception of the Rio Declaration that became known as Agenda 21. The document is a programme of the UN that is related to sustainable development and entails a comprehensive plan of action, a blueprint to be taken globally, nationally and locally by organizations, local and national governments and major groups in every area in which there are human impacts on the environment. It was accepted by 178 governments and included 40 chapters with a total of 2500 items. Chapter 28 binds local authorities to implement commitments made by the international community; the reason for the focus at local level is the belief that any impacts have to be tackled at local level – think globally, act locally. Thus, as a requirement, each local authority has had to draw up its own Local Agenda 21 (LA21) strategy following discussion with its community about what they think is important for the area. This process involves local government, private sector and local interest. While there is no prescription for the issues involved (each locality has different priorities), the partners in each area identify areas to conform to LA21 concepts to focus on sustainability. Drawing up this document meant that local authorities could create a vision that enabled ways of involving people, joining up economic, environmental and social issues, reallocating existing, and seeking new, resources. The implementation of LA21 requires co-ownership between the local authority, community and environment. It needs to be inclusive and participative, have the involvement of elected members and establish a steering committee to consider how the local authority can best promote and facilitate LA21.

However, problems with the implementation in many communities include a lack of financial support, information, expertise, support from national government and community consensus to set priorities.

Carrying capacity

Carrying capacity has been defined as the maximum number of people who can use a site without any unacceptable alteration in the physical environment and without any unacceptable decline in the quality of the experience for tourists and the local residents. It can be a simple way of deciding how many visitors an area can accommodate before the volume of tourists begins to have a detrimental effect. Most often, carrying capacity is applied in the context of the natural environment, but there are several types of carrying capacity (Table 9.4).

Carrying capacity is a positive approach intended to minimize the negative impacts of tourism and is considered to be very practical as it makes it easy to determine when the maximum capacity is reached. This can then provide the basis for tourism planning, resource utilization and the range of facilities to be provided.

However, there have also been some criticisms. The concept is seen as unrealistic, as rarely is there a single, definitive figure which indicates whether carrying capacity is reached, as there are many variables coming into play depending on the destination. A city will cope with a larger number of tourists more easily than a seaside resort. A small village might be able to cope better with a large number of tourists than the village 5 miles down the road. While the concept is easy to grasp, it

Table 9.4. Carrying capacity.

Type	Definition	Measurement
Physical carrying capacity	Number of people that can be physically accommodated	Density of development (beds per hectare), intensity of use (visitors per hectare), ratios (tourists: residents)
Environmental carrying capacity	Number of people that can be accommodated at a site before damage to that site begins to occur	Perception of crowding and spatial quality (area per user), disturbance, conflicts with other user activities
Economic carrying capacity	Number of tourists that can be accommodated before the economic life of the local community begins to be adversely affected	Changes in land use, damage to vegetation, disturbance of wildlife, pollution (environmental impact assessment)
Social carrying capacity	Volume of visitors that can be accommodated before the host community/society/culture begins to be adversely affected	Extent of interaction and tourism dominance acceptable to host community (social surveys)
Infrastructural carrying capacity	Number of tourists that can be accommodated before the infrastructure becomes incapable of coping	Benefits achieved (economic models), employment gains (direct and indirect), congestion models
Perceptual carrying capacity	Number of people a site can absorb before the quality of the tourist experience is adversely affected	Costs of infrastructure provision (cost per head), capacities available (roads, water, power, waste treatment), benefits to community

is very difficult to put into practice. Carrying capacity is a management decision and can be managed to high or low capacity. The level is often determined by the characteristics of the resource, culture and management. It is a subjective judgement, depending on the person or group of people who makes their decision based on their underlying values and stance towards tourism as well as on quantitative and forecast data and evidence. Some of the types, such as perceptual and social, rely on highly subjective assessments as well. The carrying capacity of a destination or facility may only be identifiable once it has been exceeded. Further issues associated with the concept are that the imposition of a carrying capacity may fail to take into account the associated costs, e.g. the loss of income or jobs as a result of enforced limitations. Furthermore, it might be difficult to persuade individual business owners to accept the imposition of carrying capacity limits, as it will impact on their business (McCool and Lime, 2001).

When businesses do understand and are responsive to carrying capacity then they can work within limits of acceptable change. This allows managers to quantify how much change is acceptable over a given period of time. More than just the benefit of understanding what changes can take place, it allows systems to be put in place to rectify the damage or to provide alternatives while the damaged area recovers. This type of management practice is common within heritage and conservation organizations and, as many of these are charities, the bottom line is not focused on profit because any profit is reinvested in the work of the organization.

One common system for the management and protection of fragile environments is the use of environmental impact assessment. In simple terms, this can be as straightforward or complex as necessary, from a quick cost–benefit analysis to an in-depth ecological and biological survey. Development of theoretical and simulation models to forecast the impact of any change on the environment can be used and, where necessary, may be linked to costing models to assess the real costs and potential financial gains from any combination of changes to the environment. Examples may include resurfacing a popular footpath with concrete, which may seem a heavy-handed tool, but if it limits digression from footpaths, therefore protecting the wider environment and allowing an acceptable increase in visitor figures, then there may be some justification.

To take this a step further, Geographical Information Systems (GIS) can be used. These systems rely on complex satellite photography and mapping systems and can be used to map out everything from individual properties to wide areas of countryside to assess environmental impacts. They may rely on updated satellite photography or on-the-ground research and are particularly useful in the travel sector to map out damage caused by flight paths or to support or develop reports for the development of new transport infrastructure.

Zoning

Zoning is a practice often associated with national parks, as it is a key strategy for the management of protected areas. It involves the recognition of smaller zones or units within an area, each with different levels of environmental protection or public use, and has two main purposes: first, to protect the environment; and second, to provide recreation and tourism opportunities.

S. Heitmann and P. Robinson

Zoning can be done spatially (by designating geographical areas) or temporally (zones are closed for a certain period of time). Another way of using zoning as a management technique is to create 'honeypots' – attractive points that are created with the purpose of attracting as many tourists as possible in order to avert these tourists from more fragile areas.

Similarly, some honeypots have become honeypots through historical development. In these instances, careful management is required to limit the impacts and spread of visitors to more sensitive environs. Often these honeypots exist within villages and towns within sensitive locations, such as national parks.

and sports events take place on the beach and in town (attracting several thousand visitors).

Any tourist or day visitor is asked to pay €2.50 per day in form of a tourist tax. The money earned from this income is invested in the infrastructure and redevelopment (such as a new pier bridge and promenade or leisure facilities) as well as the cleaning of the beach. Having paid the tourist tax, visitors are able to use the local bus for free, access the beach without having to pay (otherwise €2.50 per person per day) and enjoy discounted access to leisure facilities, museums and other attractions:

- The beach is divided into five main tourist areas, each with a restaurant on stilts as well as life guarding facilities and toilets.
- There is also an area between the town and the beach which is protected and, while there is no fencing, tourists are discouraged from going there in large numbers.
- Large areas of the beach are dedicated to beach sports such as beach sailing or kite buggy.
- Close to this area is the coastal line that is dedicated to water sports such as windsurfing and kite surfing.
- In the very northern part of the beach a section is dedicated to nudists.

Most discussion in recent years has been around the parking area, which several years ago was limited to the current area and has been further limited from all-year-round parking to the months of March to October, and costs €4 per car (part of this parking fee goes to the national park).

Questions

What impacts can you identify? To what extent do the impacts differ depending on the activity – sports? Cars? Events?

How is zoning implemented in this town, both temporal and spatial? Can you detect any 'honeypots'?

The car park is a fenced off area; however, what problems do you see with it being right next to the environmentally sensitive area?

There have been discussions of not allowing any cars on the beach – consider the implications for the tourists, the restaurant owners, the local businesses in town, the local council, the residents, the national park authority?

Interpretation and education

The idea of interpretation and education within areas of natural and cultural heritage is very simple: raising awareness and increasing knowledge, and thereby changing the behaviour of both tourists and locals. Within protected areas this is carried out through the provision of tour guides. These guides can have multiple roles, educating visitors about the natural and/or cultural environment and preventing tourists from leaving the designated paths or routes and thereby

S. Heitmann and P. Robinson

destroying any part of the environment. They can also be used to promote environmental good practice on behalf of a business, explaining what the airline does to reduce carbon emissions or how a train recycles energy and sends it back to the national grid.

Certification

Eco-labelling is the voluntary procedure that assesses, audits and gives assurance that a business, facility, product, process, service or management system meets specific standards. An independent third party awards a marketable logo, the eco-label, to those who meet or exceed baseline standards. From a marketing perspective, this can help attract the new, more conscious consumer, enhance the business's image and increase tourist numbers and turnover. From a consumer perspective, the tourist can be assured that the business follows the guidelines for environmentally friendly operation of the business. The issues surrounding eco-labelling, however, are that the application of the certification is voluntary and not mandatory.

One example of an eco-label is the Green Globe that was established by the World Travel and Tourism Council (WTTC) as a result of the Agenda 21 principles. The objectives of Green Globe were: to increase environmental responsiveness within the industry, including suppliers and customers; to encourage participation on a global level; and to ensure that the beneficial links between good environmental practice and good business practice are understood. In order to achieve the Green Globe brand, all operations are required to undergo an assessment by an independent third party against the standards set by the Green Globe 21 Standard. After certification, operations must undergo an annual review to ensure the maintenance of their certified status. While it is an ambitious plan, there are concerns about whether a significant proportion of the industry will embrace it. This depends on the perceived and actual benefits of participating. Further concerns arise with the effectiveness of its implementation, as organizations can receive a benchmark label (which indicates that organizations are in the process of attaining certification) without eventually receiving the certified label. The problem here is that the two (benchmark and certified) labels look very similar and consumers might not recognize the difference, thus an organization may get away with marketing themselves as environmentally conscious without being engaged in environmentally friendly practices.

Another eco-label is the Blue Flag, which is owned and run by the independent non-profit organization Foundation for Environmental Education (FEE) and works towards sustainable development of beaches and marinas through strict criteria dealing with water quality, environmental education and information, environmental management and safety.

Similar to eco-labelling is the idea of awards. Most significant among these are the Tourism for Tomorrow Award, which is given by the WTTC to destinations and companies that showcase leading examples in sustainable tourism development, and the Virgin Responsible Travel Award, which recognizes good practice in a range of categories in partnership with other travel trade bodies.

CASE STUDY 5: FROM RELIEF TO SELF-RELIANCE: COMMUNITY-BASED TOURISM IN THE NORTH ANDAMAN COAST OF THAILAND

Andaman Discoveries (AD) support tsunami-affected communities along the Andaman coast of Thailand through community-based tourism (CBT) development, with the objective of becoming a social enterprise that is financially, culturally and ecologically sustainable. Our organization evolved from North Andaman Tsunami Relief (NATR) – an NGO that has implemented over 120 projects in 12 tsunami-affected communities, since 2005. After meeting basic needs, discussions led to livelihood development. Based on the popularity of nearby Phuket and Khao Lak, communities recognized the potential of tourism. However, after several community meetings, many villagers expressed concerns that tourism would undermine and threaten their culture and undeveloped coastal region. Villagers decided that CBT would provide additional income, support the continuity of their traditions and lifestyle and support sustainable resource management.

AD worked closely with the villagers to develop meaningful and interactive activities for guests, and to provide the necessary training to the villagers. At the early stage of development, we provided a 6-month tourism and community development training for 26 motivated villagers. AD encouraged local women to participate in CBT through homestay and handicraft production, especially for those who lost their husbands in the tsunami. Some of the women who previously had no jobs now can utilize their existing skills to make a living. This has significantly improved the livelihood for families that have lost the male head of household, who is traditionally the main income source, during the tsunami. We also helped the local soap cooperative, which was formed by tsunami widows, in marketing and promotion.

AD currently works closely with two villages. We offer responsible tours and volunteer placements in these communities, which have created numerous employment opportunities through homestay, handicraft production and guiding. AD maximizes the financial contribution to these villages by ensuring that the majority of the activities, lodging and meals take place in these villages. Part of the proceeds of guests' payment is donated to the community fund, which supports various in-village initiatives such as sponsoring the local community centre, recycling, youth-led conservation programmes and adult education. The establishment of the community fund helps to spread the benefits of CBT to the entire community, since not all families participate in CBT. We meet with the villagers every month to discuss any CBT-related issues. We collect mandatory post-trip questionnaires from guests and their feedback is discussed with villagers to improve the quality of the experience. We meet with the villagers regularly to ensure that volunteer activities are worthwhile and serve a real need.

To minimize cultural impact, a code of conduct for visitors was established by villagers with our assistance to ensure that visitors respect the traditions and cultures of the communities. A pre-trip briefing with the visitors by AD staff provides visitors the information about the communities and their cultures and norms. We encourage visitors to communicate with the villagers with the assistance of our English–Thai phrasebook, interactive homestay kit, staff translator and a local guide. From the visitors' perspective, our programmes promote cultural and environmental awareness and understanding of the local way of life through an interactive homestay experience.

Continued

S. Heitmann and P. Robinson

An Andaman Discoveries short-term volunteer assisting the Ban Talae Nok Tsunami Soap Cooperative to make soap for sale in the community shop. Craig Lovell, Andaman Discoveries.

The Andaman coast remains largely undeveloped, with many communities developing community-based tourism as an alternative to mass tourism. Craig Lovell, Andaman Discoveries.

Children helping the homestay host family to prepare a delicious Thai meal. Andaman Discoveries.

(Case Study provided by Kelly May, Andaman Discoveries, www.andamandiscoveries.com)

Questions

What other examples of this type of innovative project exist? What are the components of management that make a project like this so successful?

Codes of conduct

The WTO Global Code of Ethics in Tourism includes nine articles that outline the principles for destinations, governments, tour operators, developers, travel agents, workers and travellers themselves. It is an example of codes of conduct aimed at a global level, but there are further examples at national (Caring for Australia – Code of Conduct for Tourism) or local (Moroccan High Atlas Tourist Code) levels as well as for specific forms of tourism (Code of Conduct for the Protection of Children from Sexual Exploitation in Travel and Tourism, Code of Conduct for Arctic Tourists, International Cultural Tourism Charter – see Chapter 10, this volume), sectors for the travel industry (Orkney Tourist Guides Association Code of Conduct, Australian Tourism Export Code of Conduct, Australian Code of Conduct for Inbound Tour Operators), and aimed at particular customer segments (Tourism Concern's Exploring the World – Young Travellers Code).

Codes of conduct are effective, as they can convey messages to both tourists and the travel industry in short and understandable ways, initiate conversation between the parties involved, raise awareness, assist in creating partnerships and encourage cooperation between the stakeholders. A range of companies have started to collaborate with not-for-profit organizations to help communicating ways of responsible travelling. (British Airways (BA) provides a guide for responsible travelling.) However, because codes of conducts are voluntary and not binding, some are questioning the usefulness of this tool and its effectiveness as a form of education. Tourists may be reluctant to change their behaviour, as codes of conduct are seen as rules that restrict their freedom.

Corporate social responsibility

Similarly to codes of conduct, the industry has seen a rise in the number of organizations adopting a wider focus towards their operations and including all stakeholders instead of focusing on shareholders. Corporate social responsibility has come to play a major role not only with tourism-related companies but across all industries.

One cooperation between several organizations is the Tour Operators' Initiative for Sustainable Tourism Development (www.toinitiative.org) in which tour operators (including the big companies such as TUI Travel plc, Accor and Kuoni) commit themselves to sustainable practices and concepts of tourism. Examples of good practice include, among others, a paperless but multimedia experience travel agency for customers, contracting hotels that follow green practices, promoting codes of conduct and responsible travel, staff training on sustainable tourism development, using environmentally friendly transport services, supporting local communities and local regeneration within destinations.

Task

Check a company, such as TUI or BA – what is their involvement in sustainable tourism initiatives? How much do they do, and to what extent do they follow the guidelines/ underlying philosophy as outlined above?

S. Heitmann and P. Robinson

Demarketing

Demarketing is the technique of withdrawing marketing activity from a product or service in order to dissuade demand and can be a useful tool to apply to destinations that have become too popular, resulting in damage to the environment. There are three different types of demarketing:

- General demarketing involves the withdrawal of any marketing activity.
- Selective demarketing is the withdrawal of marketing activities aimed at certain market segments while maintaining marketing activities aimed at those market segments that are considered to be more conscious consumers.
- Finally, ostensible marketing involves marketing techniques that give the impression that the product is rare, thus encouraging consumers to pay premium prices.

These techniques can be very successful in order to reduce demand or change demand. However, a reduction in demand obviously results in fewer visitors and, therefore, less income. Companies with the primary objective of making profit might resist this, as it affects profitability.

> **Question**
>
> How would you convince your line manager that demarketing would in fact be a feasible option for your company?

Pricing

Related to marketing is pricing, which can be an effective tool as the prices charged to consumers can be used to preserve and conserve the attractions. Pricing is a useful tool to restrict visitor numbers and to cover the environmental costs of tourism, through higher entrance charges and restricted access to protected areas. During high season, when pressure on resources is highest, higher prices are charged. Another way of differential pricing is to charge more affluent consumers higher prices. While it could be argued that this is an unjust system, it is a widespread technique.

Benefits to the Business

Although much of what has been discussed may seem to restrict businesses and limit operations, much of what has been discussed can actually represent an opportunity to reduce operating costs or increase profitability. It is also a useful promotional tool to consumers who are increasingly aware of environmental issues. Consider the idea that an airline business currently flies five times each day to Egypt but none of the flights is full. By reducing this to four flights there is a very real cost saving, while making little difference to bottom-line productivity and creating a piece of news that will play well within the media. Advances in technology further assist the reduction of costs and increase in profitability while continuing to deliver incremental changes in environmental management.

Summary

This chapter has provided a strong overview of sustainability as it pertains to the travel industry. However, there are some points to note. Not least, sustainability is a subject often considered to be a contemporary issue, something that is current and debated now and is very much a 1990s and 2000s discussion. In many sectors it is being seen as an increasing part of the notion of corporate social responsibility. However, the issues it raises and the holistic nature of the travel industry lend it more weight within this industry because it ultimately represents a very real need to consider the environment. While some manufacturing industries can pay homage to the idea, it may not really matter. Increased energy costs and the need to work with new raw materials are unfortunate but sometimes necessary. In the travel industry, however, very often people are choosing to visit based upon motivations to see or experience new places. If those new places fail to be preserved or cared for then the very resource people seek to visit will disappear, with potentially huge ramifications for host communities.

It is crucial, then, that there is a recognition of the need to strive for sustainability throughout the travel industry and that sustainable management needs to be a core part of each function in the organization. This should not be confused with the opportunity to develop environmentally sound holidays for niche market travel, valuable though the market and its altruism are, but a recognition of environmental good practice is essential throughout the business.

Acknowledgements

Kelly May, Andaman Discoveries; Katie Fewings, www.responsibletravel.com; Paul Geiss, Baobab Travel; Tourismus Zentrale St Peter-Ording.

Further Research

For a detailed discussion on tourism impacts:
Wall, G. and Mathieson, A. (2006) *Tourism – Change, Impacts and Opportunities*, Prentice-Hall, Harlow, UK.
For a detailed discussion on tourism planning:
Hall, C.M. (2008) *Tourism Planning – Policies, Processes and Relationships*, 2nd edn. Prentice-Hall, Harlow, UK.
For a further overview of sustainable tourism management:
Swarbrooke, J. (1999) *Sustainable Tourism Management*. CAB International, Wallingford, UK.

Web Sites

WTO: Available at: www.world-tourism.org
WTTC: Available at: www.wttc.org
Fair Trade Tourism South Africa: Available at: www.fairtourismsa.org.za
ProPoor Tourism: Available at: www.propoortourism.org.uk
Tourism Concern: Available at: www.tourismconcern.org.uk
National Parks: Available at: www.nationalparks.gov.uk

Review Questions

1. Consider either your hometown or your last holiday destination as a case study – investigate the impacts tourism may have and categorize them into economic, environmental and sociocultural. What are the negative and positive impacts? What is done to minimize the negative impacts, or to enhance the positive impacts? What practices can you find that support the idea of sustainable tourism development?

2. Investigate a large transport company (e.g. coach operator, airline, train network) – how is it addressing sustainability?

References

Bahaire, T. and Elliot-White, M. (1999) Community participation in tourism planning and development in historic city of York, England. *Current Issues in Tourism* 2(2&3), 243–276.

Hall, C.M. (2008) *Tourism Planning – Policies, Processes and Relationships*, 2nd edn. Prentice-Hall, Harlow, UK.

McCool, S. and Lime, D. (2001) Tourism carrying capacity: tempting fantasy or useful reality? *Journal of Sustainable Tourism* 9(5), 372–388.

Propoor Tourism (PPT) (2005) ProPoor Tourism partnership. Available at: http://www.propoortourism.org.uk/

Swarbrooke, J. (1999) *Sustainable Tourism Management*. CAB International, Wallingford, UK.

Weaver, D.B. (1998) *Ecotourism in the Less Developed World*. CAB International, Wallingford, UK.

World Travel and Tourism Council (WTTC) (2008) World – Key Facts at a Glance, Tourism Satellite Accounting. Available at: http://www.wttc.org/eng/Tourism_Research/Tourism_Satellite_Accounting

WTO (1999) Approval of the Global Code of Ethics for Tourism. Resolution, General Assembly, Thirteenth Session, 27 September–1 October 1999, Santiago, Chile. Available at: www.world-tourism.org

WTO (2002) Québec Declaration on Ecotourism. Available at: http://www.world-tourism.org/sustainable/IYE/quebec_declaration/eng.pdf

10 Travel, Society and Culture

GHISLAINE POVEY AND SINE HEITMANN

Objectives of the Chapter

This chapter addresses the nature of culture and societies in the travel context. The cultural and sociological impacts and consequences of travel for tourists and host communities are explored, and the implications of these for the travel industry are discussed. The nature of the relationships between travel industry stakeholders is also examined. The character of the travel experience is investigated from the viewpoints of the various participants, with issues including authenticity, value of heritage and the impacts of tourist behaviours. A diverse range of case studies is included as exemplars of the diversity of the travel experience and the cultures and societies involved in the tourism industry. The objectives of the chapter are:

- to foster an appreciation of the importance of culture and heritage in relation to travel;
- to demonstrate an understanding of tourist motivation and typologies; and
- to explain the tourist–host relationship and sociocultural impacts of travelling.

Introduction

Culture makes society; our culture is central to our tastes and perceptions, how we think and how we act. The interaction of culture with tourism can be seen as threefold. First, our culture influences our thinking and our behaviour in many situations and thus is particularly important when we consider the implications of tourists on holiday. As outlined below, our society and culture have a significant impact on the types of holidays we choose to go on. Second, culture not only influences our demand for certain tourist activities, but is also a resource for tourism – most tourist attractions are influenced by their cultural environment or offer some form of cultural experience. You cannot separate the attraction from its cultural and societal environment. Within this context, the role, value and context of heritage need to be considered. Tourism is at its core about that which is out of the ordinary or 'other' – if we are not engaged in activities from our society and culture, we like to explore other societies and cultures as part of our holiday and sightseeing. Finally, tourism leads to two societies and their cultures meeting. The consequences of this meeting can be very different depending upon the way the interactions are managed and the basis of the guest–host relationship. This chapter explores the connection of travelling, society and culture, consequences of two societies or cultures meeting, which happens when people visit, through travel, a new society or culture different from their own. It discusses locals' culture as attraction and also tourists' society as an influence on why they travel and their behaviour while on that trip.

Society and Culture

Societies are made up of small groups or large populations; what makes them a society is the interrelationship that connects them; they are united by structured social relationships and share a unique culture. The British society shares the British culture, which distinguishes it from the culture of the French society. When we refer to the study of society and culture in relation to tourism, we are investigating tourism activities from a sociological, anthropological and psychological point of view. Why do people travel? Why do many British travel to Spain, but not many Spaniards to Britain? Why are Germans number one in international travelling, but only a small percentage of Americans own a passport? Why do Afro-Americans travel to African countries and many South Americans to Spain? Why do women prefer shopping while on holiday? Why does it seem that American and Japanese tourists travel the whole of Europe in only 2 weeks? Why do only young people travel to Lloret de Mar in Spain? These are just some of the many questions that we are seeking answers for when studying travel activities from a sociological and psychological point of view. The influences on travelling behaviour come from the societal and cultural environment, as will be explored below.

No society exists without culture, but no cultures exist without societies; therefore, the two terms are linked together very closely. Culture can be defined as a system of human activity, imbued with symbols and meanings that give the activities undertaken their relevance. It is generally considered to include aspects of human life including language, religious practices, dress codes, behavioural codes and rituals. All aspects of our lives are based on our culture, such as our definition of what is beautiful and ugly, and what is eaten at different times of the day. How we celebrate the birth of our children and mourn the death of our friends is also governed by the culture in which we live. It becomes clear that culture is an important aspect when discussing tourism; however, culture is a concept that is not easy to grasp, as not all cultural manifestations are visible. What is visible is just the tip of iceberg – buildings, fashion or artefacts can immediately tell us about the differences between societies, but what we cannot see is the development of these cultures and how deeply rooted these cultural manifestations are. Furthermore, it is difficult to grasp all the historical influences that have gone into the forming of a culture. Finally, the most complex issue with regard to culture is that most of it is subconscious. Think about the English drinking tea – it is something that you take for granted and that you are used to doing, but you do not question why it is this way. In the same way, the Italian (in general) does not think about why he/she prefers coffee to tea. Thus, discussing culture in the context of tourism is a complex, yet fascinating subject which results in a lot of debates – these debates themselves are influenced by culture and society; depending on the way you grew up your ideas and your way of thinking have been shaped in a different way from someone from the other end of the world.

Having outlined some of the ideas surrounding culture, the relationship between culture and tourism has to be explored further. As outlined above, the relationship can be threefold: the cultural background that influences the tourist's choice for a holiday and the behaviour while on holiday (see tourist typology and tourist motivation below); the consequences of two different cultures (tourist and host) meeting as well as the relationship between the two societies (see host–guest relationship); and culture as a resource for tourism destination and tourist attractions. The last point leads to answering the question: What is cultural tourism?

According to McKercher and DuCros (2002), cultural tourism is a form of tourism which involves the use of cultural heritage assets of a society for the consumption of experiences and products by tourists. This is a rather simple definition but captures the key essence. When discussing cultural tourism, heritage has to be included in the discussion. Culture and heritage are often associated, as heritage is part of cultural landscapes. According to the United Nations Educational, Scientific and Cultural Organization (UNESCO), heritage is 'Our legacy from the past, what we live with today, and what we pass on to future generations. Our cultural and natural heritage are both irreplaceable sources of life and inspiration' (UNESCO, 2008). Heritage is linked to history and the past, it represents what has been handed down from past to current generations. Beyond that which is passed on, heritage can be considered to define who we are and it can impart to inhabitants their cultural identity. It is perceived by some to be fundamental to an understanding of the present. Often, heritage is used interchangeably with history; however, while history is the accurate recording of the past based on facts, heritage includes more aspects such as language, culture and identity. In other words, history is the activity of producing knowledge about the past and heritage is a means of consumption of that knowledge (Cassia, 1999, in Timothy and Boyd, 2003). Cultural heritage, however, is dynamic and constantly evolving, regarded differently as our current viewpoint changes over time. Thus, that heritage which is adopted and preserved in modern culture is subjective. It is reliant upon the preferences and whims of the individuals who comprise a particular social group, subject to their biases and reliant upon their recognition and appreciation. When tourists arrive they also bring preferences and idiosyncrasies of their own, which are sometimes different from those of the local population. This can cause a gap to arise between the groups. What the tourist appreciates and values may be different from that which is pleasing to the local population. For this purpose, the International Cultural Tourism Charter, developed by Pederson (2002), can be useful.

International Cultural Tourism Charter's five key principles (Pederson, 2002)

Due to the role that tourism plays in international cultural interaction, conservation needs to provide low-impact and well-managed opportunities for tourists and host communities to experience and understand the local culture and heritage at first hand.

Sustainable management of the dynamic and sometimes conflicting relationship between tourism and heritage sites is essential for present and future generations.

Planners need to ensure that tourists visiting heritage sites can have an enjoyable and meaningful experience.

The inclusion of hosts and indigenous peoples in the planning processes for tourism and conservation of sites is essential.

The host community at any heritage site should benefit from tourism and the conservation of that site.

Heritage can be classified in different ways (Timothy and Boyd, 2003). One way would be to differentiate between tangible and intangible heritage:

- tangible and immovable: historic buildings but also natural areas and landscapes;
- tangible and movable: objects in museums, documents in archives, artefacts, etc.; or
- intangible: values, customs, ceremonies, lifestyles and experiences like festivals and cultural events.

Another way of classifying heritage is by type of attraction:

- natural heritage, for example, national parks;
- living cultural heritage, for example, fashions, foods and customs;
- built heritage, for example, historic cities, cathedrals, castles, monuments;
- industrial heritage, for example, leather, coal, textiles or other elements of a region's past that had an influence on its growth and development;
- personal heritage, for example, cemeteries, religious sites or other aspects or elements of a region that have a value to individuals or small groups; or
- dark heritage, for example, places of atrocity, death or a generally 'dark' past that some would prefer to forget.

Following on from this, we can further divide the scales of heritage. Sites can be of:

- world status – think of UNESCO World Heritage Sites (WHS) such as the Great Barrier Reef (Australia), Stonehenge (UK) and Cologne Cathedral (Germany) which are deemed of international importance;
- national importance – because they are representative of a collective, national past and might evoke feelings of patriotism, such as the Liberty Statue in America; or
- personal importance – a good example is the rise of family history research that has become popular over the past years, including activities such as Americans with Irish ancestry travelling to Ireland to find their roots or track down grandparents' houses.

CASE STUDY 1: WORLD HERITAGE, BUT FOR WHO?

The 1964 Second Congress of Architects and Specialists of Historic Buildings in Venice adopted 13 resolutions, the first of which is now known as the Venice Charter, also known as the International Restoration Charter; the second, proposed by UNESCO, was the creation of the International Council on Monuments and Sites. In 1968, the International Union for Conservation of Nature (IUCN) developed proposals very similar to, and strongly influenced by, those derived by the 1965 White House Conference, recognizing the balance between humans and nature. In Stockholm in 1972, these were presented to the United Nations Conference on Human Environment. On 16 November of that year the Convention concerning the Protection of World Cultural and Natural Heritage was adopted by the United Nations Educational, Scientific and Cultural Organization (UNESCO) General Conference.

Since then the preservation and conservation of heritage has changed how we view monuments and sites. Since 1982, we have even had 18 April as the international day for monuments and sites with the theme for 2008 being Religious Heritage and Sacred Places. UNESCO today has a world heritage mission which essentially seeks to get nation states to identify and protect their heritage sites. It also seeks the inclusion of local populations and public awareness raising, while asking for international cooperation. It will provide emergency assistance for sites with immediate danger, encouraging nation states to set up management plans and providing technical assistance and training.

The World Heritage Committee consists of representatives of the 21 States Parties to the Convention, elected by their General Assembly, who meet annually. They implement the World Heritage Convention and decide if a site is included on the World Heritage List. The World Heritage List consists of 851 sites which have been chosen to be representative of the full range of cultural and natural heritage sites around the world. There are ten criteria for inclusion on the list, ranging from being representative of human genius to facilitating *in situ* conservation of biodiversity.

In addition to the general list, UNESCO has a World Heritage in Danger List which includes those sites most at risk of damage, either potential or actual. Inscription enables the World Heritage Committee to use resources from the World Heritage Fund to help conservation and preservation. Listed sites include, for example, Bamiyan Valley in Afghanistan, which is suffering the effects of military action, dynamite explosions, anti-personnel mines and (understandably) abandonment by its population. UNESCO is working with the Afghan Government to preserve cultural heritage here. More information about the sites currently listed are at http://whc. unesco.org/en/danger/.

Of particular importance to tour operations professionals is the World Heritage Tourism Programme, which promotes sustainable tourism at WHS. If tourism to those world sites is not properly managed it can cause degradation of the sites. If the tourism is well managed, however, it can act to enhance the sites and bring in the much-needed resources for ongoing preservation and conservation. The spin-off benefit of these guidelines is that their application to sites not listed can only further enhance the preservation of the human environment.

There are three advisory bodies to the UNESCO committee.

The IUCN provides technical evaluation of natural heritage sites and reports on the state of conservation of listed properties. This is a non-governmental, international organization, founded in Gland, Switzerland, in 1948.

Continued

G. Povey and S. Heitmann

The International Council on Monuments and Sites (ICOMOS) is again an international, non-governmental organization, with a base in Paris. ICOMOS evaluates cultural and mixed properties proposed for inscription on the World Heritage List. The origins of ICOMOS are outlined above.

The International Centre for the Study of the Preservation and Restoration of Cultural Property (ICCROM), which is based in Rome, was set up in 1956. It is an intergovernmental organization providing expert advice on conservation of properties on the World Heritage List, and training in techniques of restoration.

Questions

Considering what you have read so far in this chapter, and from Chapter 9 (this volume), answer the following questions:

1. What value do WHS have to the travel industry from a marketing perspective?

2. Does the WHS status conferred upon sites contribute to their preservation, or increase the pressure from tourists wanting to see these key heritage sites?

3. Consider sales of excursions. How could these be enhanced by including visits to WHS on itineraries?

4. From the UNESCO web site, choose two national or international examples and investigate them further: have they benefited from the WHS status? Have there been any conflicts surrounding their designation?

5. Can you think of any attraction that in your opinion should get WHS status? Would it fit the criteria?

CASE STUDY 2: THE ASWAN DAM – THE VALUE OF CULTURAL HERITAGE

The urgency of the need for an international view of heritage was sparked by events in North Africa. Egypt, along with most of the other northern African countries, was looking to develop. It wanted stability in power and water supply and came up with the plan to build the Aswan Dam to provide both. Construction was started in 1960 and the dam itself was finished by 1971. The long-term benefits have been proved to the Egyptian people, providing crop irrigation and preventing Egypt suffering from floods. It also has proved to be a source of green hydropower. Underneath the site of the dam, however, was the ancient temple of Abu Simbel. It is reckoned by scholars that the site was first built around 1244 BC. This 'Temple of Rameses, beloved of Amun' was rediscovered in 1813 by the Swiss explorer Burckhardt, and eventually entered by the Italian Giovani Belzoni in 1817. Legend has it that the site is known as Abu Simbel after a young local boy who guided the explorers to the site.

When the world at large realized that the Egyptian Government intended to flood the site of Abu Simbel they set up a donations campaign to save the monument. The project cost US$80 million, 40 million of which was raised from 50 countries around the world. The rescue and relocation began in 1964, when the site was cut into large segments and literally moved to a new location, some 65 m above the river and 200 m away. Some parts of the temple even had to be moved from under the

Continued

---

rising waters of the man-made Lake Nasser. This accomplishment is considered by many to be one of the greatest feats of archaeological engineering ever undertaken.

Questions

Considering the point of view from the various stakeholders involved, what were the arguments for and against the Aswan Dam?

Considering the value of the cultural heritage that was to be lost beneath the waters of Lake Nasser, should the Aswan Dam have been built?

We all have a cultural heritage and our tastes and actions are largely guided by this. We undertake particular activities, such as sport, cooking, artistic endeavours and religion, largely based on our cultural heritage. Culture and heritage are important to each individual as a integral part of life, and this has significant implications for the travel industry as a whole. First, an individual's culture and heritage influence travel behaviour, travel motivations and the decision-making process, as will be discussed below. Second, as a result of these influences on travel and tourism demand, cultural tourism and heritage attractions have become central features within tourism supply and are among the most visited attractions around the world. Having discussed the key concepts surrounding culture and heritage, we now have to pay more attention to the tourist. Investigating tourist motivation and understanding tourist typologies helps us to link the ideas of culture and heritage to travelling behaviour and, consequently, the tourist–host relationship.

Tourist Motivations

Studying motivation with regards to travelling seeks answers to the question: 'Why do people travel?' Motivation to travel can result from a psychological need (one the tourist might not even be aware of) or might be explained through the purpose or choice of the trip. Investigating travel motivation can be a complex area of research; however, motivation plays an important part in the decision-making process. In order to examine the motivation for tourists to travel, we can take two different approaches: extrinsic and intrinsic motivation. Extrinsic motivation is the analysis of travel motivation from a sociological perspective and results from influences external to the tourist, whereas intrinsic motivation includes the personal needs of a tourist, thus taking the psychological angle towards tourist motivation.

Extrinsic motivation

Within this model, theorists explain motivation first through the tourism–work relationship. Three different approaches have been elaborated:

1. **Work and tourism in opposition:** Work is placed in contrast to holiday. It is argued that a holiday compensates for the work or even lifestyle, i.e. if someone has a rather busy, challenging job, she/he seeks relaxation while on holiday. Vice versa,

G. Povey and S. Heitmann

other people might want to escape from constraining rules and norms in everyday life and look for novelty, thrills and challenges when travelling.

2. Tourism as an extension of work: In contrast to the opposition/compensation model above, the extension model proposes that work and holiday are interlinked and that patterns of work and patterns of holiday are hardly any different. People with challenging jobs search for a stimulating type of holiday; people with a highly regulated work adopt a similar attitude during holiday. Consequently, changes in the patterns of a job will change patterns of a holiday.

3. The third approach suggests that the job has nothing to do with the chosen type of travel; hence, people on an exciting holiday could have either a challenging or a regulated job.

While the tourism–work relationship can be very useful as a basis for analysis, we have to consider a second framework for extrinsic motivation, namely the social determinants that influence an individual to travel and to make the decision to purchase a holiday. These factors include:

- **Cultural:** the cultural (White, Black, Asian, etc.) or religious (Christian, Muslim, Hindu, etc.) background; subculture (may be determined through linguistic, aesthetic, religious, political, sexual, geographical or a combination of factors); and social class (working class, middle class, upper class);
- **Social:** family, reference groups (friends, colleagues, etc.), roles and status;
- **Personal:** age, lifestyle, occupation, economic circumstances, personality.

All these factors can have an impact on motivation and the incentive that leads someone to book a holiday. These social influences are not mutually exclusive; it is more a combination, while one pressure can be more explicit than the other. We can call those economic, technological, social, cultural and political factors within any society determinants, as these drive or set limits to travel demand, they determine the volume of a population's demand to travel.

The extrinsic motivations are useful to explain tourist motivations in general; however, for a better picture we should also have a look at the psychological, intrinsic motivations as they contribute considerably to the explanation and analysis of travel motivations.

Intrinsic motivations

Some argue that motivations are a purely psychological concept and not a sociological one as described above. When we refer to the internal factors within individuals, expressed as needs, wants and/or desires that influence tourism choices, we speak of motivators. No two persons are the same – each individual has a different attitude, different personality and thus a different motivation to travel. This makes the study of motivation difficult and challenging, but interesting at the same time as we can make some generalizations. However, one has to bear in mind that the motivation to travel is very often subject to societal values, norms and pressures which are internalized and then become psychological needs. Thus, you can find some overlaps in the sociological approaches, mentioned above, and the psychological concepts, which will be examined now.

Push/pull factors

A first attempt to explain motivation might be the identification of push and pull factors. Pull factors can be described as destination-specific attributes or outer motivations – particular attractions or the destination as a whole is so attractive that it is 'pulling' the tourist towards it. The push factors in turn are internal or inner motivations and the factors that influence an individual into making a decision. These are described as person-specific motivations (needs, preferences, etc.). Accommodation, restaurants, entertainment facilities, etc. are not of much relevance to the tourist, instead the person just feels the need to 'get away' from his current whereabouts.

Motivation by purpose

Travel motivators can also be explained in relation to the purpose of the holiday taken. For example, Swarbrooke and Horner (2007) suggest a typology of six motivators (see Table 10.1).

For example, linking these ideas back to the discussion on cultural heritage and its influence on travel behaviour, heritage itself is a suitable example for a motivator by purpose. Tourists might travel to sites because they consider it to be part of their

Table 10.1. Travel motivation.

Travel motivator	Explanation
Physical	Physical motivators indicate the need for physical activities. This can be either the need for rest, relaxation and simple things like getting a suntan or for active participation in exercises and health-related activities – any activity motivated by the desire for reducing tension or refreshing the body while on holiday
Emotional	Emotional motivators indicate the influence of emotions on travel behaviour, and could include travelling activities related to romance, adventure, spirituality, escapism or nostalgia
Cultural	Cultural motivators indicate the need or desire to explore and learn about the destination, its culture, its heritage, or to generally expand one's horizon and knowledge through travelling to new places
Interpersonal	Interpersonal motivators indicate the need for maintaining existing relationships or developing new relationships. This includes visits to family, friends and relatives, or the holiday is taken in order to meet new people
Personal development	Motivators of personal development indicate the need for increasing knowledge or learning new skills
Status and prestige	Travelling is motivated by the desire for enhancing one's status, receiving attention and appreciation from others, but can also include travelling for the purpose of personal development

G. Povey and S. Heitmann

heritage or they might travel to heritage sites that are not necessarily connected to their own heritage. Italian tourist visiting the Colosseum in Rome might have different motivations to travel there than German tourists.

Questions

1. Go to Chapter 3 (this volume) and look at Maslow's hierarchy of needs – how does this compare to the six travel motivators proposed in Table 10.1?
2. Safari in Kenya, 2 weeks in Blackpool with family, a week in Newquay with friends, 10 days in a Kibbuz in Israel, hen night in Prague, cookery course in France, backpacking through Eastern Australia, volunteering in Indonesia – using Table 10.1, which motivators influence these types of holidays? Are there any overlaps?

Further to motivations, travel behaviour is also explained with the use of tourist typologies.

Tourist typologies

Plog (1974) divides tourists into three simple categories (see Table 10.2). First, the allocentric tourists are confident and adventurous people who are seeking challenges and new experiences. They can be found in long-haul destinations or off the beaten track. A large number of tourists are mid-centric in their nature and, as the name suggests, situated between the two extremes. These tourists prefer package or guided holidays – you come across these in Europe and some long-haul destinations. Finally, psychocentric tourists are home loving and prefer familiar surroundings and safety. Thus, they prefer a home from home environment and you will find them in domestic destinations or within Europe.

Cohen's typology of tourists identifies four different categories based on the tourist's relationship with the tourism industry and the destination (Table 10.2). The organized mass tourist prefers highly organized package holidays, while the individual mass tourist tends to rely heavily on the tourist infrastructure but is more independent than the previous type. These first two types are also described as institutionalized tourist types, indicating the heavy influence of the tourism industry in organizing, planning and controlling the travel. The next two are non-institutionalized tourist types, indicating the individual nature of travelling and its organization. The explorer is an independent traveller who every now and then makes use of the tourist infrastructure but prefers to travel off the beaten track and engage more with the locals. Finally, the drifter is completely independent and in close contact with locals, he even tries to avoid any tourism honeypots as much as possible.

Smith (1989) identifies seven tourist types and can thus be considered an extension of Cohen's typology, but the establishment is based purely on numbers and the frequency by which these tourist types can be observed. The explorer is the smallest segment, which is not seen very often. This tourist accepts local traditions and cultures fully. The elite tourist as well is rarely seen, and he is able to adapt fully to any local traditions and cultures. The off-beat tourist is rather uncommon and adapts well. The unusual tourist occurs occasionally and adapts in part. The incipient mass is more common than the previous types of tourists who seek, while the mass is arguably the

Table 10.2. Tourist typologies. (Adapted from Cohen, 1972; Plog, 1974.)

Cohen (1972)	Plog (1974)	
Organized mass tourist		Familiarity
Depends on the 'tourist bubble' – the environment and infrastructure created, supplied and maintained by the tourism industry		
All-inclusive, fully packaged	*Psychocentric*	
Seeks familiarity, avoids novelty (unless highly controlled)	Less adventurous, visits popular mass tourism resorts at home or abroad, comfortable	
Individual mass tourist	when surrounded by other tourists	
Use institutionalized facilities (e.g. scheduled flights, tour operator and travel agency services and bookings, transfers)	- Near-pyschocentric	
Arranges as much as possible before leaving home	- -	
Visits same sights as mass tourists but maintains control of itinerary	*Midcentric*	
Explorer	- -	
'Off the beaten track' – inspiration from travel articles rather than a brochure	Near-allocentric -	
Moves back to the 'tourist bubble' if it gets too tough	*Allocentric*	
Drifter	Adventurous, prepared to take risks, prefers exotic/unusual	
Seeks novelty and excitement at all cost, might even look for danger and discomfort	destinations	
Avoid contact with tourists as much as possible		
Spending will benefit locals rather than larger companies		Novelty

most common tourist nowadays who expects. The last type, the charter appears in massive numbers and demands.

Having outlined the different typologies, we have to take a critical stance towards these. The typologies can be very useful to understand the behaviour, characteristics and personal traits of tourists. Furthermore, they are useful from a marketing perspective, as it can help to segment markets and develop various products that are tailored for each market segment. However, you should bear in mind that these typologies are rather simplistic and tend to make assumptions about characteristics as well as personality traits. In some cases, you might even find that they tend to be stereotypical. Social influences such as travel experience, age, gender or income are not taken into account. Finally, the models should not be considered as static, as the tourist is likely to move between the different classifications, thus the models are more like continuums. Quite often, the more allocentric tourists (or what Cohen labels as drifter and explorer) pave the way for mass tourism to be developed. For

G. Povey and S. Heitmann

Table 10.3. Psychocentric and allocentric travellers. (Adapted from Poon, 1993.)

Psychocentric/old tourist	Allocentric/new tourist
Impose values on host environment	Happy to explore
Security in numbers	Spontaneous
Everything prepaid and arranged (mass)	Niche products
Escape from home and work	Vacation as an extension of life
West is best	Venture further afield
Search for the sun	See and enjoy
Lie in the sun	Get up and get active, like sports
Get sunburned	Keep clothes on
No special interests	Special interests

example, Goa in India used to be visited only by few travellers but has now become a mass tourism destination. This has two implications.

First, tourists nowadays are more experienced – they have more and easier access to information (about destinations, products, ways of travelling) through the Internet and they have more experience as a tourist as tourism is more accessible than it used to be (through improvements in transport infrastructure and technology resulting in travelling being cheaper than a couple of decades ago). Second, and closely related to this last point, is the concept of the travel career ladder – the more experienced the tourist is in travelling, the more likely he will change his preferences and travel behaviour. Taking Plog's dichotomy as an example, Table 10.3 outlines how the 'old tourist' had more resemblance to the psychocentric tourist, while the 'new tourist' (or the modern traveller) shares more characteristics with the allocentric tourist.

Questions

1. Ask your friends and family why they decided to go on their last holiday – can you match their responses with any of the motivators and typologies above?
2. Compare the type of holidays that your grandparents have taken to the ones your parents and yourself have taken – what are the key differences? How does this relate to the changes proposed above?

Having discussed some key concepts of travel motivation and tourist typology, it is worth pointing out two further concepts which will be discussed in the next section. First, the tourist gaze, a concept proposed by Urry (2002), has received substantial attention. The tourist gaze can be argued to form part of tourist motivation, as it results in a need to gaze on sights, places and people that are unusual. Second, we will be discussing the concept of authenticity, which argues that tourists today are in a constant search for the authentic (believed to be found either in other cultures and their heritage or within own heritage). Thus, it has been argued that authenticity itself can be considered a motivator for travelling.

The tourist gaze

Urry's (2002) idea of the tourist gaze originates from the activity any tourist engages in when being on holiday, namely the importance of the visual gaze: we look at

---

places, we look at people, we look at landscapes and buildings, we look at performances. Tourists choose to travel in order to see and experience something different from our usual daily routine, and the visual consumption is inherent to any travel experience. Why do we decide to travel to Paris? We want to see the Eiffel Tower, the Mona Lisa in the Louvre and, ideally, two people kissing, as they represent the romantic Paris. Why do we decide to travel to London? We want to see the attractions and museums that London is famous for. Why do we travel to the Amazon? We want to see the natural landscape of the jungle and hopefully catch a glimpse of some Indian tribes living there. Niagara Falls? You have to see them. Central to the concept of the tourist gaze is the distinction between the ordinary and the extraordinary. Attractions are marked as being worth seeing – they have undergone a process of what MacCannell refers to as site sacralization – a sight is named, framed and elevated, enshrined and reproduced mechanically (in forms of souvenirs) as well as socially (in forms of new sights being established and naming themselves after the original sight). Attractions could be unique objects, such as the Eiffel Tower, the Grand Canyon, Buckingham Palace or the Tower of Pisa. But there are also particular signs the tourists are looking for: the typical English village, the typical German beer garden, the typical Italian trattoria, the typical Amsterdam coffee house. Another example listed by Urry is seeing ordinary aspects in an unusual context, such as everyday routines in China as a communist country. Finally, even carrying out everyday activities on holiday (like shopping, eating, drinking, etc.) is extraordinary, as these are influenced by the visual gaze of an unusual environment.

Urry differentiates between the romantic and collective gaze. The romantic form of the tourist gaze is characterized by the solitude, privacy and personal relationship with the object of the gaze. In contrast, the collective gaze places emphasis on the people who are present when looking at the object. For example, if you travel up the mountains and see a beautiful landscape, you can enjoy it on your own – in fact, if there were too many other people present, it would affect the quality of the experience and people would be rather disturbing (this has some overlaps with perceptual carrying capacity, see Chapter 9, this volume). Thus, this type of attraction necessitates a solitary, romantic gaze. The collective gaze in turn necessitates the presence of other people – if you were to attend a festival, all the other visitors would be essential to the atmosphere and attractiveness of this event. Or travelling to larger cities, whose unique attractiveness is the cosmopolitan character – it would feel eerie if you were there on your own and you would not enjoy the experience; only if people (tourists) are present would you enjoy it.

The idea of the tourist gaze has been criticized and developed over the years. Much emphasis is placed on the visual aspects, whereas travelling obviously includes physical and corporeal experiences, touching all senses (think of the importance of eating local food to some tourists, going on wine-tasting trips or the soundscapes when travelling to Latin American countries because of interest in music). Furthermore, limiting the tourist experience to the gaze could also fail to identify the 'second gaze' which goes beyond the superficial experience and realizes that there are things unseen and unsaid that are part of the experience. In contrast, as travelling is inherently about being mobile and on the move with limited time available, tourists have been criticized for not even gazing, but just glancing – for having become even more superficial in their holiday experiences (think of the American and Japanese tourists travelling through Europe and visiting 12 countries in 3 weeks because of their tight schedules).

Sociocultural Impacts

A quick overview of key sociocultural impacts is provided in Chapter 9 (this volume). This section intends to go into more detail about some of the concepts that are used to analyse the extent of sociocultural impacts and the character of the host–guest relationship. Sociocultural impact studies are concerned with changes that occur to the society and culture of local communities as a result of tourism. These could be changes in collective and individual value systems (i.e. moral conduct), changes in behaviour patterns (i.e. dress, food, social relationships, individual behaviour), changes in community structures (i.e. family relationships, gender roles), changes in lifestyle (i.e. religion, traditional ceremonies, production of cultural practices and artefacts) or changes in the quality of life (i.e. crime, safety levels).

Tourist–host encounters (Fig. 10.1) happen in three major forms: when tourists purchase goods and services from locals; when tourists and locals find themselves side by side (e.g. at an attraction, in a bar, at a show, in public places); and when tourists and locals come face to face for information exchange. The tourist–host encounter has some specific characteristics, though, that differentiate it from other encounters. First, it is temporal and transitory in nature. It might be unique to the tourist, but to the local it can be business as usual – thus, the two parties get together with different expectations and perceptions. It is also rather shallow and superficial as the tourist resides at the destination for only a limited period of time before a new tourist arrives – the tourist faces changes, while the local stays. Second, the encounters have spatial characteristics,

Fig. 10.1. Tourists at a local street market in Hluhluwe, South Africa.

as in some destinations the encounter is controlled through the creation of so-called tourist ghettos (e.g. in the Ecuadorian capital of Quito one part of the city is referred to as Gringolandia – the name implicating that it is dominated by foreigners who are not venturing much beyond the boundaries of this district). Third, tourists and locals come from different cultural backgrounds with different values and attitudes, which have an immense influence on the communication between the two. Both verbal and non-verbal communication can be a deciding factor whether the encounter is a positive or negative one. While different languages might result in obvious difficulties in communicating with each other, there are also facial expressions, eye gazes, territorial behaviour, touching of the opponents and gestures which are acceptable within the tourist's culture but not within the local's culture (or vice versa). Further examples include rules and patterns of personal interaction such as greetings or making/refusing a request. Finally, one important aspect has to be taken into account – tourism is an economic activity, thus the tourist–host encounter is primarily a commercialized relationship.

The host–guest relationship

Beneviste (1969) studied the way that host communities dealt with tourists in Greece. In greek, the word *philoxeno* means to offer hospitality. It is made up of both the word *xeno*, meaning stranger, and the word *philo*, which means friend. In ancient Greece, the word meant stranger, enemy and guest. In fact in many Indo-European languages, there is little distinction between these states. This is very different from the clear distinction found in English-speaking cultures between:

1. Friends, to whom hospitality would be offered;
2. Strangers, who would probably be treated with suspicion and who would be treated courteously, but not offered hospitality; and
3. Enemies.

By contrast, traditionally in Greece, *o xenos*, someone from outside the host community, is considered to be special. They could be a messenger from the gods, or even a god themselves, sent to test the individual. To help a stranger could well bring great rewards in later life or in heaven. According to Zarkia (1996 in Boissevain, 1996), this behaviour could have implications for relatives who may be in peril or the souls of family who have died. According to Beneviste, however, the traditional host–guest relationship has a set of strict rules and codes. The host is clearly the one in charge. The guest is stripped of their rights and is expected to graciously accept what is offered, which traditionally would often be the best that was available anyway. At the same time, they could not make specific demands. The host would try to make the guest feel at home, not for monetary reward but as a moral obligation.

This relationship has now significantly changed as the guest is now a customer and not a guest in the true sense of an offer of friendship. The host is selling a service not gaining moral merit. The relationship is a commercial transaction and thus governed by laws of commerce. The guest, the tourist, is in the superior position as the one who is paying. It is now a transaction not an interaction. The gain for the hosts is monetary not moral.

Tourist–host relationship in Greece

Tourists in Greece in the 1950s and early 1960s often reported that they were not allowed to pay for services such as the use of local boats for trips. They had to leave the money for rooms surreptitiously, as hosts did not want to charge them for their stay. Sardine barbeques with local fishermen and their families on the beach were often free. Time however has gone by and 50 years later this has all changed, and tourism in Greece is a very professional, profit-oriented business.

Host societies, however, were still sometimes shocked by tourist behaviour. In Cyprus, by the 1970s, the elderly were deeply shocked by the tourists dressed in beach wear walking through the villages. This became outright horror when they viewed the topless women tourists of the 1980s. From the tourist perspective many beaches were so remote (or perceived to be so) that tourists felt they could sunbathe naked without giving offence to anyone. These isolated spots, however, were often observed by shepherds and locals going about their daily business. Another example was the tradition that churches were never locked, despite often being crammed with offerings of gold and silver. Thefts from these churches were unheard of until the proliferation of tourism. Host societies have developed strategies to deal with this. Churches are now locked. Certain beaches have been designated as 'nudist' beaches. Those observing these beaches know what they will find there. Another area of great concern for many of the host communities has been the influence of tourist behaviour on their own community, particularly the demonstration effect (see below). Zarkia (1996 in Boissevain, 1996) cites the case of Skyros, where festival feasting at their monastery takes place after the last bus of tourists leaves at night. If the tourists remained, they would be treated as guests and would be served first, with the best food and drink. The monks for whom the feast is prepared would get none.

Questions

Search the news and the Internet – has the relationship between hosts and guest changed in Greece? How? Can you find another destination that had similar experiences?

For many host communities the reality is that big parts of their lives are lived out on a stage created by the observations of the culture-seeking tourists. Imagine going to your local club and finding bus loads of people standing around looking at you and taking pictures while you dance. Imagine going to your local supermarket just as three coaches of tourists arrive, who walk around very slowly, looking at everything but only buying one or two small items, while they block all the aisles and create a shortage of trolleys. Communities have retreated from the main tourist areas and often develop recreational facilities for themselves that are not easily accessible to the tourists. Bars, for example, still exist, even in tourists hot spots such as Agia Napa, where only Greek is spoken, all the menus are in Greek and very few non-Cypriots are ever seen. Those who are there are real friends of local people, and often do speak and read some Greek.

This chapter focuses upon the relationship between host and visitor communities, so it is important to consider that many visitors to a new destination, if not looking for a resort or club-based holiday, are likely to visit museums and other cultural heritage sites. This can have significant impacts on the sustainability of a site (Chapter 9, this volume). Aspects of group visits to heritage sites, such as group size, can have severe impacts. As a whole, the larger the group the greater the impacts are likely to be, particularly on vegetation and wildlife, although conversely some naturalists argue that frequency of disturbance is also a factor and that one large group has less impact than several small ones. Less obvious are the impacts associated with various more normal tourist activities such as rock climbing and photography, which can affect wildlife. Vegetation and soil damage can be caused by activities such as hiking and camping. Scuba diving and cruise boats can damage marine environments. Mechanized aquatic activities can be even more damaging to natural heritage and disrupt breeding patterns and feeding among some species. In the Everglades, for example, tourist motorboats frequently damage the manatees. Motor boats are also very polluting. Conscientious tour operators limit impacts on natural heritage by having viewing policies. Cultural sites can ask visitors to respect local culture by wearing suitable clothing, or being quiet or silent. Tour operations professionals have a clear role in helping to limit problems by educating their clients and teaching low-impact visit strategies. Just making tourists aware of the protection and preservation problems can have very significant implications. They can also help by ensuring that tourists understand the importance of keeping within zones allocated to activities and ensuring that tourists are aware of what facilities are available at various sites.

Questions

Reading Chapter 9 (this volume) on sustainability, which sustainable tourism initiatives would be useful here to minimize any potential negative impacts that tourism might have on local societies and their cultural/natural heritage?

The severity of impact also depends on the stage of tourism development within a destination. Butler's tourist destination life cycle (1980) adopts the idea of the product life cycle (see Chapter 4, this volume) and applies it to destination. During the stage of exploration, a country or region is being discovered by a small number of visitors. The restricted number of visitors is mainly due to the explorer-type nature of the travellers, but also due to lack of access, facilities, promotion and awareness of the region. During the second stage, involvement, visitor numbers rise and communities start to decide whether they plan to encourage further tourism development and, if so, what type and scale of tourism is planned. They might start to build small properties for tourism, promotion is encouraged and pressure is on the public sector to cater for infrastructural needs. The third stage, development, sees an increasing number of travellers and, in some instances, the rising number of tourists might lead to changes in the organization of tourism. The rising popularity of the destination attracts outsiders (e.g. international tourism companies) that move in to provide additional facilities and to get a share of the profits. Land values may increase. Outsiders buy up spare land and set up tourism-related businesses, often on a larger scale than the locals. Local people still benefit economically; however, the revenue is generally spread among a smaller group. This could result in locals having difficulties in competing with these companies, and

G. Povey and S. Heitmann

the public sector is now under pressure to cater for both internal and external stakeholders to avoid any conflict. By the fourth stage, consolidation, visitor numbers rise less but still increase and the destination has become a fully fledged part of the tourist industry and tourism system. When a destination has reached its peak number of visitors, it is in the stage of stagnation. The destination might lose its appeal, and major promotional efforts are needed to attract both new and repeat visitors. After this fifth stage, there are two different scenarios for the destination: if it loses visitors, it is in a stage of decline; if it manages to relaunch by attracting new markets or developing new products through new facilities, it is in a stage of rejuvenation.

Doxey's irritation index

Following on from the discussion of the sociocultural impacts and the implications of tourism on the host–guest relationship, Doxey's irritation index (1976; Fig. 10.2) is a useful tool which identifies four different stages that happen alongside tourism development within a destination. Throughout the exploration stage of tourism development, tourists and investors are very welcome and encouraged to visit, as they present new contacts and new sources of income. Doxey refers to this as the stage of euphoria. Once tourists have become taken for granted and the contacts between locals and tourists have become more commercialized, the stage of apathy is reached. Once the saturation point is reached and locals do not perceive tourism as a positive development anymore, as tourists are disrupting day-to-day life, we can observe the stage of annoyance. This can turn into antagonism, which indicates that local people have no control over the situation anymore and become openly hostile towards tourists – irritations are openly expressed as tourists are seen as the cause of all problems.

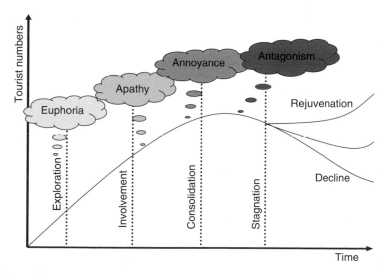

Fig. 10.2. Doxey's irritation index. (Adapted from Doxey, 1976 and Butler, 1980.)

Demonstration effect

Demonstration effect is known as the process by which alien values and ways of life are being introduced to the host community. This is particularly relevant in the context of tourism within developing countries where tourists from 'rich' developed nations spend their holiday and money in poorer countries. While the tourist is on holiday, away from work and constraints at home, he/she enjoys the 2 weeks he/she has as much as possible, not caring about the money he/she spends or the activities he/she engages in, thereby showing levels of affluence that locals cannot afford. Problems arise if the locals witness this behaviour and aspire to copy it. Once local communities begin to adapt and change their values as a result of the tourist's demonstration, the acculturation process kicks in. However, when talking about these kind of impacts (as well as those outlined above and in Chapter 9, this volume), it is often easy to blame tourism as the main culprit; on the other hand, it would be wrong to accredit all changes within a community to tourism activity. Historically, the era of colonialism has brought changes to formerly traditional communities. Nowadays, media (particularly television and the Internet) have a considerable influence on communities all around the world. While tourism contributes to changes, it could be argued that it rather intensifies the changes that are inevitably going to happen.

Authenticity

Authenticity within tourism has received much attention from academic scholars and the discussion surrounding this concept is endless. As a basis for this section, we should understand what 'authentic' means. If we take the classical Greco-Roman origin it indicates a sense of a true, sincere or original element in a historical context. At its simplest, authentic means the genuine, the unadulterated or 'the real thing'. Authenticity was originally used in the context of museums and referred to the authenticity of an object. If the cultural element is material (e.g. exhibit, products, works of art, architecture, dress) the authenticity of this element is easy to judge through experts, certificates of origin, certificate of authenticity or other official documentation that proves that this element has been untouched since its creation and has not been subject to any modern influence. But how do we judge the authenticity of immaterial elements such as language, festivals, rituals or even tourism experiences in general? In this case, something is considered to be authentic if it is made, produced or enacted by local people according to custom and tradition. Similar to material elements, authenticity here connotes traditional culture and origin, a sense of genuine, the real or the unique – it is 'made by local hands'.

Within tourism academic literature the discussion surrounding authenticity has a range of key actors. The two main scholars are Boorstin (1961) and MacCannell (1999). Both of these authors argue that modern society is inauthentic. In other words, it is argued that people nowadays are alienated by the fast developments in the modern world and that reality is not bearable. Boorstin (1961) takes this point further and argues that this results in people, as tourists, not being able to experience reality directly but thriving on pseudo events. As they are used to modern society, which is fast-changing and thrilling, they seek further thrills or fake reality on holiday. Take Disney theme parks as an example. These theme parks create a new reality for the visitors and promise action, thrills and excitement. That most of the experience is constructed and fake is irrelevant to the tourists; they enjoy it nevertheless. MacCannell (1999) in turn, and many other scholars, argues that the fact that people are alienated from the modern way of life results in a constant search for authenticity. He compares tourists to a kind of contemporary pilgrim who is seeking authenticity in other times and other places, away from that person's everyday life and modern reality. This authenticity is believed to be found in other times (away from modernity), i.e. in historic periods and cultures that depict purer and simpler lifestyles. Authenticity connotes the traditional/pre-modern, hence to be found in traditional/pre-modern cultures – either in our own past and in our own heritage, or in other cultures which are considered to be less developed than our own such as Indian tribes, African villages and Aborigine communities. It can be argued that authenticity itself has become a motivator to travel.

As a result of these arguments and the behaviour of tourists who are in a search of authenticity, hosts/locals put their culture (including themselves) on sale in order to create an appealing package, and historical sites or heritage put on display is framed and packaged. This can happen to the degree that this packaging alters the nature of the product – the authenticity sought by the visitor becomes 'staged authenticity' provided by the host. Staged authenticity, according to MacCannell (1999), is whereby locals create the illusion of authenticity in order to satisfy the tourist's desire to experience their culture, but put it on stage (perform it) in order to save their own culture and its meaning.

This model of staged authenticity can be expanded into a continuum whereby the divisions of stages are blurred (Table 10.4). A tourist's quest for authenticity can progress along the continuum until she/he reaches the final stage of participating in the local's life, which is unlikely – she/he will rather encounter 'staged authenticity' (stages 2–5) with some glimpses into the back region if allowed.

However, as authenticity is not a given, measurable quality applicable to a particular event or product nor a fixed or static concept, as it can change over time, Cohen (1988) took MacCannell's one-dimensional framework and added another dimension. He argues that there are two types of settings (staged and authentic) and two tourists' impressions of the setting – equalling four different relationships. In other words, the following are the four different relationships:

1. A setting can be authentic and the tourist perceives it as such.
2. A setting is staged but the tourist perceives it as being authentic.
3. A setting is authentic but the tourist suspects it to be staged.
4. The setting is staged but the tourist perceives it to be authentic.

Table 10.4. Continuum of staged authenticity. (Adapted from Sharpley, 2008.)

Stage 1	Front region, a social space the tourist attempts to overcome or penetrate
Stage 2	Still a front region, decorated to appear as a back region in some aspects
Stage 3	A front region that is totally organized in order to resemble a back region
Stage 4	Tourists are permitted to move into a back region that is open to outsiders
Stage 5	A back region, somewhat altered/cleaned up, as occasionally some tourists are allowed to glimpse in
Stage 6	The back region, the ultimate goal of the tourist but rarely, if ever, reached

This shows the complexity of authenticity – it is negotiable and socially constructed, depending on the individual tourist and his/her knowledge and his/her frame of reference. Different tourists have different criteria depending on their travel behaviour and travel frequency. We should not forget that authenticity is not necessarily reality (although we have very simply defined it as the real thing above), but the image of a destination; any stereotypes and clichés can have an influence on the tourist's perception as well. Think about yourself travelling to France: you expect to see snooty waiters, people wearing berets, eating baguette and cheese, drinking red wine, etc. Or travelling to Germany, you expect someone wearing leather trousers, drinking beer, etc. You cannot help but feel disappointed if you do not see these things that you consider authentic to these cultures – the French and Germans might not consider it to be an authentic part of their culture. In much the same way, visitors to London are sometimes surprised that it is not always foggy, and that people do not walk around the streets dressed as beefeaters.

If we take heritage as another example, we also encounter somewhat of a contradiction. If we follow MacCannell's argument that the tourist is in a constant search for authenticity, we would assume that the tourist expects the authentic and real thing. However, quite often you will find that they want a sanitized image of the past – when visiting a living heritage museum about the industrial era, the tourist is interested in the way that people lived during that time, but they do not necessarily want to see (or smell) dirt, depression or death. Undoubtedly, these were aspects of everyday life back then, but given the intrinsic nature of holidays being something enjoyable, too much reality might put the tourist off and affect his/her enjoyment of the experience. Furthermore, referring back to some of the difficulties with heritage that we discussed above, the heritage which is adopted and preserved in modern culture is subjective. It is reliant upon the preferences and whims of the individuals who comprise a particular social group (tourists or locals), subject to their biases and reliant upon their recognition and appreciation. When the tourist arrives they also bring preferences and idiosyncrasies of their own, which are sometimes different from those of the local population. What the tourist appreciates and values as being authentic may be different from that which is pleasing to the local population.

CASE STUDY 3: BLACK COUNTRY LIVING MUSEUM

This open-air museum is based near to Dudley in the West Midlands, in the heart of the area known as the Black Country. Authenticity is very important to the team at the Black Country Living Museum. Museum staff and volunteers dress in authentic clothes and interpret the lives of the residents of their open air village. The village sweet shop makes and sells sweets, the bakery shop sells traditional cakes, and the fish and chip shop even fries their products in traditional beef dripping. Sights, smells, sounds and experiences are as close as they can reasonably and legally achieve.

The interpretation is lively and the characters are believable, even to those who grew up locally. In the kitchen of one of the artisan cottages, the lady interpreting clearly explains realities of life in the area at the turn of the century, and

Continued

G. Povey and S. Heitmann

shows how kitchen gadgets worked at the time. She calls attention to the outside toilet (which you can go and look at) and asks visitors to imagine the smells when the family of eight or ten used it, and the fact that there were no really comfortable chairs, only hard wooden ones. To really bring home to visitors how different life was, she reminds them that they do not have their televisions, telephones or music centres. The modern is referred to, and not hidden at the back of the exhibit.

(Source: Case study provided by the Black Country Museum)

Questions

Does referring to modern items, to enhance appreciation of exhibits, really detract from authenticity? Can it be justified in terms of its ability to enhance visitor experiences?

Taking Cohen's idea further, it is not only the setting, but also the persons gazed upon that are part of the tourist experience and thus influencing the perception of authenticity. Authenticity is also determined by the relationship between hosts and guests.

Taking the supplier's point of view, authenticity often appears in tourist brochures, advertisements and other travel publications to describe, and of course to sell, different types of travel, certain journeys or even entire holidays. It is often used to distinguish between specialist/niche-market and mass tourism products (implying that the latter is inauthentic). Looking at brochures you will find various methods to emphasize the authenticity of a tourism product. Producers use authenticity in marketing to make tourists believe that a commodity is exclusive and hard to find, and to make a product expensive to emphasize its authentic qualities.

Case Study 4: Authenticity at the Peter and Paul Festival, Germany

The Peter and Paul Festival is one of the largest festivals in south-east Germany, which attracts more than 100,000 visitors each year. The theme of the festival is 'A city relives its history', and most locals engage in activities that re-enact local life as it used to be in the past 500 years. The festival area can be divided into three main parts. First, there is an amusement area with rollercoaster, carrousels and tombola booths. The second part is the area around the market place, where different activities are carried out and presented to the public throughout the 4 days, for example concerts, comedy and the two highlights of the festival – the parade and the battle (both involving all participants). Finally, another part is dedicated to various activities and presentations, such as jugglery, medieval dances and children's plays, but also where most of the camps are located.

Continued

G. Povey and S. Heitmann

Locals form into groups with a mediaeval theme (e.g. lancers, archers, washer-women, farmers, etc.) and establish camps all over the city centre, wearing mediaeval dress and engaging in typical historic activities, all based on extensive research into the town's social history (e.g. handcrafting, manufacturing of weapons, production of daily products or simply daily life). While the participants either carry out these activities or just 'hang around' in the camp (drinking, eating, chatting), the visitors are merely allowed to glimpse into these camps and watch what happens in them. Access to camps is only allowed when dressed appropriately. While those participants belonging to militia groups wear mainly uniforms, the vast majority wears mediaeval dresses, mingling with the visitors and attending different performances, but by being dressed differently they separate themselves from pure visitors.

Questions

1. To what extent does the festival cater for the romantic or collective gaze?
2. Consider the concept of authenticity (see above) applied to the festival – how authentic is it? How would you apply 'staged authenticity' here?
3. Taking the discussions on culture and heritage into account – what are the motivations of locals to participate in the festival? What are the motivations of tourists to attend the festival?
4. The festival has different meanings to the visitors and to the locals – what do you think these meanings are? What are the key differences? Could you consider any potential conflicts?

Commodification/commoditization

Referring back to MacCannell's concept of staged authenticity, the packaging of tourist experiences can result in commodification, which refers to the packaging, promotion, presentation and institutionalization of an object, event, place, performance or idea for commercial gain. Consumerism has changed the basis on which we perceive the world: we attach a monetary value to everything. We treat cultural or natural tourist attractions as a resource or as a commodity over which tourists have rights – paying for a holiday often results in tourists having the attitude that every single part of their holiday experience has been bought, including performances by locals and cultural experiences. Immaterial things like language, dances, religious rituals, etc. become 'things to be consumed' with a money value attached to them. The more tourists visit cultures perceived to be more authentic than their own, the more the visited culture becomes commodified. This has two major implications. The more commodified a culture becomes, the less attractive it becomes to: (i) the tourists, as the culture has been spoilt and therefore becomes more fake; and (ii) to the locals, as the culture loses its intrinsic meaning – they are being paid to perform their culture; if they are getting paid they have to deliver in order to satisfy the tourists – even if that means modifying their sacred rituals.

There are examples where academics have lamented the loss of cultural meaning as these performances became modified for tourists' sake. Such an example is the festival of San Fermin in Spain, which used to be a locals' festival but, because of the popularity of the Bull Run and the parade, more and more tourists were attracted to the festival. Subsequently, the festival changed over the years – for example, the parade was to be repeated several times in order to allow as many tourists as possible to attend. This of course brought some resistance from the locals, but it was changed nevertheless (Greenwood, 1989). Another example is religious dances in Indonesia, where tourists started to attend these ceremonies that could last up to several hours – too long for the schedule of the tourist, and thus a more tourist-friendly version of half an hour was offered (Picard, 1996). However, we should not be too negative on this issue. When revisiting these cultures several years later, people could observe that the 'tourist version' was accepted by the locals and in parts even adopted into local life (this is what we would call 'emergent authenticity'). As you can see from the discussion above and these examples, authenticity is a very fluid subject, as it can change over time. You could say that authenticity is like jelly in your hand – depending on the way you look at it, it always changes.

Summary: the Challenge of the Future

The future holds terrific challenges for travel, societies and our cultures. The tour operations industry has a key role in facilitating positive intercultural exchanges between tourists and their hosts. Tour operations professionals need to understand the nuances of the host–guest relationship, whatever stage of the destination's life cycle that tourism is part of, and work to ensure the ongoing societal sustainability. There is also a role for the tour operations industry in educating tourists about the sensitivity of heritage sites to degradation by them. They also need to ensure that they work with heritage site managers, both to ensure the long-term integrity of the site and to provide meaningful, enriching experiences for those visitors.

Acknowledgements

The Black Country Museum; Paul Geiss, Baobab Travel; Kelly May, Andaman Discoveries; Katie Fewings, www.responsibletravel.com; Tourismus Zentrale, St Peter-Ording.

Further Research

AlSayyad, N. (2001) *Consuming Tradition, Manufacturing Heritage*, Routledge, London.
Dann, G. (1981) Tourist motivation: an appraisal. *Annals of Tourism Research* 8(2), 187–219.
Pedersen, A. (2002) *Managing Tourism at World Heritage Sites: A Practical Manual for World Heritage Site Managers*. UNESCO World Heritage Centre, Paris.
Sharpley, R. (2008) *Tourists, Tourism and Society*, 4th edn. Elm Publications, Huntingdon, UK.
Urry, J. (2002) *The Tourist Gaze*, 2nd edn. Sage Publications, London.

G. Povey and S. Heitmann

Web Sites

UNESCO: Available at: www.unesco.org
British Museum: Available at: www.britishmuseum.org
SAFE: Available at: www.savingantiquities.org
Black Country Museum: Available at: www.bclm.co.uk

Review Questions

1. Look at the last question of the case study of Sani Pass in Chapter 9 (this volume) – consider it from the locals' perspective and from the tourists' perspective – what are the sociocultural impacts? How do you see the host–guest relationship evolve in case of future tourism development?

2. While working as a resort representative you are accompanying a group to a very important historical site. How would you ensure that their visit has a low impact at the site?

References

Beneviste, E. (1969) *Le Vocabulaire des Institutions Indo-Europeennes*. Les Editions de Minuit, Paris.

Boorstin, D. (1961) *The Image: A Guide to Pseudo-events in America*. Harper & Row, New York.

Butler, R. (1980) The concept of a tourist area cycle of evolution: implications for management of resources. *Canadian Geographer* 24(1), 5–12.

Cohen, E. (1972) Towards a sociology of international tourism. *Social Research* 39(1), 64–83.

Cohen, E. (1988) Authenticity and commoditization in tourism. *Annals of Tourism Research* 15(3), 371–386.

Doxey, G. (1976) When enough's enough: the natives are restless in old Niagara. *Heritage Canada* 2, 26–27.

Greenwood, D. (1989) Culture by the pound: an anthropological perspective on tourism as cultural commoditization. In: Smith, V.L. (ed.) *Hosts and Guests. The Anthropology of Tourism*, 3rd edn. University of Pennsylvania Press, Philadelphia, Pennsylvania.

MacCannell, D. (1999) *The Tourist – A New Theory of the Leisure Class*. University of California Press, London.

McKercher, A. and DuCros, H. (2002) *Cultural Tourism: The Partnership between Tourism and Cultural Heritage Management*. Haworth Press, Binghamton, New York.

Pedersen, A. (2002) *Managing Tourism at World Heritage Sites: A Practical Manual for World Heritage Site Managers*. UNESCO World Heritage Centre, Paris.

Picard, M. (1996) *Bali: Cultural Tourism and Touristic Culture*. Archipelago Press, Singapore.

Plog, S. (1974) Why destination areas rise and fall in popularity. *Cornell Hotel and Restaurant Administration Quarterly* 14(4), 55–58.

Poon, A. (1993) *Tourism, Technology and Competitive Strategies*. CAB International, Wallingford, UK.

Sharpley, R. (2008) *Tourism, Tourists and Society*, 4th edn. Elm Publications, Huntingdon, UK.

Smith, V.L. (1989) *Hosts and Guests: The Anthropology of Tourism*, 3rd edn. University of Pennsylvania Press, Philadelphia, Pennsylvania.

Swarbrooke, J. and Horner, S. (2007) *Consumer Behaviour in Tourism*. Butterworth-Heinemann, Oxford.

Timothy, D. and Boyd, S. (2003) *Heritage Tourism*. Prentice Hall, Harlow, UK.

UNESCO (2008) World heritage. Available at: http://whc.unesco.org/en/about/

Urry, J. (2002) *The Tourist Gaze*, 2nd edn. Sage Publications, London.

Zarkia, C. (1996) Philoxenia: receiving tourists – but not guests – on a Greek island. In: Boissevain, J. (ed.) *Coping with Tourists: European Reactions to Mass Tourism*, Berghahn Books, Oxford.

G. Povey and S. Heitmann

Concluding Remarks:
the Future of Travel

Operations management is arguably the most important aspect of travel management. Businesses rely heavily on effective operations management to deliver a high-quality end product. Operations management affects all aspects of the business, and all aspects of the business influence operations management. This synergy has been demonstrated in the preceding chapters that have built to create a holistic overview of the industry. However, much of what has been discussed is only an evolution of business and tourism theories that have taken place over the last decade. As the industry and its external environment change and develop, greater opportunities will exist for the industry and much greater changes may yet take place over the next decade.

So, what are the key messages for the future of travel? It is certainly likely that travel will continue to grow, although the industry will also face existing and new challenges. Inevitably, there will be external influences which are new to the industry or which may not be predictable. It is only necessary to look. Just looking at the impacts of 9/11 it is easy to recognize how quickly the world as a whole can change, and the measures businesses need to take to adapt to new and uncertain environments. Strategists will consider some of these changes, and most businesses will have developed pre-emptive contingency plans, but there are many issues which are operational in nature and which require a much quicker and immediate response.

The economic threats over the next few years are many and will impact on leisure and business travel alike. As fuel and energy prices become less stable this will impact on operators from all sides. Increased fuel costs will eventually drive up the ticket prices of even the most resilient of operators. There is only so long that operators can absorb increases before they risk financial instability. However, while some operators can resist these changes, those that fail to do so or lack the resources necessary to withstand these impacts will struggle to compete, giving a competitive advantage to those with greater resistance. Predicted increases in energy prices are a threat to operators of infrastructure. Imagine, for example, the energy costs at airports. These have to be passed on to shop lessees and airline operators, representing further increases in operating costs and ticket prices for the consumer. After a decade of rising profits, low-cost airlines now have difficulties keeping their ticket prices low for customers, thus jeopardizing their own competitive advantage. For business travellers considering the impacts of rising costs, there may be technological alternatives that reduce the need for travel. Satellite and video conferencing make meetings possible without travel.

However, it is not an entirely gloomy outlook. Airline operators investing in new equipment, such as the Airbus A380, can carry greater capacity in more fuel-efficient aircraft, and train companies such as Virgin that operate Pendolino tilting trains are able to produce electricity under braking, which can be sold back to the National

---

Grid. In fact, as much as technology can be a threat to the industry, it also provides new opportunities to respond to global issues.

The much greater risk may be more political in nature. There has been consistent if not increased terrorist activity in recent years, quite often aimed at tourist destinations and travel infrastructure in order to receive as much attention as possible. Not only does this have significant consequences for the image of the destination and the local governments in terms of political actions required, it also affects tourist consumer behaviour and travelling activities. Travellers need to feel safe to use transport. Although Maslow's hierarchy of needs is discussed within the Human Resources chapter (Chapter 3), those same basic needs must be catered for, whatever activity people are involved in. Travel operators have much work to do in maintaining and enhancing safety and security in the current political climate. Within the European Union there are further developments that facilitate travelling, through the abolition of border control and visa requirements, while at the same time other countries are considering stricter visa regulations, be they for workers or tourists. There will always be strengths and weaknesses in the external environment.

The good news, however, is that the World Travel and Tourism Council and World Trade Organization forecast growth in this sector over the next few years, and industry growth translates into job opportunities and profitability, subject to the concerns identified above. Furthermore, there is substantial evidence that global demographics are changing. Much attention is now paid to the emerging markets of India, China and Brazil, industrialized countries where recently enhanced prosperity is offering people greater levels of disposable income are seeing a growth in outbound travel. In established markets, consumers are becoming more sophisticated and have a greater awareness of the opportunities travel can offer.

This ties in well with sustainability and a desire to get away from the traditional concept of mass tourism. The market for sustainable travel is still growing, but the supply of these holidays still comes primarily from the smaller businesses in the sector. However, many larger businesses have acquired niche market operators to increase their share of these new markets with a relatively risk-free approach. Alongside a greater awareness of the protection of the environment is the growth of new niche-market tourism products, which include, for example, dark tourism and ethical or responsible tourism, and a general industry shift away from commoditized package travel to diversification and individualization of even the more traditional holiday. Indeed the industry we discuss in this book as the service economy is fast becoming an experience economy, with consumers seeking much deeper and more enhanced travel experiences.

Reflecting then on the notion that many operators may struggle over the coming years with economic influences and global changes, it should be noted that at the opposite end of the scale exciting new opportunities are developing. Space tourism, expensive though it is now, is starting to 'take off'. New technology also brings with it new markets. While the high-street travel agent has seen a decline in user numbers over recent years, the online marketplace continues to grow. It is unlikely the high-street travel agent will disappear altogether, because they cater for a less technology-minded market, and they stock brochures that are commonly preferred to Internet-based browsing; however, there may be a need to radically redesign the service offering within these retail units.

In summary then, much like any other industry, the travel business faces exciting yet challenging times ahead. As the industry continues to grow and be shaped by external influences, so will the shape and scope of operations management be changed. Research in the sector will continue to analyse performance and propose new systems, models and approaches for operations management; staff training and development, the very seed from which this book grew, will similarly become increasingly important as the industry becomes increasingly professionalized.

Index

Page numbers in **bold** refer to figures and tables